REAL-WORLD ADVICE FROM
TEEN TIPS

PLUCK A BUCK ◇ I used to spend a great deal of time nagging my kids to do their household chores, but that has changed since I started plucking money from their allowance for neglecting their work. Now, every Monday morning I place my children's allowance, all in single dollar bills, in an envelope with their name on it. The envelopes are taped on the refrigerator. They can't take the money until the following Sunday evening. In the meantime, if they forget or refuse to do their chores, I pluck a buck from their envelope. I don't nag; I just pluck a buck. On Sunday, they can keep what's left. After the first two weeks of watching their needed allowance dwindle away, they started being much more diligent about their responsibilities. Occasionally I even pluck a buck when they fight with each other. *Shelley McKinzie, Fremont, California*

THE ALARM ENFORCES CURFEW ◇ Before our two teens went out with friends for the evening or on a date, my husband and I would negotiate a reasonable curfew for their return. Instead of waiting up for them past our own bedtime, we would set our alarm to ring at their curfew time. Then my husband and I would retire to bed at our normal time. If our children came home before their curfew, they would tiptoe into our bedroom and shut off the alarm before it went off. If, however, they were late and the alarm woke us up, we would know that they missed their curfew. We always encouraged them to call us if they were going to be late. We preferred waking up to their voice on the phone rather than being startled by the alarm going off and not knowing where they were. *Patty McMillan, Long Beach, California*

NO MORE HOMEWORK COP ◇ My husband and I used to quiz our daughter nightly regarding the completion of her homework. It was like playing cops and robbers. So now, instead of hounding her about her homework each evening, we review a semiweekly progress report from each of her teachers. Since her privileges depend on a good progress report, she is now motivated to complete her homework and get good grades—without our pestering. *Teresa Dulberg, Hayward, California*

Also by Tom McMahon

KID TIPS: Proven Child-Care Tips from Experienced
    Parents Across the Country—For Newborns to Ten-Year-Olds
    (Previously published as IT WORKS FOR US!)

Available from POCKET BOOKS

TEEN TIPS

A PRACTICAL SURVIVAL GUIDE FOR PARENTS WITH KIDS 11 TO 19

Tom McMahon

POCKET BOOKS
New York   London   Toronto   Sydney   Singapore

The tips in this book have all worked for the parents who submitted them. Children and teenagers are individuals, however, and not all tips will be suitable or safe as described herein for you and your child. If you have any questions at all, please check with your doctor. In applying these tips, the author and publisher advise you to use your common sense and your intimate knowledge of your own child, and to be sure to keep safety in mind at all times. We cannot be held responsible for the use or misuse of any information in this book.

An *Original* Publication of POCKET BOOKS

POCKET BOOKS, a division of Simon & Schuster Inc.
1230 Avenue of the Americas, New York, NY 10020

Copyright © 1996 by Thomas L. McMahon

All rights reserved, including the right to reproduce
this book or portions thereof in any form whatsoever.
For information address Pocket Books, 1230 Avenue
of the Americas, New York, NY 10020

Library of Congress Cataloging-in-Publication Data

McMahon, Tom (Thomas L.)
    Teen tips : a practical survival guide for parents with kids 11 to 19
    Tom McMahon.
       p.   cm.
    Includes index.
    ISBN: 0-671-89106-5 (pbk.)
    1. Parent and teenager—United States.   2. Teenagers—United
States.   3. Parenting—United States.   I. Title.
HQ799.15.M33   1996
649'.125—dc20   96-1614
                                                          CIP

First Pocket Books trade paperback printing August 1996

10

POCKET and colophon are registered trademarks of
Simon & Schuster Inc.

Cover design by Jeanne Lee
Front cover photo credits: top, Dale Durfee/Tony Stone Images; middle
    left, Jon Riley/Tony Stone Images; middle right, © Telegraph Colour
    Library/FPG International; bottom, Lori Adamski Peek/Tony Stone
    Images
Text design by Stanley S. Drate/Folio Graphics Co., Inc.

Printed in the U.S.A.

To the memory of
Kevin Patrick Norton
who soars on wings like eagles

ACKNOWLEDGMENTS

A heartfelt thanks to the hundreds of parents who contributed tips to this book. You are the real authors of this work to whom I will always be grateful. A special thanks to all the families who opened up their homes to me and shared their secrets of success in parenting. Each of you will surely have a positive influence on the many parents who read the pages to follow. For them, I also thank you.

I am especially grateful to my family for their love, support, and encouragement while I worked on this manuscript. I thank my wife, Nancy, for her advice and editing, and my daughters, Kelly and Amber, for their tolerance of this major project and for teaching me every day what is important in life.

I want to acknowledge a number of friends and colleagues who directly contributed to this book: Susie Anderson, Dr. Carol Becker, Paul Dulberg, Jim Klent, Dr. Neil McCallum, Dr. Daniel Meyer, Sheldon Nagel, and Dennis Ean Roby. I also want to thank all the individuals at Pocket Books who have worked on this book, especially Claire Zion, Danielle Dayen, and Anne Cherry, whose thoughtful and insightful editing of the manuscript has made this a much better book.

CONTENTS

9

VALUES

10

SEXUALITY AND DATING

11

DRIVING

12

DRUGS AND ALCOHOL

13

PROMOTING A HEALTHY SELF-CONCEPT

14

TEEN-FAMILY RELATIONSHIPS

15

DIVORCE AND STEPPARENTING

16

LOOKING TOWARD THE FUTURE: COLLEGE AND CAREERS

You have a wonderful child. Then, when he's thirteen, gremlins carry him away and leave in his place a stranger who gives you not a moment's peace. You have to hang in there, because two or three years later, the gremlins will return your child, and he will be wonderful again.

—JILL EIKENBERRY

"On Raising Teenagers," *Parade*, July 12, 1987

✖◆◆◆◆◆◆◆◆◆◆◆◆◆◆◆◆◆◆◆◆◆◆◆◆◆◆◆◆◆◆◆◆◆◆◆✖

A PERSONAL INTRODUCTION

✖◆◆◆◆◆◆◆◆◆◆◆◆◆◆◆◆◆◆◆◆◆◆◆◆◆◆◆◆◆◆◆◆◆◆◆✖

With teens, there are times when you wonder who that kid is sitting across from you at the dinner table, the one in baggy pants with an attitude—and perhaps an earring dangling from one ear. The transformation from childhood to adulthood takes our teenagers through many stages and changes and at times causes us to feel that we don't know them anymore. It's also common to doubt our abilities as parents during the teen years. Sometimes our parenting tactics that got results just a few months ago don't work anymore. Our love is the same, and we still want the best for our children, but things just don't click as easily now as they once did.

Relax. You are not alone. The majority of parents have these same thoughts and frustrations about the teen years. Adolescence is challenging for most parents, even if there are no major problems. One thing that I have learned after writing my last book, *It Works For Us! Proven Child-Care Tips from Experienced Parents Across the Country,* is that other parents can help. There are many experienced parents who have not only survived the teen years but enjoyed them, and became closer with their children as a result. What did they do that worked? What can they tell us that can make our job as parents easier and more effective? For the past three years I have been on a quest to find the answer to these questions— something that, to my knowledge, no one else has ever done on such a large scale.

A good portion of my time during the last three years has been spent sitting at kitchen tables and in living rooms with families who had something to share with all of us about the teen years. I asked them to share their secrets of success. They did. And now I have a chance to share these secrets with you. I am certain that many of their practical tips will make a positive difference in parenting your own teens.

I first began interviewing families in my own community, ones that I personally admired, followed by families that were recommended by other parents and educators in nearby cities. Later in the project, I expanded my interviews to other states and once even interviewed families along the route of our family vacation.

Most of the families I interviewed began the conversation with a comment such as "We're not experts at parenting, we just tried to survive the teen years one day at a time." But as my questions probed into their strategies for building relationships, increasing self-esteem, providing boundaries, and administering discipline for their teens, they began to share their magic—little tidbits of parental innovation and creativity that make you wonder, "Why didn't I think of that?" My laptop computer could barely keep up with their many ideas.

In the meantime, newspapers printed articles about my quest for tips, and radio stations interviewed me about my early findings. Tips began trickling in through the mail, on my "parenting tips" answering machine, and even through cyberspace via the Internet, America Online, and Prodigy.

The many parents who share their advice with you in this book are a true cross-section of parents like you. They come from two-parent, single, and blended families; from poor to wealthy communities; and from a diversity of beliefs, lifestyles, and ethnicity. The common thread that binds them is their claim that they have learned something valuable in parenting their teenagers. And they wanted to share it with you.

You will find the best of their tips throughout the chapters of this book, plus some of the latest surveys and research about teens, comments from teens themselves, and quick, easy parenting lessons called Skill Builders, all with the goal of making the teen years a rich and valuable time for you and your teenager. (For suggestions on how to get the most out of this book, please read "How to Use This Book" on page xxi).

There is no magic formula for parenting teens. About the best we can do is to use our good common sense and judgment, and to learn from other parents who have been there before. Of most importance, we also need to spend time with our teens, who, because of their complex developmental needs, desperately need our understanding and attention. Just how much teens need parental attention was brought home to me by several mothers who stressed that they felt their children actually needed them more now that they were teens than when they were younger. I agree. Although there are exceptions, many of the teen problems—violence, gangs, suicide, and drug abuse—that we witness now are not a result of these children being overnurtured by our society. Quite the contrary.

With teens, there will be wonderful times and rocky times. You may occasionally feel as though your life has been turned upside-down. But trust me, normality will return. No matter how tumultuous the journey is, the vast majority of teens make it to adulthood in fine shape and eager to tackle the rest of their life.

The more I learn about adolescent development, the more I marvel at what a rich time it is, and the deeper my respect for teenagers grows. Adolescence is an important part of life's journey; it sets the tone for our future. The investment we make in our children now will be blessed in a thousand ways in the years to come.

—Tom McMahon
January 1996

PARENTS' BILL OF RIGHTS AND RESPONSIBILITIES

This Parents' Bill of Rights and Responsibilities was created by a group of parents, educators, counselors, law enforcement personnel, and an assortment of community leaders—collectively known as the Tri-City Substance Abuse Coalition—in response to questions and concerns expressed by parents in their community. The fifteen items listed below address many of the legal and moral obligations we have to our children. The pages that follow are dedicated to helping you achieve these ideals with practical solutions and succeed in dealing with the many other issues of adolescence.

1 We, as parents, have a right to be treated with respect.

2 We have the right to say no and not feel guilty.

3 We have the right to know where our kids are, who their friends are, and who they are with at any time.

4 We have the right to demonstrate we care by occasionally verifying or spot checking our children's whereabouts. We may, for example, call host parents on parties or overnight stays.

5 We have the right to set a curfew and enforce it with restrictions and loss of privileges.

6 We have the right not to condone any alcohol or drug usage and to say no to attendance at activities where alcohol or drug usage may occur.

7 We have the right to make mistakes and/or change our minds.

8 We have the right to ask questions and expect answers about all things which may affect our children.

9 We have the right to monitor all school-related activities: academic, behavioral, and social.

10 We have the right to know and consult with adults who influence our children's lives, i.e., coaches, employers, teachers, youth group leaders, ministers, and counselors.

11 We have the right to know what is happening within our own home, to set "house rules," and know the identity of guests who come into our home.

12 We have the right to assign our kids chores and other family responsibilities appropriate to their ages.

13 We have a right to promote time together, as a family, which may include meals, outings, study time, and other planned activities.

14 We have a right to be authoritative when logical explanation and reason have not succeeded.

15 We have a right to have family rules and consistently enforce them with appropriate consequences.

Printed with permission of the Tri-City Substance Abuse Coalition (Fremont, Newark, Union City, California)

HOW TO USE THIS BOOK

Teen Tips: A Practical Survival Guide for Parents with Kids 11 to 19 contains the following features:

Practical Parenting Tips ◇ The best practical parenting advice ever collected from the real experts—other parents—are listed in chapters 2–16 after the chapter introductions. Each tip is credited with the name or initials and the city of the contributor. Some contributors asked to remain anonymous because of the personal nature of their tips or to protect the anonymity of their family members. Use your own intimate knowledge of your child to select tips that are most promising and which fit into your own value and belief system. Some will be more applicable to you than others and, of course, not all tips will work for all teens. Some tips may seem similar to others in the same section, but they have a new or unique twist.

Adolescent Research ◇ Each chapter begins with an introduction that includes important, current information about the topic. Chapter introductions typically include surveys and research-based studies on adolescent development, as well as quotes from some of the top developmental researchers.

Parenting Skill Builders ◇ Fifteen parent skill builders on a variety of subjects, such as what to look for if you suspect your teenager is using drugs, how to improve your listening skills, and how to handle confrontation successfully, have been placed throughout the book. These skill builders are quick lessons—usually a paragraph or two—on useful skills for parents.

Teen Talk ◇ Teens sent me some of their own advice for parents after hearing that I was seeking parenting tips.

Their comments and feedback to us have been placed in the appropriate chapters and offer a fresh slant on parenting as seen by teens themselves.

Recommended Reading and Further Information

⋄ At the end of many of the chapters is a list of books and reference materials for further information. Some chapters also list the phone numbers and addresses of organizations that provide further information or assistance for parents and/or teens.

Other Items of Note

- Before you begin reading Chapter 1, don't miss the Parents' Bill of Rights and Responsibilities, (page xix) and also take a moment to reflect on your own teen years (see page xxiii).
- Besides being a good parent, there are other ways to improve the lives of teenagers in our society. For a list of suggestions, see "Ten Things You Can Do to Improve the Lives of Teens" (page 226).

S T O P !
DON'T TURN THE PAGE YET
BEFORE YOU BEGIN READING ABOUT TEENAGERS, TAKE A MOMENT TO REFLECT ON YOUR OWN TEEN YEARS.

You will be surprised at how this brief exercise will help you understand your own teenager(s). Although many aspects of teen life are different now, many are the same or similar to your own experiences.

Close your eyes for a few minutes and think back to

... when you were thirteen years old.

1. Recall in your mind's eye the home you lived in, your bedroom, and your neighborhood. What was a typical day like for you?

2. Think about your best friend and the clique or group of friends you spent time with. What did you enjoy doing together?

3. Try to visualize your school, some classrooms, where you ate lunch, etc. Recall some memories about your teachers and activities at school.

4. How did you feel about your parents? Recall some of the good and bad times. How would you have liked your parents to be different in how they treated you?

5. Had you started puberty? Were you an early or late developer compared to your peers? How did you feel about all the changes going on with your body? Recall your feelings about the opposite sex.

... when you were seventeen years old.

1. Refer to questions 1–4 above.

2. Recall your thoughts, feelings, and perhaps even fears about your future. What were your plans at this point? Did they change over the years?

3. If you dated at this age, recall your memories about your boyfriend(s) or girlfriend(s). Did you experience one or more breakups? Recall your feelings and experiences about sexual thoughts or experiences.

4. Did you have a driver's permit or license? Recall some of the memories about learning how to drive, your driving test, and other driving experiences.

Briefly repeat this exercise for the specific age(s) of your teenager(s).

TEEN TIPS

WHAT IS A TEENAGER?

"Who are you?" said the Caterpillar. Alice replied, rather shyly, "I—I hardly know, Sir, just at present—at least I know who I was when I got up this morning, but I must have changed several times since then."

—LEWIS CARROLL, *Alice in Wonderland*, 1865

Welcome to the exciting new world of adolescence—the teen years—one of the most interesting and challenging phases of life. Adolescence is a time of change, a time to gradually shed one's protective childhood for a new identity and a world of new responsibilities and independence. The transition from childhood to adulthood has never been easy, but there are few times in history when the adolescent years have been more challenging than in the closing years of the twentieth century.

Our life span, from conception to late adulthood, has distinct and somewhat predictable phases through which we pass on life's journey. Infancy, childhood, adolescence, and adulthood are the main developmental phases, each of which can be broken down into even smaller periods of time. For example, childhood includes the toddler, preschool, and elementary years, and adulthood can be divided into young adulthood, middle age, and late adulthood. Each segment offers new challenges, behaviors, and tasks, and many of these help us prepare for the next phase of life.

Adolescence is one of the more lengthy developmental phases. Spanning approximately ten years, it usually begins at the age of eleven or twelve and ends between the ages of eighteen and twenty-one. Like the other major developmental phases, adolescence can be divided into distinct stages, in this case three: early adolescence (eleven to fourteen years old) roughly covers the junior high or middle school years; middle adolescence (fifteen to eighteen years old) includes the senior high years; and late adolescence (nineteen to twenty-one years old) covers the college years or the beginning of a full-time job or career. Each stage has its own unique issues, potential problems, and important tasks to complete. For instance, the onset of puberty is a significant issue in early adolescence, dating is of importance in middle adolescence, and career decisions play a key factor in late adolescence.

Being a teenager in the 1990s has the ups and downs of a roller coaster ride: it's exciting, fun, risky, and scary—all at the same time; and the anticipation of the next blind curve is often better than the real experience. The journey to adulthood in this decade has an unprecedented number of potential dangers—including violence, car accidents, suicide, and sexually transmitted diseases. Caught between childhood and adulthood, wanting to be grown-up but reluctant to give up the security of childhood, teens frequently take two steps forward and one back. In the eyes of many teenagers, the road to adulthood looks unfriendly. And in many ways it is. One fifteen-year-old girl sums up the feelings of many teens in the 90s as she unleashes her frustration on past generations:

> Parents should think back to when they were teenagers, then watch the evening news to see how much has changed. Kids are confronted with drugs, sex, and violence all the time. And we have to solve all the problems that your generation started. Parents had it easy when they were teens. They did everything they wanted to and barely had any consequences for their actions. Everything we do has a consequence, and most of them are deadly.

Teenagers also feel misunderstood and maligned by our society. The media and a small percentage of troubled teens have caused the image of teens to be seriously tarnished. Teens are frequently portrayed in news reports and depicted in movies as being lazy, deviant, promiscuous, self-centered, disturbed, and delinquent. One large metropolitan newspaper recently uncovered through its own investigation that teenagers are pictured more negatively than any other group in their newspaper, and have made plans to portray them more fairly in the future.[1]

Although there has been an increase in delinquent behavior by teens, this negative stereotype still represents only a small percentage of all teens. Research findings clearly demonstrate that the vast majority of adolescents are not as troubled and disturbed as their stereotype suggests. Researcher Daniel Offer and his colleagues found that almost three-quarters of the adolescents they studied had a healthy self-image. They perceived themselves as able to exercise self-control, they expressed confidence about their sexual selves, they valued work and school, they expressed positive feelings toward their families, they felt they had the capability to cope with life's stresses, and they reported enjoying life.[2]

One issue that many teens do worry about is their future. They know that adulthood will not meet them with open arms. They will face significant increases in college tuition, extraordinary competition for jobs, a struggling economy, continuing changes in the family structure, high divorce rates, and a future full of problems left over from previous generations. For teens living in poverty, especially those in the inner cities, the outlook is much bleaker and, in their eyes, almost hopeless.

Adolescence is also a time of extraordinary changes. Your teen is changing in many ways, physically, cognitively, socially, and emotionally. The specific purpose of this chapter and many other parts of this book is to help you understand and anticipate these changes, and, most important, to help you and your teen cope with these changes. This chapter describes three of the most important aspects of adolescent development—physical changes, including puberty and its emotional aspects; cognitive (intellectual) changes; and the process of identity development.

PHYSICAL DEVELOPMENT

One of the biggest milestones of adolescence is the onset of puberty, a series of events lasting on the average of two to five years, that gradually transform an adolescent's physical characteristics into those of a man or woman. The onset, rate, and ending of puberty are controlled by the central nervous system, which commands various glands to begin secreting hormones. The hormones travel through the bloodstream to certain organs and tissues causing specific changes to take place. Although most teens begin puberty in early adolescence, there is considerable individual variation in both the timing and tempo of puberty, depending on factors such as genetics, health, nutrition, and body mass. There is such a wide normal range for individuals to start puberty (see below), that it is possible for some teens to complete the pubertal sequence before others their same age even begin.

When asked to describe puberty, one teen replied, "It's when your body goes crazy." In many ways, that's close to the truth, especially from a teen's perspective. There are changes in the genitals; further development of the sex glands; growth of facial, pubic, and body hair; changes in the quantity and distribution of fat and muscle; and increased strength and stamina. There is also a rapid growth and weight gain called the adolescent growth spurt, which typically lasts for two years. During this period, both boys and girls can grow as much as four to five inches in a given year. Girls begin their growth spurt around the age of ten or eleven, two years before boys. This helps to explain why many girls tower over their male counterparts in sixth and seventh grades.

Girls usually begin puberty between the ages of eight and thirteen, with the entire cycle lasting from one and a half to six years. It is widely believed that menarche, the first menstrual period, marks the onset of puberty for girls, but, in fact, menarche occurs relatively late in the pubertal cycle, typically around age thirteen, but with a wide normal range from nine to fifteen. Body weight can also be a factor in determining the onset of menarche. It usually occurs within a body weight of 103 to 109 pounds, with fat making up approximately 17 percent of the girl's body weight.[3]

The first sign of puberty for girls is either the slight elevation of the breasts (typically called breast buds) or the appearance of pubic hair. As puberty progresses, the pubic hair becomes coarser and darker, and the breasts continue to develop through a series of five distinct stages. Regardless of breast size, the final stages of breast growth are marked by the areola (the nipple and area around it) receding to the contour of the breast with only the nipple elevated. Internal changes include growth and development of the uterus, vagina, and other aspects of the reproductive system.

Boys usually begin puberty between the ages of ten and fourteen, and end between the ages of thirteen and seventeen. Sex characteristics also appear in a predictable order in boys. First, there is rapid growth of the scrotum and testes and the appearance of pubic hair. Next, the penis enlarges and the pubic hair becomes coarser and darker. Later in the pubertal process, facial and body hair appear, the voice deepens, and the ability to ejaculate seminal fluid occurs.[4]

Adjusting to Puberty

It is not surprising that the plethora of physical changes brought on by puberty cause some adjustment problems as well. It takes time for teenagers to adjust to these changes and accept their new appearance. It is both understandable and normal for them to become preoccupied with their bodies during puberty. They will probably spend an inordinate amount of time looking in the mirror, wondering where the next change will take place. Most teens also have bouts of being overly sensitive or even embarrassed about their "new" body, causing them to have a poor body image and frequent complaints about their appearance. However, by the end of puberty and the beginning of late adolescence, most teens have an improved, if not proud, body image.

Since one of the unwritten laws of pre- and early teens is

to not appear too different from their friends and peers, those who don't develop along the average timeline often experience a more turbulent time during puberty. Judy Blume's endearing character Margaret in *Are You There God? It's Me Margaret* typifies a young adolescent who can't wait to blossom as some of her peers have. Impatient with her lack of development, Margaret takes up her issue with God:

Are you there God? It's me, Margaret. I just did an exercise to help me grow. Have you thought about it God? About my growing, I mean. I've got a bra now. It would be nice if I had something to put in it.[5]

Being the first or last peer to develop physically can accentuate the general adjustment problems of puberty mentioned earlier. Developing breasts too early or too late can cause some girls to be embarrassed about their appearance and to have a negative self-image. The same is true for early or late maturing boys, who may be teased in the showers for appearing different. Early maturing girls may receive newfound attention from older boys, but may become the object of nasty rumors instigated by their peers. It is quite normal for early or late developers to become extremely preoccupied with their development, secretly wishing that their peers would either catch up to them or that they would catch up to their peers.

Although obviously stressful at times, most teens successfully weather the occasional stormy seas of puberty and enter late adolescence with a more positive body image and acceptance of self. Parents can play a key role in minimizing the stressful aspects of their child's puberty cycle by being understanding, accepting, and tactful. Stress can be minimized if teens know what to expect and have a positive attitude about their forthcoming changes. Girls should learn about and be prepared for the onset of menstruation and boys should learn about ejaculation and be prepared for their first wet dream. Information about puberty and sexual maturation should be presented in a manner that is positive and builds pride, not shame.

For further information, parenting tips, and recommended reading about puberty and sexuality, see Chapter 10, "Sexuality and Dating."

COGNITIVE DEVELOPMENT

As one's body develops over the course of adolescence, so does one's intellectual ability. With improved memory, attention span, and the ability to process information faster and with a greater capacity, teenagers become capable of thinking in more advanced ways. They gradually move from the limited ability to think only in concrete ways, things in the here and now and events they can see, into the world of abstract thought and reasoning. This new ability allows them to think in multiple dimensions that are more advanced, efficient, and effective.

One aspect of a teenager's new thinking skills is the ability to think hypothetically, to explore the consequences of various propositions. The power of hypothetical reasoning opens up many new horizons for their cognitive development. They can now solve logical and scientific problems. And, according to many parents, their ability to argue reaches new heights. They no longer only consider what they can see, they begin discovering the many alternatives of a situation that *might* be.

The ability to think abstractly also enables teens to be more introspective, to think about their own thoughts and feelings. It's common for teens to spend hours pondering new ideas and thinking deeply about issues of importance to them: What does love mean? What do I want out of life? Is there really a God?

It's also very common for this type of thinking to lead to periods of intense preoccupation with one's self, what psychologists call adolescent egocentrism. David Elkind, a developmental psychologist, believes that an adolescent's egocentrism is usually expressed in one of two ways, what he calls "imaginary audience" and "personal fable."[6]

The term *imaginary audience* is used to describe egocentric behavior by a teen who erroneously believes that his behavior is the focus of everyone else's concern and attention, similar to an actor on a stage. It is most common in early adolescence when one's feelings of self-consciousness are at a peak. For example, a teen can obsess about a small pimple on her face or a hair out of place to the point where she believes everyone in her class or the cafeteria is looking directly at her.

The personal fable evolves out of a teenager's erroneous belief that his or her experiences are unique. It is a belief that no one in the world could possibly understand what they are feeling or experiencing. For example, after a breakup with his girlfriend, a young man tells his father that neither he nor anyone else could ever understand his pain. Of course, in reality his father and most other people have experienced such a heartbreak more than once and can feel empathy.

There is a growing belief among psychologists that adolescent egocentrism and its frequently erroneous belief system may account for much of the reckless behavior of teenagers, including unsafe sex, suicidal behavior, and drug use. In their minds they have created the illusion that they are unique ("I'll never get caught") and invulnerable ("Other people get AIDS, not me").

IDENTITY DEVELOPMENT

Who am I? Where am I going? Adolescents spend a great deal of time pondering these and similar questions in their quest for an identity. According to the famous theorist Erik Erikson, establishing a sense of who you are is the major task of adolescence.

Finding one's identity in today's rapidly changing world is more difficult than ever before. There are more choices, from occupations to lifestyles. And with more choices there is often more confusion. For example, instead of following in the footsteps of a parent and becoming a farmer, blacksmith, homemaker, and so on, as young people did for centuries, there is now almost a limitless array of occupations and careers to choose from.

Erikson writes about the choices adolescents will make in forming their identity, "[F]rom among all possible and imaginable relations, [the young person] must make a series of ever-narrowing selections of personal, occupational, sexual, and ideological commitments."[7] Using their expanded cognitive and social skills, and new knowledge, adolescents keep pieces of their childhood identity while shedding others in exchange for new beliefs, directions, and ways of looking at the world. During late adolescence, when it becomes clearer every day that they will soon be responsible for themselves, teens begin to narrow their focus on career goals. Much of their identity formation at this stage involves the question, "Where am I going?"

An adolescent's identity is developed through experimentation; they explore different roles and "try on" new personalities, hoping to find one that fits. This is a normal and necessary aspect of identity development, but one that can be trying at times for parents. Teens can be quite moody and rebellious in their search for identity. They may be friendly one moment and argumentative the next moment. Personalities, clothing styles, and friendships can change frequently. Parents often talk about these times as being "phases" their teens are going through. These phases, or periods of experimentation, can be as brief as one day or can last for an extended period of time.

Chances are, some of the phases will be undesirable from the standpoint of the parents. Stay calm and wait for the phase to pass, recommend experienced parents. The more you fight it, the deeper the foothold will become. Remember that these are phases and that phases pass. Talk to other parents who have been through this; you will discover that they have experienced situations similar to yours.

Parents can support their teen's quest for identity by giving them the time and the space to explore their options, roles, and personalities. That does not mean that you should allow your teen to get involved with individuals, groups, or activities that you believe to be dangerous or illegal. Instead parents can be helpful by promoting their teen's sense of individuality. Many psychologists, including noted developmentalist Catherine Cooper, believe that parents should promote their teen's individuality while at the same time maintaining the family connectedness, which provides a secure base from which to explore one's identity.[8] Studies also show that a democratic parenting style (one that allows teens to be involved in family decisions) fosters identity development more than an autocratic or permissive style.[9]

The identity that your son or daughter chooses to enter young adulthood with will be tweaked, revamped, and revised over the years. Identity development is a lengthy and ongoing process, one that Erikson believes is constantly lost and regained. But its foundation is established in adolescence. So watch in wonder—and patience—as your child's new sense of self emerges. Those of us who are older and wiser know that there will be many mysteries and surprises around each corner of our children's ongoing development.

2

MILK AND COOKIES DON'T WORK ANYMORE

*Before I got married I had six theories about
bringing up children; now I have six children and
no theories.*

—LORD ROCHESTER (1647–1680)

SWITCHING GEARS FOR
THE TEEN YEARS

Where is that small, charming, and helpless kid I once
knew? You know the one; he used to come in with a scraped
knee and ask me to put on a Band-Aid. We used to have milk
and cookies together in the afternoon. He used to listen to
my advice. I was his champion.

As a parent, you may feel that your child does not need
you as much. But he does—just in a different way. There will
be conflict and disagreements at times as your relationship
evolves, but chances are, if you were close during childhood,
the two of you will continue to have a positive and warm
relationship. The vast majority of teens and their parents do.
A recent survey revealed that the majority of teens consider
their mom or dad, or both, as their best friend.

Adolescence is a time to move forward, to try on new parenting approaches, and to get to know and understand that new creature who is emerging from childhood. Parents need to keep in mind that a new relationship is forming because slowly but surely, your "old" style of parenting will not work anymore. The goal is to keep in step with your child, and gradually replace your milk-and-cookie approach for one that will promote and encourage a growing need for independence.

Some parents become very threatened by their teen's newfound quest for independence and react by pulling in the reins even tighter. They may fight to hold on to the child they know so well. "Where is that nice young boy we used to know?" they ask. The problem does not rest with the changes the teen has made—that's who he is now—rather it's the lack of changes the parents have made to adjust to the new relationship. The sooner parents establish changes in their own behavior that are more appropriate for an adolescent, the less conflict they will have during this transition. In other words, when we refocus our attention from our child's behavior to our own behavior, the relationship will turn the corner for the positive.

Saying good-bye to the childhood years is difficult for all parents. But our job now is to move on. With every ending there is a new beginning. And don't fret about the milk and cookies! Teens love them just as much as young kids do, but they will probably want to eat them alone or with their friends.

These tips are offered by other parents who survived the transition to adolescence. They are followed by three related sections: Letting Go: Encouraging Independence, Pick Your Battles, and Making Those Tough Decisions.

ASK FEWER QUESTIONS ◇ When my son was thirteen, he complained that I asked him too many questions. After some reflection, I had to agree that he was right. I would often ask him twenty questions when he came home from school. So one day, I made a point to ask him fewer questions. It was surprisingly hard; I had to bite my tongue a few times, but I did it. After a few days, it became more natural for me. And I noticed that my son began to initiate the conversation more and talk about things that he wanted to chat about. He seemed to appreciate not having so many questions. *V.P., San Jose, California*

A TWO-WAY STREET ◇ Respect is a two-way street. Let it begin with you. *Bill and Teresa Higgins, Marion, Kansas*

INDIVIDUALIZED APPROACH ◇ Parenting strategies and approaches need to be tailored to the individual child. Even my identical twin boys, as similar as they are, have different needs and respond to different parenting styles. I believe that there are as many individualized parenting approaches that work as there are people. *B.O., Ventura, California*

PARENTS NEED TO TAKE LEAD ◇ As parents, we sometimes expect our kids to change their behavior, but we tend to forget that we need to alter our own thinking and behavior, too. It takes two to tango. If the dance is going to happen, the parent has to take the lead. Otherwise, you will probably never even reach the dance floor. I have personally learned that relationships are best changed by changing yourself and hoping that the other person will follow your lead. It's worked for me. *Anonymous, San Diego, California*

PARENTING PLANS AND STRATEGIES ◇ We make business plans and financial plans, but what about parenting plans? I recommend coming up with a parenting plan for the teen years. Ask yourself, What do I want out of adolescence with my children? What can I do that will make that happen? Outline a strategy. Then prepare to be flexible as you go. *Michael Stahler, Niles, California*

LETTING GO: ENCOURAGING INDEPENDENCE

It has been said that the two most important things we can give our children are roots and wings. Beginning in early adolescence, or even earlier, and continuing throughout the teen years, the adolescent's quest for independence often becomes an arena for conflict. Although both parents and teens have the same goal in mind—autonomy by the end of adolescence—the rate of change and how it is to be achieved are frequently points of contention.

Most adolescents want to put as much space between themselves and their childhood as quickly as possible. They see glimpses of the future and they want it. Teens constantly push their boundaries to experience new things and try on new personas. They strive to be independent and self-sufficient.

Parents, on the other hand, are more cautious and slow in granting independence. One of the toughest aspects of parenting an adolescent is determining the right amount of autonomy to extend to a child at any one point. It becomes a balancing act between underparenting (not having enough boundaries) and overparenting (having too many boundaries). A good rule of thumb is to increase a teen's privileges and independence at a rate commensurate to his track record for maturity, reliability, and dependability. Keep in mind, however, that a teen's safety is an important factor in granting more freedom and independence.

Overparenting may occur if parents try to equate their love for their teens with how much they can do for them. For example, many of us have heard someone comment, "She's the most wonderful mother. What she wouldn't do for those children!" But when we do too much for our children, we deprive them of necessary life experiences. We deprive them of learning how to solve their own problems.

There are many ways that parents can encourage their teens to be independent. Knowing that teens usually live up to the expectations of significant others such as parents and teachers, let them know that you have confidence in them and that you trust their judgment. Begin treating them more like an adult and less like a child. Allow them to do things for themselves. Give them as many opportunities as possible to make independent decisions and choices. And let them learn from their mistakes.

Don't expect major changes to occur overnight. Being an adult in training involves lots of practice and trials and errors. But gradually, over the years and with your guidance and encouragement, your son or daughter will have the tools and experience necessary to enter the next phase of development—adulthood.

$$\diamond$$

A DIFFICULT THING FOR A PARENT TO DO ◇ As parents, we must learn to gradually let go of our teenagers. Although it's difficult to do, we must learn to trust them to act with the morals and values we have taught them. *Laura S. Petelle, Northbrook, Illinois*

CHOICES AND DECISIONS ◇ Give all children, especially teenagers, as much freedom as possible in making decisions about their lives. Then when you have to say no, they will value your opinion and generally listen without resistance. Teens are eager to be independent. The experience they get in making their own decisions as teens will be of value to them in their adult life. *Virginia Bourgeous, Syracuse, Utah*

IT'S YOUR CHOICE ◇ My wife and I offer our teenage daughter more and more privileges as she demonstrates to us her ability to make mature choices and good judgment. For example, when she showed she could make safe choices as she drove with her learner's permit, we allowed her to get her driver's license. Privileges can also be taken away if we don't think she is using the type of judgment that is appropriate for a specific activity. Reinforcing good choices by offering new privileges is a great way to teach responsibility to teens. *Paul Dulberg, Hayward, California*

ORE FREEDOM DURING SENIOR YEAR ◇

Knowing that my daughter would be going off to college in less than a year, I gave her more freedom during her senior year in high school. I let her attend functions and go to places that I had previously disapproved of. In doing so, I was permitting her to experience some of the freedom she would have the following year, but with the safety net of being close to home instead of being thousands of miles away from her family. She made some mistakes that senior year, but we were there to help her pick up the pieces. She went on to college the next year and has been quite successful in her studies. Just the opposite happened to two of her friends who had always been kept on a very short leash by their parents during high school. They went so wild with the newfound freedom at college that they were forced to drop out and return home. *L.M., Honolulu, Hawaii*

TEEN TALK

Let us make as many of our own decisions as you can. Parents think of us as being young, but remember that we see ourselves as being quite old and mature. (Kelly, New Jersey)

◇

I really appreciate my mom for allowing me to learn from my own mistakes. She freely offers her advice and opinion, but ultimately allows me to make many of my own decisions. I have learned a lot from the mistakes I made because they were my responsibility—not my mom's. (Alicia, New York)

A WONDERFUL NEW RELATIONSHIP DEVELOPED ◇

At a certain point I realized that my kids didn't need milk and cookies anymore. Not only did our relationship mature from that point on, but I started doing some things for myself. I decided to enroll at the local community college. It was great to realize that it's never too late to live your dreams. *F.E.S., San Jose, California*

LIFE'S LESSONS COME FROM LIFE'S EXPERIENCES ◇

Be cautious, but don't be overprotective.

Some of life's best lessons come from life's experiences. *Marilyn Tipp, Omaha, Nebraska*

MAINTAINING A BALANCE OF "LETTING GO"
◇ One of the most difficult aspects of parenting teenagers is to maintain the delicate balance between being overprotective and underprotective. There are dangers at both ends of the continuum. I know of one situation where a mother was too protective of her teenagers; she tried to shield them from everything. She justified her strict rules on the basis that "she was doing it for their own good." Her teens felt so smothered by her protectiveness that they moved out of the family home as soon as possible, and their relationship with their mother remains estranged even today. *Bob Wadley, Spanish Fork, Utah*

DON'T OVERMANAGE
◇ I learned with experience that parents can overmanage their children by nagging about homework, reminding them about time, and being overinvolved in their projects. If I had to do this over again, I would have let him fail with smaller items and projects at a younger age. It would have been hard to do, but it would have taught him about the consequences of his actions. *Dolly Hickey, Clearwater, Florida*

✦✦✦✦✦✦✦✦✦✦✦✦✦✦✦✦✦✦✦✦✦✦✦✦✦✦✦✦✦✦✦✦✦✦

PICK YOUR BATTLES

✦✦✦✦✦✦✦✦✦✦✦✦✦✦✦✦✦✦✦✦✦✦✦✦✦✦✦✦✦✦✦✦✦✦

You and your teen will differ on many issues. Some issues will be of fundamental importance to you; others will be only semi-important or trivial. Experienced parents recommend ignoring as much as you can and saving your strength and thunder for the issues that you have decided are nonnegotiable.

◇

DON'T SWEAT THE SMALL STUFF ◇ My husband and I sat down and figured out which behaviors we could tolerate from our teen and which ones we wouldn't. We chose not to sweat the minor stuff, but we agreed to come down hard on potential problems such as drug use or poor grades. We even agreed on constructive ways of dealing with these issues in case they occurred. Afterward, we talked to our teen about the issues that were of importance to us and the consequences that we would follow through on if any of them occurred. We believe that knowing the consequences of specific behaviors—long before there are any signs of them—is a deterrent for them to ever occur. *Leith Harris, Windsor, California*

IS THIS ISSUE WORTH A BATTLE? ◇ Years ago my teenage daughter and I had a big argument in front of one of my friends. I had just told my daughter that she couldn't get her ears pierced. After my daughter left the room, my wise friend said, "Why not let your daughter get her ears pierced? Is this issue really that important? Let the child win sometimes—on issues that are not really that important. Pick your battles for those few, but really important issues that you won't compromise on. And maybe your child will let you win sometimes!" *Glinda Goodwin, Fremont, California*

SOME ISSUES ARE WORTH FIGHTING OVER ◇ Some teenagers like to test their parents and fight over just about everything: makeup, hairstyles, body piercing, homework, chores, etc. Since you can't battle over everything, I decided which issues were really important to me. They are school, drugs, and alcohol. Things like hairstyles are not an issue; if my daughter can live with it, so can I. *Anonymous*

WILL IT MATTER NEXT YEAR? ◇ Be selective in deciding what is worth fighting about. As much as possible, concentrate on those things that affect the long-term development of mind, body and soul. Apply the "long-term rule of thumb": Will it matter next year? If not, forget it. For example, will the messy state of her room matter to her long-term development? Probably not. Close the door. *Linda Sanderson, Garland, Texas*

SPIKED HAIR IS HER CHOICE ◇ When my daughter came home with spiked hair, I shared my dislike for it but told her that her hairstyle was her choice. Hair is far too insignificant to allow it to come between us. I did ask her to consider if the teasing and ridicule she might receive from others would be worth it. I told her that as long as she didn't complain about the teasing to me, I would defend her right to wear her hair in any style she wanted. For six months, she wore her hair spiked and took lots of ribbing, some of it mean and threatening. Looking back, she has some regrets because that's what her classmates remember about her. But she did learn how difficult it can be to live with a decision. She also learned that she couldn't use her appearance to get to her mom. *Anonymous*

MAKING THOSE TOUGH DECISIONS

Parents make countless decisions that help guide their teenagers through adolescence. But achieving that delicate balance between underparenting and overparenting can be challenging!

◇

LOVING THEM ENOUGH TO SAY NO ◇ Loving children doesn't mean never saying no; it means loving them enough to say no. *Anonymous, Pittsburgh, Pennsylvania*

"I NEED TO THINK ABOUT THAT" ◇ Occasionally, when my daughters would ask me for permission to do something that I wasn't sure about, I would respond, "I need to think about it," or "I need more information to make my decision." Frequently, during the few days I asked to ponder the idea or gather more information, my daughters lost interest in that activity or the plans fell through. So by asking for more time to consider their request, I found myself saying no much less than I did in the past. The extra time or information also helped me arrive at the right decision most of the time. When I did say no, my daughters knew that my decision was final. *Holly Frei, Mission San Jose, California*

"LET ME GET BACK TO YOU ON THAT" ◇ On any major issue involving our children, my husband and I talk it over together before we make our decision. Whenever our children request something from us that requires consultation with each other, we simply say in a friendly tone, "Let me get back to you on that." This comment usually appeases our children, because we didn't say no. This also works well if it appears that a child is playing one parent against the other. *Maureen Powell, Gahanna, Ohio*

"I'M GOING TO RELY ON YOUR GOOD JUDGMENT" ◇ I hated to say no to a request from one of my seven children, but I usually did if I didn't have enough information about a situation to feel comfortable saying yes. Now, if I don't feel totally comfortable making a decision, I'll ask the child making the request to help me with the decision. I'll say, "I don't feel like I have enough information to make a decision about this, so I am going to rely on your good sense and best judgment to make the decision." Although the children usually hated to make the final decision, it made them take some responsibility for their decisions. *Barbara Johnson, Reno, Nevada*

TRUST YOUR HUNCHES ◇ Experience as a parent has taught me to trust my hunches when I feel strongly about something. After I base a decision on one of these feelings, I tell my teenagers something like, "I am doing my best to make decisions that will protect you or are in your best interest. I don't always have all the information that I need, but often my feelings and hunches are right. I base my decisions on what is good for you." Even though they may not like my decision, they realize that I made it out of love and concern for them. *Cathy Jones, Santa Ynez, California*

"WHAT'S THE WORST SCENARIO?" ◇ Before deciding if one of our three daughters could do a specific activity or go somewhere new, we asked her to think of some of the potential dangers and things that could go wrong. If she and I thought that she could handle that situation, we usually let her go. We also thought of solutions to many of the potential problems before she left. Teenagers will react better and quicker to real-life situations if they have an opportunity to plan a strategy in advance. *L.W., Richmond, British Columbia*

TEEN TALK

We don't mind hearing no as much when we're given a reason. No is harder for us to accept when we hear, "Because I said so!" or "Because I'm the parent, that's why!" (Aimie, Ohio)

"STOP ME, PLEASE STOP ME!" ◇ When our daughter tells my wife and me about certain things that she knows with no uncertainty that we will not approve of, we think that it's her way to ask us to stop her before she does it. And we do! It's easier, we believe, for our daughter to tell her peer group that her mean parents won't let her do something, than it is to tell them that she doesn't think it's a good idea or something that she doesn't want to participate in. As parents, we need to be aware of these cues and to respond accordingly. *P.D., Queens, New York*

"ARE YOU ASKING FOR MY OPINION OR FOR MY PERMISSION?" ◇ After many years of trying to keep my daughters safe by refusing to allow them to participate in what I perceived to be risky activities or go out with friends who tended to get into trouble, I realized that they often lied to me and did what they wanted, no matter what I said. So now, when they ask for my permission to do something that I don't approve of, I simply say, "Are you asking for my opinion or for my permission? Don't lie to me, just tell me what you are going to do. I'm not going to stop you from doing it, because you've proven to me and your father that you're going to do it anyway. You get to live with your consequences, not me!" *F.E.S., San Jose, California*

"YOU DON'T TRUST ME, DO YOU?" ◇ Whenever I hear that comment from one of my teens in response to hearing that they can't attend a specific activity, I reply, "I trust you, but I don't trust this situation for your age group. I'm going to listen to my instincts this time." Even though they may still argue about my ruling, I believe that they at least understand my concerns. *T.A.R., Tucson, Arizona*

"HERE'S MY REASON" ◇ Never beat around the bush about your reasoning for a particular decision or fail to explain it at all. Teens especially dislike hearing "Because I said so," as an explanation. Teenagers are more apt to accept the decision if your reasoning is explained clearly and truthfully. For example, an explanation for not buying another car would be, "There are many reasons why your mom and I will not buy another car at this time, but the main one is that we can't afford the payments right now. We also feel that we can get by fine if we continue to share the two cars we have. We just need to do some good advance planning and each volunteer to use public transportation occasionally." *C.E., New London, Wisconsin*

WHY AM I SAYING NO? ◇ Sometimes, when I have the inclination to say no to a request of one of my children, I question my own reasoning first. I ask myself, "Why not?" If I have some strong reasons to deny their request, I stick with my inclination to say no. Otherwise, I usually give in and allow their request. For me, the inclination of saying no is because of my difficulty in letting go of my teens. This simple process has helped me to evaluate if I am being overprotective or reasonable in my response. *R. Merrill, Orem, Utah*

LET SOMEBODY ELSE RAIN ON THEIR PARADE ◇ A few years ago, a relative's son, age thirteen, came home one October afternoon and announced that he and his friends had decided to go to Florida (from California) for March break. An older brother would be driving, and they would be sleeping on the beach, etc., etc. My relative said nothing, except "That's interesting, we'll have to sit down and discuss it when we have more time." In the meantime, one of the other parents blew his top and nixed the proposed trip. My clever relative was not seen as the one to rain on the parade. *S.S., Toronto, Ontario*

MOM TAKES THE HEAT ◇ My teens frequently felt pressure from their friends to do things that they weren't comfortable participating in. So they frequently took me up on my offer to take the blame for them. For example, it was easier for them to say "My mom won't let me," instead of saying, "I don't want to." I didn't mind being the "bad guy." I remember all too clearly the powerful tug of peer pressure during my own adolescence. *Holly Frei, Mission San Jose, California*

DIVIDE AND CONQUER ◇ It's best if both parents are in accord with the major decisions concerning their teenagers. Talk with your spouse and try to come to an agreement before you announce the decision to your teen. Otherwise, you will undoubtedly hear comments such as, "But Dad said I could!" Teenagers are masters at playing one parent against the other until they get their way. *A.B., Bountiful, Utah*

AUTHOR'S NOTE: *Much of the conflict between parents during the teen years comes from disagreeing with each other over the answer to a teen's request or the solution to some issue or problem. One way to avoid much of this conflict is to allow the parent who will be most affected by the outcome of a request to be the one to make the final decision, or the parent with the most expertise in a particular area can have the final say. It helps to agree in advance about these issues as to which parent will take the lead on a particular issue.*

3

TALKING AND LISTENING TO YOUR TEEN

I have come to think listening is love.
— BRENDA UELAND

THE GIFT OF LISTENING

When you are troubled or need advice, to whom do you turn? Think about it. Is it the person who is always quick with advice and seems to know what's best for you and most other people as well? Is it someone who can lecture you about your problem? Or is it someone who will listen with quiet enthusiasm while you sort out your own answers? Chances are, you'll choose the good listener. So will your teenager.

Everyone wants to be listened to. We love the attention, the feeling of being valued, and feeling important enough for someone to take the time to listen to what we have to say. We appreciate those instances when a listener gives us undivided attention—for at that moment in time nothing is more important to the listener than what we have to say. Unfortunately, these moments don't happen as frequently as we would like.

If your household is like ours, most conversations take place between two or more individuals, each involved in a

24

different activity while simultaneously keeping one eye on the stove, in a book, or on television. But there is a need in our families for active listening, a time when we listen to each other with all of our attention and concentration. Teenagers desperately yearn for this kind of attention from their parents. The teenage years are a time of turmoil and change, a time when teens need a sounding board to help them cope with their new experiences.

In my travels and talks with parents, I was struck by the frequency with which parents shared how the simple act of listening had helped to transform their relationship with their son or daughter. The tip most frequently offered by parents to other parents for the teen years was "listen to your teenager." One mother commented, "When I take the time to concentrate on what my daughter is saying, I understand her world better." For parents to understand their child's world—his or her thoughts, feelings, dreams, and fears—is high on the wish list for most teenagers. But according to teens, it often doesn't happen.

Although many teens feel extremely close to their parents and feel listened to by at least one parent, some said that what little communication they do have with their parents is negative. They report more nagging, lecturing, advising, and negative criticism than listening. Some teens report feeling totally estranged from their parents. Many of these couldn't remember the last good talk they had with their parents. "They're too busy with other aspects of their life" was an all too common explanation.

Busy or not, we need to listen. The rewards are worth it. By listening, you will better understand your child's view of the world, the issues of importance to her, and problems she may be facing. The more you understand her feelings, the better you can respond to her in a helpful way. Your relationship will grow closer, and you will teach each other new things. But the greatest reward of listening to your child is what she will tell you. My daughters share their innermost thoughts with me when I take the time to listen to them. I feel a closeness, a oneness to them as I travel through their uncharted world. And each time that I experience this, I tell myself that I must take the time to do it more often.

Listed at the end of this section are two parent skill builders that offer simple guidelines for becoming a better, more empathic listener. Once a day, at dinnertime, bedtime, or some other special time, use these listening skills with your teen—even if only for a few minutes. And at least once a week have an extended listening time (thirty to sixty minutes) with him or her. We only have one chance to know our children as they advance through each stage of development. Don't miss out. The time to start, if you haven't already, is today.

◇

DROP EVERYTHING WHEN THEY NEED TO TALK ◇ Listen to your teenager. Drop whatever you are doing, even if it's important, whenever your child tells you that she needs to talk to you. *Linda Robinson, Lincoln, Nebraska*

TUNING IN TO NEW BEHAVIORS ◇ As parents, we sometimes ignore obvious signals from our teenagers that point to a problem or issue affecting their life. Tuning in to little indicators and signals and checking them out with our children can help us to nip things in the bud before they become big problems. A reassuring comment like, "You seem to be more pensive than usual. If you ever need to talk about a problem, you know I'm here for you," will demonstrate your empathy and caring to your child. Also, some new behaviors may be caused by drinking or drug abuse and should be checked out with your child. Similar to how only a small portion of an iceberg can be seen above water, these little indicators and signals can point to a bigger and deeper problem below the surface. *Susie Anderson, Mission San Jose, California*

DON'T OVERREACT ◇ In dealing with my teenage daughter, I have found it helpful to be careful not to overreact or show panic or shock to anything she says, especially when she is talking about a concern or problem. It's even more difficult to do when you hear about something she or her friends have done, or a sticky jam she has gotten herself into. I freely offer my advice and share my feelings about certain issues, but I try to remain calm. I believe that when parents overreact to something their teenagers tell them, there's a good chance that they won't hear too many more concerns and problems that their children may be dealing with. The teens will probably clam up or share their concerns with someone else, probably their friends. *N.L. Colvin, Chapel Hill, North Carolina*

TEEN TALK

Listen when we need to talk to you, even if it's something you don't want to hear. (Aileen, California)

◇

I hardly talk to my parents anymore because they blow up when I tell them things. I wish that I could be more open with them and not have to worry about how they will respond. (Julie, Nevada)

◇

My mom tells me that I can talk to her about anything. But when I do, she gets mad and starts yelling. (James, Oregon)

◇

My parents don't have a clue as to who I really am. They never take the time to even ask me about my day, let alone my life. (David, New York)

VALUABLE LESSON LEARNED ◇ Raising nine children, I have learned some valuable lessons. One significant lesson, after much trial and error, was that teens often just need a parent to listen to them without offering advice or counsel. Just talking about a problem or issue often helps to clarify things. I learned that the less I offered my advice, the more my children asked me for it. *Pat Deggelman, Fremont, California*

MOM AS FRIEND ◇ Occasionally one of my four daughters would say, "Mom, I need some advice as a friend, not a mom." I would always listen to them carefully and try to answer from a friend's perspective. But sometimes, when I had a comment or two to add as a mom, I would ask them if I could also respond as their mother. They always seemed interested in getting both perspectives. *Edith Schuette, Ukiah, California*

A PARENT'S PRESENCE IS COMFORTING ◇ I've realized that my teenage daughter sometimes prefers not talking at all when she's upset. My presence alone seems to be comforting to her. *A.P., Des Moines, Iowa*

LISTENING WITHOUT JUDGMENT ◇ As I reflect back on parenting my five children, with two already grown, the one thing that I wish I had been better at is listening to my children—really listening—and without prejudgments. *B.B., Bountiful, Utah*

EVERY TEENAGER NEEDS AN ADULT CONFI-DANT ◇ There's usually some topic, issue, or dilemma that a teenager is confronted with, but which they don't feel comfortable talking to their own parents about. Therefore, it's a good idea for every teenager to have a

---

PARENT SKILL BUILDER

Active Listening

The purpose of this exercise is to practice listening with your undivided attention. Although this sounds simple, it's not. It takes much more energy than a typical conversation. A good time to practice these skills is when your child expresses an interest in talking or whenever you are alone together (in the car, at your child's bedtime, etc.) Take the phone off the hook or shut the door for privacy if needed.

1. Give your child your full attention.
2. Maintain eye contact with your child.
3. Concentrate on what your child is saying.
4. Nod your head occasionally to show your involvement without interrupting.
5. Don't change the subject. Let your child lead the conversation.
6. Do more listening than talking. This is why we have two ears and only one mouth.

Notice how your child reacts to your new listening skills. Did she seem more talkative than usual? Did she seem pleased by your attention? What other observations did you make? After you feel comfortable with active listening, go on to the next skill builder, Empathy.

PARENT SKILL BUILDER

Empathy

Now that you have practiced active listening, it's time to add empathy to your communications repertoire. Empathy goes beyond active listening. It involves understanding the deeper meaning and feelings of an individual. It's listening with your third ear.

1. Use all of the listening skills listed in the previous skill builder, Active Listening.
2. Try to put yourself in your child's shoes. If you were your child right now, how would you be feeling? As she talks, what are her words and body language telling you about her feelings?
3. Instead of telling her "I know how you feel," let her know that you understand her feelings with a comment such as, "You must feel so *confused* after getting conflicting messages from your friends."
4. Communicate to her that you acknowledge and accept her feelings.
5. Don't deny or minimize her distress by saying "You shouldn't be so upset" or "It's not really that bad."

Note: A helpful way to understand someone's feeling is to listen to her words and respond to the feeling (emotional meaning) behind the words. For example, if your daughter tells you, "I caught my boyfriend holding hands with Marie today at school," what would be the feeling or emotion behind that statement? Depending on how she said it, she could be feeling outraged, hurt, furious, threatened, etc. A simple empathic comment could be, "You must have been so hurt when you saw them together."

special trusting relationship with a responsible adult outside of the immediate family. That person could be a
teacher, counselor, neighbor, minister, aunt or uncle, etc.
Ideally, it's usually best if the youngster can talk to his/her
own parents, but it's better to talk to another responsible
adult rather than not talk to anyone at all. If you sense
that your teenager is dealing with a dilemma that they're
not willing to talk to you about, encourage them to talk to
someone else that you trust. *Glinda Goodwin, Fremont,
California*

BEST PLACES FOR TALKS

THE BEST PLACE FOR HEART-TO-HEARTS ◇ I
have noticed that some of the best heart-to-heart talks
that I have had with my two teenage sons did not take
place in our home. They most frequently take place when
I'm alone with one son during a walk after dinner or in
the car as we drive to one of their activities. Now that I
know this, I try to make myself even more available for
these kinds of activities. *D.C., Dublin, California*

A "GOOD NIGHT" TALK ◇ Never underestimate the
value of saying good night to your teenagers, no matter
how old they are. I still will lie down next to my daughter
on her bed for a couple of minutes in the evening and
contemplate the shadows on the ceiling. It's kind of like
lying in the grass and looking at the clouds. I'm not stand-
ing over her, I'm on her level. You can't fall asleep,
though—you have to listen! *Donna J. Carlyle, Austin,
Texas*

TALKS IN THE DARK ◇ When my son was younger, I
used to tuck him into bed each evening. But now, as a
thirteen-year-old, he thinks he's too old for that, and I
agree. So we started what we call "check-in time," a time

(usually once a week) when I sit in a chair next to his bed and we just talk. We've had some of our best talks and discussions sitting there in the dark together. It's a great way to check in with each other and have an uninterrupted half hour together. *Charly Kasal, St. Paul, Minnesota*

TEEN TALK

The best talks I have had with my dad were when we went fishing or hunting together—just the two of us. (T.A., Arizona)

LATE NIGHT TALKS ◇ Some of the most precious, heart-to-heart talks I have had with my teenagers were late at night after they came home from an evening activity. I would usually wait up for them. They always seemed more eager to talk about their evening activities immediately after they came home; they weren't as talkative the following day. They often opened up during these late-night chats and talked freely about their boyfriends and girlfriends, their hopes and dreams, their fears, or whatever was on their minds. I looked forward to these heart-to-heart talks. *R. Merrill, Orem, Utah*

SWING TALK ◇ There's something magical about front porch swings—or so it seems. Some of the best moments with my family have been on our front porch swing. As I sit with my teenagers on the swing, they talk. We communicate better there. They relax and tell me what they are thinking about. They ask me questions. Parents of teens know how rare this sort of thing can be, but it's not rare on our front porch swing. Perhaps it's a teen version of being rocked by the mother. Whatever it is, it works! *Denise Rounds, Tulsa, Oklahoma*

KNOW WHEN TO BACK OFF TOO

DON'T FORCE COMMUNICATION ◇ Don't try to force communication with your teenagers when they are moody or not talkative. They will probably clam up even more if you do. Instead, be patient and wait for a time when they are more willing to talk. Learn their cues and times for when they want to talk. The result will probably be more positive. *Bob Wadley, Spanish Fork, Utah*

LEARNING THEIR SIGNALS ◇ Teens fluctuate between needing your attention and not wanting anything to do with you. With experience, you can learn the signals that mean to back off or become more involved. *Patricia Stahler, Niles, California*

DON'T FORCE THEM TO TALK ◇ Whenever I sensed that my oldest daughter had a problem, I would force her to talk about it. Later, after she had graduated from high school, she told me that she had appreciated my concern, but she didn't like being forced to discuss an issue when she didn't feel like talking. This was good feedback for me to hear, and I have since learned to know when to pursue a talk and when to back off with my other children. *A.B., Bountiful, Utah*

KNOWING WHEN TO BE LESS INTRUSIVE ◇ During my daughter's early teen years, I gradually learned the importance of allowing her to be silent when she wanted to be. If I ask her many questions about her day and school, she often clams up and is sullen. However, if I make myself less intrusive into her life but available to listen, she soon comes in to talk. I have witnessed her friends' parents nag their teenagers a lot, and I know how much teens hate that. *Patricia Tolbert, Baton Rouge, Louisiana*

COMMUNICATION STOPPERS: NAGGING AND LECTURING

Teenagers are no different from the rest of us—they hate being nagged, lectured to, and criticized. They were quite vocal about this in my talks with them. Here is a small sampling of their comments.

TEEN TALK

Teenagers hate when parents nag them. (Emily, Utah)

◇

Teens hate to hear a parent begin a sentence with something like, "When I was a teen . . ." Life as a teenager in the 90s is very different than life was as a teen in the 50s, 60s, or even the 70s. Sure, there will always be some commonalities between teens from different eras, but there are always differences too. We want you to recognize those differences. Stop comparing us to your teen years. It doesn't work. Instead, try to understand us as unique individuals with unique dilemmas and issues. What worked for you twenty or thirty years ago may not work for us in the 90s. (Aileen, California)

◇

Teens hate negative criticism. It's like another slap in the face. Instead, encourage us and compliment us when we do something right. (Kim, California)

◇

Don't tell us that something isn't important. It probably is to us. (Arinn, California)

DEALING WITH MOODINESS
AND DEPRESSION

One of the most frustrating aspects of living with teenagers is dealing with their frequent mood swings. This is especially true for pre- and early adolescents. Rest assured that your child is not becoming a social misfit when she becomes uncommunicative, sullen, or fixated on something that seems trivial to you, such as her hair. Moodiness is very common among teens. Mood changes are often unpredictable and seem to come out of the blue and for no reason. Luckily for all, sour moods usually disappear as quickly as they came.

Since younger adolescents seem to be more prone to bouts of moodiness than older teens, some individuals believe that mood swings are brought on by puberty and its related hormonal and physical changes. Teens at this age also seem to be more fragile psychologically. Trivial issues and minor disappointments, real or imagined, can turn into major predicaments in the eyes of a teen.

Parents often become frustrated when they try to find a reason for their child's moodiness or try to solve the problem themselves. Neither of these tactics works. Chances are, even your teen doesn't know the reason for her behavior. The best advice for parents is to back off and give some space to your moody teen. Be as understanding and supportive as possible and tell him that you are available to listen when he needs to talk. Dealing with a teen's mood swings is not easy on family members, but remember, it's a much worse experience for the teen.

There is a big difference between occasional mood swings and a major depression, and parents should be able to know the difference. A major depression could lead to suicide, which, along with accidents and homicides, is one of the leading causes of death for teenagers. Review the information about teen suicide in the parent skill builder at the end of this section. Be especially observant of your teen's behavior after she experiences a perceived negative event in her life such as divorce or separation of parents, breakup with a friend or of a romance, or failure in achieving an important goal.

Here are a few other good ideas from parents in dealing with teen moodiness:

BACK OFF WHEN MOODY ◇ I have learned to back off and respect my daughter's need for privacy when she's in a low mood. At the most, I'll let her know that I'm available to talk to if she wants. She usually bounces back to her cheery self in a matter of hours. *S.B., San Diego, California*

TEEN TALK

Eleven is a tough age. We have to worry about lots of new things: boys, clothes, appearance, and harder work at school. Until this year I have not been moody at all. It is like eleven is some magic mood age for teens. (Kate, Pennsylvania)

THE BEST ADVICE ◇ A long time ago a friend gave me the best advice for dealing with a teenager's moodiness. She told me that in most situations it's better to do too little than too much. *Anonymous, Salem, Oregon*

DON'T ARGUE WHEN MOODY ◇ My advice is to not argue with a teen who is irritable; it will only make matters worse. Wait until his mood shifts so he will be more open to what you have to say. *M.L., Boise, Idaho*

PROFESSIONAL HELP FOR DEPRESSION ◇ For a long time I attributed my teen son's moodiness and depression to typical turbulence caused by hormonal levels. Then he was diagnosed as being manic-depressive. I felt terrible finding out that he had a major illness all along. I encourage parents to have their child examined by the most appropriate professional for any prolonged depression. *D. Curiel, Antelope, California*

PARENT SKILL BUILDER

Recognizing Suicidal Behavior

EARLY WARNING SIGNS OF SUICIDE AMONG ADOLESCENTS

1. Direct suicide threats or comments such as "I wish I was dead"; "My family would be better off without me"; "I don't have anything to live for."
2. A previous suicide attempt, no matter how minor. Four out of five people who commit suicide have made at least one previous attempt.
3. Preoccupation with death in music, art, and personal writing.
4. Loss of a family member, pet, or boy/girlfriend through death, abandonment, breakup.
5. Family disruption such as unemployment, serious illness, relocation, divorce.
6. Disturbances in sleeping and eating habits and in personal hygiene.
7. Declining grades and lack of interest in school or hobbies that had previously been important.
8. Drastic changes in behavior patterns, such as a quiet, shy person becoming extremely gregarious.
9. Pervasive sense of gloom, helplessness, and hopelessness.
10. Withdrawal from family members and friends and feelings of alienation from significant others.
11. Giving away prized possessions and otherwise "getting affairs in order."
12. Series of "accidents" or impulsive, risk-taking behaviors; drug or alcohol abuse; disregard for personal safety; taking dangerous dares.

WHAT TO DO WHEN YOU SUSPECT THE DANGER OF SUICIDE

1. Ask direct, straightforward questions in a calm manner: "Are you thinking about hurting yourself?"
2. Assess the seriousness of the suicidal intent by asking questions about feelings, important relation-

ships, others with whom the person has talked, and the amount of thought given to the means to be employed. If a gun, pills, rope, or other means has been procured and a specific plan has been developed, the situation is very dangerous. Stay with the person until help arrives.

3. Listen and be very supportive, without giving false reassurances.

4. Encourage the young person to get professional help and provide assistance.

WHAT NOT TO DO

1. Do not ignore warning signs.

2. Do not refuse to talk about suicide if a young person approaches you about the topic.

3. Do not react with horror, disapproval, or repulsion.

4. Do not give false reassurances ("Everything is going to be all right") or platitudes and simple answers ("You should be thankful for . . .").

5. Do not abandon the young person after the crisis has passed by or after professional counseling has begun.

Reprinted from *Living With 10- to 15-Year-Olds: A Parent Education Curriculum*, Center for Early Adolescence, Univ. of North Carolina at Chapel Hill, Carrboro, NC, rev. ed. 1992. Used with permission

For Further Information or Assistance

National Adolescent Suicide Hot Line, 1-800-621-4000. Available twenty-four hours a day for teenagers contemplating suicide. Parents may also call for assistance or information.

Local parental stress and suicide prevention crisis lines are available in most cities. Contact your local directory assistance for these phone numbers.

Recommended Reading

Adele Faber and Elaine Mazlish, *How to Talk so Kids Will Listen and Listen so Kids Will Talk* (New York: Avon), 1980.

Kathleen McCoy, *Understanding Your Teenager's Depression* (New York: Perigee), 1994.

Gerald Oster, *Helping Your Depressed Teenager: A Guide for Parents and Caregivers* (New York: Wiley), 1995.

Louise Felton Tracy, *Grounded for Life! Stop Blowing Your Fuse and Start Communicating with Your Teenager* (Seattle: Parenting Press), 1994.

4

RESPONSIBILITIES

Misery is when you make your bed and then your mother tells you it's the day she's changing the sheets.

— SUZANNE HELLER, *Misery,* 1964

Responsibility, having to account for one's actions, goes hand in hand with a teen's growing need for autonomy and independence. As parents gradually let go and offer more independence during the course of adolescence, they should also expect more responsibility from their teen. Maintaining a reasonable balance between the two is important. A teen who has a great deal of independence without responsibility can quickly get out of control and into trouble. On the other hand, a teen who has many responsibilities and little independence will lack many important life skills and experiences as he enters adulthood.

Experienced parents talked often about four areas of teen responsibilities. Their parenting tips are divided into those four areas: chores and allowance, clothing allowance, part-time jobs, and money management.

CHORES AND ALLOWANCE

It is not only reasonable to require your teenager to share in the household chores, it is also an important responsibility for him to learn. The more you involve him in the decisions about chores, the less chance you will experience the dreaded chore battles. For example, instead of arbitrarily assigning weekly chores and a time limit to complete them, sit down with your son and ask him if he has a preference from a list of chores you created. If his request is reasonable, the next step is to agree on a time line for specific chores to be completed. Once again, give him some leeway to make the decision himself. So what if the lawn is mowed on Friday instead of Wednesday or the dishwasher is unloaded in the afternoon after school instead of the morning? Experienced parents know that if a teen feels in control of his destiny, there will be less conflict about requests from the parents.

A tip I learned for younger children is also appropriate for teenagers: use the term *community service* instead of *chores.* "Chores" and "housework" are heavy-sounding words that are best not uttered around teenagers.

Listed below are some creative ways to involve your teen in "community service," and tips for dealing with the hot topic of allowances.

PLUCK A BUCK ◇ I used to spend a great deal of time nagging my kids to do their household chores, but that has changed since I started plucking money from their allowance for neglecting their work. Now, every Monday morning I place my children's weekly allowance, all in single one-dollar bills, in an envelope with their name on it. The envelopes are taped on the refrigerator. They can't take the money until the following Sunday evening. In the meantime, if they forget or refuse to do one of their scheduled chores, I pluck a buck from their envelope. I don't nag anymore; I just pluck a buck. On Sunday, they can keep what's left. After the first two weeks of watching their needed allowance dwindle away, they started being much more diligent about their responsibilities. Occasionally I even pluck a buck when they fight with each other. It works great! *Shelley McKinzie, Fremont, California*

"FAVOR JAR" ◊ As our children reached their teen years it seemed that they were always requesting time-consuming favors from us, without a "payback." To make this situation a bit more equitable, we established a job jar of simple chores. Whenever there was a request to "drive us to the mall" or the like, we required that a job be chosen from the favor jar and that the job be completed before the favor was granted. It helped to give the kids more of a sense of "give and take" in relationships and cut down on some of the less important requests for favors. *Vanetta Hayhurst, Farmington, Connecticut*

JOB JAR ◊ In addition to their regular chores, our teens sometimes enjoy the variety of choosing jobs from the "job jar." The job jar is a medium-size jar in which I have placed small strips of folded paper with easy 1- to 5-minute chores (clean the smudges on the refrigerator, sweep the front porch, etc.) listed on them. Once you pick a chore, you can't put it back into the jar; you must complete the chore. My kids complain more about their regular chores than the ones they pick out of the job jar; the idea of picking a chore at random is appealing to kids. *JoAnn Wadley, Spanish Fork, Utah*

COLOR-CODED CHORE LIST ◊ Our household chores used to be a major pain, lots of complaining from our three children and nagging from me, until I started a new and better-organized system. First, I called a family meeting and together we made a list of both daily and weekly chores. Second, we picked out those chores for which our children would be responsible. Then we divided those chores into three color-coded lists, each with morning, evening, and weekly chores. The lists are posted on the fridge and are rotated among the children each week. One week the child will be responsible for the yellow list, next week the green list, etc. All weekly chores must be done by noon on Saturdays. Now, because the children were involved in the planning and implementation of the project, the bickering about chores has been greatly reduced. *R.P., Houston, Texas*

CHOICE OF CHORES ◇ I've learned that my daughter responds more positively to household chores if I let her choose (within reason) which chores she wants to be responsible for. *Teresa Dulberg, Hayward, California*

WRITTEN CHORE LIST ◇ My teenagers respond better to a written list of chores than if I just tell them what to do. With a list, it's up to them to decide when to work the chores into their plans as long as they complete them by the deadline that I set. As they complete each chore, they cross it off the list. *Anne Kirby, Salem, Oregon*

BONUS OR PENALTY FOR WEEKLY CHORES ◇ My two children receive a weekly allowance for chores they do around the house. They each have an average of three chores to do each day. I subtract $1 for every chore not completed or if I had to nag them to do it. Occasionally, I'll also award a bonus buck for an extra chore completed on their own initiative. We use a chore chart on the refrigerator to help us keep track of the money earned. Chores not done are highlighted with a marker. It's been a fun way to get chores done each week. *Anne Scheidler, Indianapolis, Indiana*

LIST OF CHORES FOR PAY ◇ Our teenagers complained that they didn't have enough pocket change, so I posted a list of household chores and the amount I would pay for each one. They picked various chores, depending on how much money they wanted to earn. At the end of the week, they presented me with a bill describing the jobs they completed and how much I owed them. I always checked their work, then paid them. This was good training for the real world of work. *Donna Ruiz, Huntington Beach, California*

WEEKLY CHORE SCHEDULE ◇ If you have more than three children, I recommend posting a weekly chore schedule so you and your children can keep track of their responsibilities. Each Sunday I would post a schedule on the refrigerator for my six children to follow for the week. Each child's name was listed along the left-hand side of the poster and the various chores were listed along the top. A big X under a specific chore and in a child's column denoted a specific chore for the week. The chores would rotate each week. The children added some rules to help with coordination of the chores. For example, if one child didn't unload the dishwasher by dinnertime, he or she would get the added responsibility of loading the dishwasher after dinner. That alone was incentive to complete the chore in a timely fashion. *Mary Hopkins, Sacramento, California*

SEPARATE CHORES FOR EACH CHILD ◇ I have learned that my teens argue less with each other about their chores if they work independently of each other. In the past, when they both shared kitchen responsibilities, one child would complain that they couldn't wash the dishes because their sibling hadn't cleared the dirty dishes from the table. Now, I assign all related chores to one child for one week. They rotate chores and responsibilities every week. There is less finger pointing and blaming with this new practice. It really works! *Susie Anderson, Mission San Jose, California*

TEEN BEDROOM ◇ Instead of always nagging our teenage daughter to clean her bedroom, my husband and I decided that it's her private room and she's responsible for it. We provided a desk, lots of bookshelves, and a large closet to store all her things. Now, there are no big arguments about the state of her room. If it's tidy enough for her, then it's tidy enough for us. She has a sense of privacy and control about her room. Without any nagging and reminding, she has learned about responsibility and has gained a sense of independence. *Anonymous, Pleasanton, California*

WEEKLY ALLOWANCE EQUALS AGE ◇ A good rule of thumb that I use to determine the amount of weekly allowance for my daughter is one dollar for each year of her age. My daughter is thirteen years old now so she receives $13 a week for allowance. It provides pocket money for entertainment and personal necessities. *James Greenblat, San Francisco, California*

OPPORTUNITIES TO EARN MONEY ◇ In addition to their weekly chores, our children have ample opportunities to earn extra money for activities and items they want to buy. We pay them for ironing shirts, mowing the lawn, and other odd jobs around the house. Teenagers value things more if they pay for it themselves. *JoAnn Wadley, Spanish Fork, Utah*

TEENS RESPOND TO A SMILE AND HUMOR
◇ After all other approaches have failed, and if the issue is not serious, try humor. It's less threatening and controlling than a direct order or command. For example, after asking my son to pick up his bedroom, I'll tease him by saying, "In the meantime, please keep your bedroom door closed. I don't want the bacteria to invade the rest of the house," or I'll say, "My biggest fear is to be in your room and fall into one of your socks." My son usually responds with a sheepish smile. The message—clean your room— gets across, but in a lighthearted way and with a smile. *Anonymous, Ventura, California*

CLOTHING ALLOWANCE

There are two developmental stages in life when the issue of clothing turns into battles between parents and their offspring: the toddler and the teenager. As parents we have now survived the toddler years, and experienced parents of adolescents say it's even easier to survive the teen clothing battles. Parents of teens have solved the problem by not making clothing a big issue (see "Pick Your Battles" on page 17). They also recommend giving a monthly clothing allowance to teens along with full responsibility for their own wardrobes. Not only will there be fewer arguments about what's appropriate and what's not, but parents also claim they save money with this approach and that their teen learns some responsibility about clothing and money management.

It's a rite of adolescence to wear the "uniform" of the peer group. Every generation of teens had its own style of dress and parents who were aghast at it. My parents were no exception; two and a half decades ago, they voiced their disapproval of my bellbottom pants, tie-dyed shirts, long hair, pork chop sideburns, and necklace. I'm a little appalled now myself whenever I look at my once favorite necklace, a string of alternating wooden beads and cloves, hanging in my study as a reminder of a past life. These beads and the memories from my own youth help to put the current fashion trends in perspective for what they really are—a passing phase expressing youthful independence and individuality. Besides, two decades from now, this current "hip" generation will be just as appalled as I am now at what will be hanging in their closet and once hung from their neck, nose, or ears.

MONTHLY CLOTHING ALLOWANCE ◇ When our daughter entered adolescence it seemed as if her wardrobe was never large enough or fashionable enough to please her. We decided to establish a monthly clothing allowance so that she could have some control over the situation. At the beginning we sat down together to determine the amount we could afford each month, and exactly what items were to be purchased from the allotment. She became a careful shopper (always aware of sales), and sometimes even decided to forgo expensive designer labels in favor of greater quantity. *Vanetta Hayhurst, Farmington, Connecticut*

SOLUTION TO CLOTHING BATTLES ◇ Clothes shopping with my teenage daughter always ended in disaster until I increased her allowance and made her responsible for selecting and buying her own wardrobe. I have had to learn to live with my daughter's choices of clothing and to bite my tongue when I feel the urge to beg her to replace her tattered socks or underclothes. It's been an adjustment for my daughter, too. She's never told me so, but I think she now understands how expensive designer clothing items are because I never see any in her closet. *Terry Rowney, Mariposa, California*

MONTHLY ALLOWANCE ◇ We give our daughter a set amount of money every month from which she is expected to pay for her own activities and buy her clothes, gasoline for the car, cosmetics, and other items she needs. As a result, she has become a frugal shopper and learned how to sock money away for big-ticket items and costly outings. Not only has this practice taught our daughter the value of money and saving, but it has probably been a money saver for my wife and me. It puts the burden of buying decisions on the teen instead of us. *Dave Hopkins, Sacramento, California*

SET AMOUNT OF MONEY FOR CLOTHES ◇ We gave each child a set amount of money in late summer for their school clothes and once again in the spring for their summer clothes. They learned to be careful shoppers and seldom bought the expensive brand names. *A.B., Bountiful, Utah*

ALLOWANCE FOR CLOTHES ◇ Give teens as many opportunities as possible to earn their own money, and then allow them to buy their own clothes. This will give them valuable money management experience that will carry over to their adult life. *Virginia Bourgeous, Syracuse, Utah*

DRESS CODES ◇ In regards to my teenagers' style of dress, I am only concerned with immorality or illegality. Otherwise, it's OK with me. If it will wash off or out, grow out, or can be shaved or cut off, I leave it alone so long as it doesn't defy a dress code at school or work. I have learned that just because I think it's ugly or tasteless doesn't make it immoral. *Linda Sanderson, Garland, Texas*

TEEN TALK

My mom used to be strict about my clothes and general appearance. But over the years she has come to realize that my appearance has not affected my personality or schoolwork. And I respect my mom for giving me the freedom to express myself in the way I dress. (Brenda, Illinois)

"IF YOU WANT TO DRESS IN THAT STYLE, BUY IT YOURSELF!" ◇ When my daughter wants me to buy clothing that I don't approve of, I tell her to buy it with her own money if she likes it that much. She usually chooses not to if she has to use her own hard-earned money. *M.J.W., El Sobrante, California*

BUYING SHOES—ALWAYS A HASSLE ◇ Buying shoes for teenagers is always a hassle, especially over cost and brand name. My solution was to allow my son to buy two pairs of shoes per year, and I would pay a maximum of $50 per pair. My son did the shopping and selecting himself, but anything over $50 was his responsibility. His first purchase was a pair of "high hype" tennis shoes—for $120. It was hard for me to accept, but he paid the additional cost. After six months, when his expensive shoes looked just like his beat-up and battered $50 pair of tennis shoes, nothing had to be said. He has since become a very selective shopper. *Margaret Watkins, Omaha, Nebraska*

PART-TIME JOBS

For the past fifty years there has been a steady increase in the number of adolescents who work part-time while they attend high school. Today, approximately 75 percent of high schoolers work at part-time jobs, compared to only 4 percent of their counterparts in the 1940s. The expansion of retail stores and restaurants during the last four decades has opened up millions of part-time jobs that were quickly snatched up by teens. As the spending power of teens has increased, so has the variety of consumer goods for the lucrative teen market. Fancy stereos, designer clothes, and many leisure activities are no longer a match for a weekly allowance, so even more teens are lured into part-time jobs.

Research confirms what many parents already know about part-time jobs for teens: too many hours of work can have a negative effect on a teen's life. Teenagers who work long hours often spend less time with their family, participate in fewer extracurricular activities, and have a difficult time balancing other important activities. They also are absent from school more often, report enjoying school less, earn lower grades, and spend less time on their homework than students who do not work long hours.[10] Most experts recommend a maximum of fifteen to twenty hours of work per week for teens during the school year.

A part-time job can be a rewarding and educational experience for a teen. Being employed can teach a teen how to get and hold a job, how to budget time, and how to manage money. The best part-time jobs for teens, however, are ones that can maintain the delicate balance between work, school, family, and social activities.

Here are some tips from parents who have been through the world of part-time employment with their teens.

AGREE ON RULES FOR EMPLOYMENT ◇ It's a good idea to discuss and agree on some rules with your teen pertaining to his employment *before* he begins his job hunt. For example, what's the maximum number of hours he can work each week, what hours of the day or evening work best for his schedule, and what types of employment are acceptable and unacceptable? By talking about these issues before your teen begins his job search, he will have some clear guidelines in which to begin his job hunt and you will have some peace of mind that he will select a job that will work with his schedule. *M.J.D., Portland, Oregon*

"HOW WILL THIS JOB AFFECT YOUR LIFE?" ◇ Teenagers seldom think about how a new job will affect their lives. Before any of my teenagers could get a part-time job, I made them convince me that they could still find an appropriate amount of time for their academics, family, and social activities. I gave them a blank weekly calendar that had a small box or space for every hour in the day and evening, and I asked them to fill in all of their current obligations (school, homework, soccer or baseball practice, piano or flute lessons and practice time, at least four family dinner hours, time for boyfriend/girlfriend, family chores, etc.). My teens were amazed at how busy their schedule already was. They either came to the conclusion that they didn't have time for a new job, or would have to cut down the number of work hours from fifteen to ten, or would realize that they would have to give up something else on their current schedule before they could get a job. It was a valuable exercise for them to do and I highly recommend it for other teenagers as well. *F.H., San Francisco, California*

PART-TIME JOBS ARE GOOD—TO A POINT ◇ There are many advantages to having your teen work part-time: they learn discipline and responsibility, they learn how to deal with the general public, and they learn firsthand about the buying power of low income wages. This last point can become a real bonus for parents who have tried unsuccessfully to motivate their child to get good grades in high school and to have aspirations for college. I've seen many teens comment that they wouldn't want to work at a fast food restaurant for the rest of their lives. And soon thereafter, many parents report, grades begin improving without any coaxing by parents. The downside of part-time work for teens is that it can interfere with family and homework. Many employers don't care about your teenagers' school and family obligations and they often put pressure on them to extend their working hours. Work should be held to a maximum of fifteen hours per week so teenagers have time to decompress with family and friends and have enough time to keep up with their academics. *Bennett Oppenheim, Mission San Jose, California*

NO PART-TIME JOBS ON WEEKDAYS ◇ We only allow our teenage sons to work at part-time jobs on the weekends during the school year. Weekday jobs tend to crowd in on after-school sports, activities, and homework. *D.H., Fremont, California*

PRESSURE TO WORK LONG HOURS ◇ Parents should caution their teenager about being pressured by her employer to work longer hours than she originally agreed on. I've seen this happen with my own daughter and some of her friends. Employers often don't care about other obligations a teen has outside of the work environment, including school and family responsibilities. Impress upon your teenager that her future is more important than a low-paying temporary job. *Anonymous, Scottsdale, Arizona*

STARTING A NEIGHBORHOOD BUSINESS ◇ Our twin boys are adults now, but when they were teenagers, they were always asking us to buy things for them. They complained about never having enough money to buy the things themselves, so I came up with a plan that they enthusiastically endorsed. I fronted the money (over $2,000) for a drivable mower that also came equipped with a roto-tiller and plow. The three of us would be co-owners, so each boy owed me $700. The maintenance and servicing were my responsibility, and the boys were able to keep all of the money they earned. We live in a neighborhood with large lawns and long driveways, so in no time at all the boys had over twenty customers per week (mowing and tilling in the summer and snow plowing in the winter). They paid me back sooner than expected. As businessmen, they gained valuable experience working with adult customers, billing, and budgeting their time and money. It was a great job considering the alternative of working for minimum wage at a fast-food restaurant. Sometimes parents need to invest their time, creativity, and resources to help their kids get started in an activity. *John Rogers, Johnstown, Pennsylvania*

◆◇

MONEY MANAGEMENT

◆◇

Money management, like parenting, is one of those important life skills to learn, but one that is seldom taught to our youth, either by parents or the schools. Many financial and educational experts say the preschool years are a good time to begin teaching children about money. As a child matures, so should his knowledge about money management. And the family is the perfect training ground to learn about it. Allowances, savings accounts, and family finances provide the natural props by which to learn about the world of finance.

Teenagers as a group have become an earning and spending power to be reckoned with. Within the next few years, they are expected to pump over $100 billion into the economy annually. Even so, research discloses that most teens have very poor money skills. These same teens will be on their own soon, making and being responsible for their own financial decisions. The beginning of adolescence provides us parents with only a few precious years in which to teach our children about the real world of debits, credits, budgets, savings, and investments.

Here are some clever money-management tips that are recommended by other parents.

LEARNING MONEY MANAGEMENT ◇ When my husband and I grant a request from our teens for more independence, we, in turn, ask for more responsibility from them. For example, as their allowance grows, so does the need to learn money management. We are currently teaching both of our children (ages fourteen and twelve) how to write checks and balance a checkbook. We have decided to give them their own checking account when they are sixteen years old and a credit card when they are seventeen. Money management is one of those life skills that is rarely taught at home or in school. We hope these early lessons in life skills will instill values in our children that will carry through to their adult life. *Denise Rounds, Tulsa, Oklahoma*

MONTHLY ALLOWANCE ◇ Adolescence is a good time to switch from a weekly allowance to a monthly allowance so your teen will learn how to budget money over a longer time period. *T.L.M., San Diego, California*

YEARLY ALLOWANCE TEACHES MONEY MANAGEMENT ◇ Eight months ago my wife and I decided to switch from a weekly allowance to a yearly allowance for our two teenagers. They were sixteen and seventeen years old, so I thought it was a good time for them to learn about long-term money management. In a few years they would be on their own and I wanted them to be prepared for the real world. I went to the bank with them and assisted with opening a savings and checking account for each of them. I deposited their allowance (their regular weekly allowance for fifty-two weeks) for the entire year and explained that there would be no more money for twelve long months. I've been real proud of the way they've handled their money so far after eight months. *Anonymous*

INCENTIVE SAVINGS PLAN ◇ To encourage our teens to save money, we began an incentive program. At the end of each year, my husband and I calculated how much money each child had saved in their savings accounts. Then we matched it at the following rate: $1–50 we matched 50 cents for every dollar, $51–100 we matched 75 cents for every dollar, and any amount over $100 we matched dollar for dollar. *Mary McKinley, Reynoldsburg, Ohio*

TEEN PAID FAMILY BILLS ◇ When my son was sixteen years old and wanted everything under the sun, including his own car, I thought it was time for him to learn about family finances. So one evening, I asked him to help me pay the monthly bills. I showed him the amount of my monthly paycheck and how it was deposited in the checking account. Then I showed him the pile of bills for that month and taught him how to read a bill. I also taught him how to write a check and enter it into the check register. I left him on his own to pay the rest of the bills. He told me later that he actually enjoyed writing the checks. This little exercise was a real eye-opener for him; he never realized how much money it takes to run a family each month. And his begging for his own car has dropped off considerably. *D.R., San Diego, California*

PRETEND STOCK PORTFOLIO—ON-LINE ◇ Many of the computer on-line services such as America Online, Compuserve, and Prodigy have a financial program that tracks your stocks and mutual funds portfolio. A great way to teach older teens about the stock market and investment strategies is to have them create a pretend stock portfolio on-line. Tell your teen to imagine that

---

TEEN TALK

One month my mother handed me the monthly bills and her checkbook and asked me to pay all the bills and leave enough money for groceries. She told me that it would be good practice for me. I worked for hours trying to make the money stretch. From that day on, I never complained about not having a new pair of shoes or the latest styles. I never realized that there were bills for everything—even hauling out our trash. (Beth, Nebraska)

---

he has $5,000 to invest for one year. Teach him some basics about investing, share some interesting newspaper or magazine articles with him, and show him how to read the daily stock page. Then he's ready to pick out his individual stocks, mutual funds, or other investments with his pretend $5,000. Create the portfolio on-line and let him keep track of his investments. He will enjoy "selling" some investments and "buying" others. My son and I enjoyed checking on his investments and comparing my real investments to his. It was a fun and educational experience for both of us. *R.O., Pasadena, California*

Recommended Reading

Neale S. Godfrey, *Money Doesn't Grow on Trees: A Parent's Guide to Raising Financially Responsible Children* (New York: Fireside), 1994.

5

FRIENDSHIPS

I get by with a little help from my friends.
—JOHN LENNON

Never underestimate the importance of friendships during the adolescent years, say experienced parents. And the experts agree. Not only do teenagers spend most of their waking moments with their friends and peers, they are also influenced by them. Chances are, friends will influence many aspects of your teen's life—her behavior and decisions, her hair and dress style, and even her sense of self-worth and happiness.

Beginning in the preadolescent years, friends will play an increasingly important role in your child's life. Although this is quite normal, parents may have a difficult time seeing themselves being at least partially replaced by their child's peers. Cliques, those small groups of friends who regularly spend time together, provide a focal point for activities and a sharing of ideas and beliefs. Laurence Steinberg, author of *Adolescence*, says "The clique is the setting in which the adolescent learns social skills—how to be a good friend to someone else, how to communicate with others effectively, how to be a leader, how to enjoy someone else's company, or even how to break off a friendship that is no longer satisfying."[11]

The desire to fit in, to be part of a group, and to be accepted by peers is extremely important to adolescents. For some, just fitting in and being part of a group is good enough. Others may strive to be well liked or even popular with their peers. According to Steinberg, "The chief determinant of a youngster's popularity during adolescence is his or her social skill. Popular adolescents act appropriately in the eyes of their peers, are skilled at perceiving and meeting the needs of others, and are confident without being conceited. Additionally, popular adolescents are friendly, cheerful, good-natured, humorous, and, you may be surprised to learn, intelligent."[12]

Making friends comes quite naturally for some teens, while for others it's a struggle. Teens who are timid or lack social skills can have a difficult time meeting peers. Getting involved in activities that a teen enjoys is a good way to meet friends. Clubs, sports teams, church groups, scouting, and extracurricular activities are good bets. If your teen has had a difficult time making friends at school, encourage activities outside of school where he can get a fresh start with new peers. According to many parents, scouting and church groups did wonders for their teens. Not only are these two sources a good place to meet peers with similar values and interests, but they also provide ample opportunities to practice interpersonal and leadership skills. For teens who are shy and seem to want to make more friends, parents can *gently* encourage an occasional social interaction or offer an occasional suggestion such as, "Say hi to five people today." But pushing teens to be more social than they are ready for or making social plans for them usually backfires.

Some teens, no matter what strategies they try, never fit in during adolescence. However, many of these teens blossom later in college or in their work environment where the social circle is larger or more tailored to their personalities. This was evident at my twenty-year high school reunion. Many of my former classmates who were considered "nerds" or outcasts in high school are now successful in both their careers and personal lives, even surpassing many of our supposedly "popular" classmates of more than two decades ago. Nevertheless, the adolescent years can be painful for teens who don't fit in and heartbreaking for their parents. Sometimes, the most parents can do is to provide a supportive, caring, and nurturing home environment.

The issue of peer influence, which can be positive or negative with potentially long-lasting consequences, is of most concern to parents. Parents have a wide variety of approaches to dealing with questionable friends of their teenagers. Most of the parents I talked to said that it is quite common for a teen occasionally to select a friend who may not be desirable according to the standards of the parents.

But, they say, there's a good chance that the teenager will realize on his own that the friendship is not a good match.

Parents do, however, recommend keeping an extra eye on any friendship that you are not totally comfortable with. The vast majority of parents recommend using a subtle approach instead of directly discouraging a questionable friendship. Ultimatums and other direct approaches often create power struggles, ones that parents seldom win. One parent commented on the risk of using an ultimatum, "The teen will just dig her heels in deeper to protect and defend her friend and to demonstrate her independence, even if she knows you are right." Other strategies and suggestions are listed in this chapter beginning on page 59 (Questionable Friends).

The parenting tips in this chapter are divided into five sections: Friends and Peers, Questionable Friends, Peer Pressure, Phone Calls, and Teen Parties. Also, don't miss the two parent skill builders: Role-Playing (page 63) and A Parent's Guide to Teen Parties (page 71).

◇

FRIENDS AND PEERS

BE FRIENDLY TOWARD THEIR FRIENDS ◇ The best advice that I can offer parents of teenagers is to become friendly with your children's friends. Invite them to your home and occasionally ask them to stay for dinner. My children always appreciated my friendly manner toward their friends. Even though it's been years since my children moved out on their own and are in their twenties and thirties now, their friends still stop by and visit with me occasionally. These friendships have been a very valuable experience for me, and I hope for them, too. *Naomi Curry, Canal Winchester, Ohio*

PARENT NETWORK ◊ Get to know and stay in touch with the parents of your children's friends. This is just as important with teenagers as it was when your children were younger. It's important to have other parents to talk to. Chances are, you will discover that other parents share many of your feelings and agree with your decisions about parenting. Sometimes your kids make you feel as if you're the only parent with certain rules. It's also good to confirm details about sleepovers and other events with the host's parents. *Susie Anderson, Mission San Jose, California*

THE TRUE MEANING OF "POPULAR" ◊ My son complained to me that he was not part of the group of kids in his high school class who were "popular." In questioning him about these classmates, I asked him if they were truly "popular" or if they just had a certain image. After some thought to this question, my son replied that they were not in fact well liked. Recognizing the difference between being "popular" in the true sense of the word and simply projecting a rather unfriendly image and attitude has helped my son with his self-esteem. *Anonymous, Sierra Village, California*

WHAT A FRIEND IS ◊ Preadolescence is a good time to talk about friendships with your child. Preadolescents often have a skewed view of what a real friend is. I asked my daughter to make a list of "What a friend is" and another one for "What a friend is not." We had a great discussion as we went over the characteristics on her two lists. This simple exercise was a real eye-opener for my

---

TEEN TALK

My parents always had a positive relationship with my friends. They never tried to be "cool," but they were always friendly toward my friends. That was very important to me. (Kim, California)

◊

Learn not to judge a person by his or her appearance. (Aileen, California)

daughter and I believe it influenced her judgments from that point on in selecting friends. *Anonymous, Chicago, Illinois*

DON'T BE QUICK TO JUDGE TEENS ◇ Both as a high school principal and a father of teenagers, I have learned not to be quick to judge youngsters by my first impression only. Occasionally I have met teenagers and been quick to make a judgment about them based on their initial behavior or the way they dressed or looked, only to find out later that they had many very positive qualities. It takes time to really know a person. If you look beyond the surface, you will be frequently surprised to discover a very solid and likable person. *Bob Wadley, Spanish Fork, Utah*

LEARNING HOW TO BE A GOOD FRIEND ◇ Teenagers sometimes need to be reminded that in order to have a good friend, you must be a good friend. In years past, I occasionally suggested little acts of kindness that my daughter could do for a friend: pick some daisies and drop them off before an important recital, a short note of appreciation for being such a good friend, or a token pick-me-up gift for a friend down in the dumps. Now she does these little acts of kindness on her own—and her friends frequently reciprocate. *A.C., Reno, Nevada*

AUTHOR'S NOTE: *One powerful but often overlooked skill that attracts friends in swarms is being a good listener. Teens often think that it's what they say and do that attracts friends, but in fact it's the good listener who is in demand as a friend. Your teen may be interested in the listening tips listed on pages 28 and 29 (Active Listening and Empathy).*

ABUSED KIDS HAVE A NEED TO HELP OTHERS ◇ Children who have been physically or psychologically abused sometimes have a tendency to be attracted to other kids who need help. This need to be an enabler can sometimes lead them to troubled kids who tend to get into mischief. Such teens need a positive outlet to accommodate their drive to feel needed in lieu of getting involved with a wrong crowd. One outlet that has been used successfully is to have them volunteer for an organization that needs an extra helping hand. Church, school, and community programs offer many opportunities for teen volunteerism. A popular choice for some teens is the animal pound or veterinarian clinic. Such an experience occupies their time in a positive way and fulfills their desire to be needed. *Anonymous, Queens, New York*

UNREALISTIC VIEW OF FRIENDSHIPS ◇ Establishing friendships and being part of a group are extremely important to every teenager. A large part of teenagers' self-images comes from the friendships they establish and the groups to which they belong. Sometimes, teenagers have an unrealistic view that most friendships will last a lifetime. One day, when one of my daughters was upset about the loss of a friend, I explained that the majority of relationships made during high school are temporary. I further explained that after high school only a few of her current friends would probably remain friends for life. She seemed surprised but also relieved to hear this. This information seemed to help her cope better with her current loss and, hopefully, for others to follow. *A.B., Bountiful, Utah*

QUESTIONABLE FRIENDS

SUBTLE BEHAVIOR SHAPING WORKS BEST ◇ My wife and I learned a valuable lesson about trying to shape a teenager's behavior: be subtle instead of direct. We learned that if you tell teenagers not to do something, they will probably do it anyway as a way to rebel against authority. But if you are subtle in giving guidance, they will be less rebellious toward your advice. For example, our daughter had two close friends in junior high school. One friend, Lyla (not her real name), was a super role model for our daughter, but the other friend, Sandi (not her real name) wasn't. If we had told our daughter not to be friends with Sandi, she probably would have rebelled and pursued the friendship with even more vigor. Instead, we subtlely encouraged time spent with Lyla, and discouraged her involvement with Sandi. For instance, if our daughter asked to spend the night at Lyla's house, we would always say yes. If she wanted to stay at Sandi's house, we would usually discourage her with various excuses (school night, family obligation or outing, etc.), but we never said that we didn't want her to be friends with Sandi. Subtle behavior shaping worked much better for our two teenagers than direct orders. *Jim Goodwin, Fremont, California*

KEEP A CLOSER TAB WITH CERTAIN FRIENDS

◇ When my daughter would spend time with a friend who I thought was not a good influence on her, I would keep a closer tab on her. There were also a few friends with whom I would not let my daughter drive in the car. *Karen Dombek, San Diego, California*

NONVERBALLY SAYING "WE DON'T LIKE YOUR FRIEND"

◇ Our teens seldom brought home friends that my wife and I didn't approve of. But when they did, we didn't greet them with open arms and we didn't say anything good about them to our children. We didn't say anything bad about them either. But our children always seemed to get our message. This tactic seemed to work much better than verbally putting down their friends, which usually resulted in our children defending them and then being at odds with us. *David Hopkins, Sacramento, California*

"YOU CAN'T HANG OUT WITH THESE PEOPLE"

◇ Since teens are heavily influenced by their friends, I told my son that he cannot spend time outside of school with anyone who smokes, does drugs, or has a police record. Unlike some rules that I occasionally bend on, there are no exceptions to this rule. *Bennett Oppenheim, Mission San Jose, California*

JAIL TOUR ◇ If your teen tends to pick friends who frequently get into trouble, and they won't listen to your advice, take them on a tour of the local jail. Explain the possible consequences of hanging out with kids who get into trouble. Many cities and counties sponsor programs that feature former criminals offering a firsthand account of jail life. It's an eye-opener! *Helen O'Leary, Indianapolis, Indiana*

AUTHOR'S NOTE: *These programs are primarily recommended for individuals who have a history of trouble with the law. They have been known to be quite effective with teens who are on the verge of escalating their illegal activities. A tour of a long-term correctional facility such as a state prison can leave an impression on a young person that has more impact than a million words from parents and probation officers.*

"YOUR FAMILY IS YOUR GANG" ◇ After watching a television newscast about teenage gangs, I turned to my son and said with a smile, "Your family is your gang. We can have colors if you want to, but this is your gang right here. Don't even think about joining any other." Although I doubt if my son would ever join a gang, this casual comment left no mistake regarding my feelings about gangs. By sharing my feelings about a potential situation before it happens, I hope to influence my child in making the right choice if he ever has to face that situation. *Anonymous, Ventura, California*

NEGATIVE INFLUENCE FROM FRIENDS ◇ We noticed an almost immediate change in our daughter's personality when she began spending time with some new friends who had a tendency to get into trouble. We fought our impulse to tell her that she couldn't be friends with these individuals because such orders had often been countered with her own demonstration of independence. Instead, we occasionally pointed out how her personality had changed since befriending this new group of kids. In a very caring manner, we told her that the influence of her new friends had the effect of pulling a dark curtain over her radiant personality. We also told her that she had lost the sparkle in her eyes. Gradually, she began to realize these negative changes herself and she stopped seeing these particular friends. A few months later she thanked us for hanging in there with her, and she began describing this time in her life as "a dark time." *Anonymous, Hayward, California*

PEER PRESSURE

During childhood and continuing throughout adolescence, parents need to remind their children constantly of the importance of believing in themselves and having the courage to stand firm in their own beliefs and values. Of course, this is not always easy to do when pressured by peers. Depending on the situation, the pressure to conform can be tremendous on a teenager. Teens often capitulate to the wishes of a peer group so they won't appear different from the rest. Sometimes these are minor issues, but often they can be dangerous and life-threatening ones such as drinking and driving (or letting someone else do it) or taking drugs. Individuals with low self-esteem are especially prone to giving in easily to peer pressure. One of the most effective methods to counter peer pressure is to role play (see next page) possible situations before they occur, which gives the teen an advantage in dealing with his friend or peer group.

DEALING WITH PEER PRESSURE ◇ Peer pressure can have an incredible influence on most teenagers. Talk to your children no later than the early preteen years about peer pressure and how to deal with it. When children are warned about something in advance, they are more likely to use better judgment when the situation arises. Ask your teen questions similar to the ones below, using the names of friends who try to negatively influence your child: Do you think that Mark will feel bad if you flunk out of school because you ditched classes with him? Do you think that Mark will feel bad if you lose your license to drive because you got arrested for drinking and driving? The answer will almost always be no to questions like these. Also, explain that the individual who provided the pressure to do certain things will almost never take any responsibility for what happens. After the damage is done he will probably say, "You didn't have to do it" or "I didn't twist your arm." It is also helpful to role-play ways of saying no in peer pressure situations. *B.W., Tacoma, Washington*

PARENT SKILL BUILDER
Role-Playing

No one can always use good judgment on the spur of the moment when pressured to do something. But if a person rehearses similar situations in advance, he will be more likely to make a safe and wise choice.

Take time to role-play possible situations where peer pressure may occur, such as ones involving the subjects of alcohol, drugs, or sex. The more realistic the situation, the more helpful the role-playing will be for your teen. Also, role-playing is more effective if it involves a real upcoming situation such as a party, date, or outing. Usually a parent plays the role of his teenager's friend who is likely to try and manipulate the teenager to do something like try drugs or sex. The teen plays himself. Many parents also claim that it's fun to switch roles. For example, here's a typical conversation that could take place between a father and a son:

Father: "You and three friends are watching a movie at the drive-in theater when the driver pops open a beer for himself and hands one to you and your other friends. You're sitting there holding the unopened can as your friends pop open their beers. What do you do?"

Son: "I'd tell them that I'll be the designated driver."

Father: "That's one possibility. What if they begin teasing you about being too weak to be able to handle a beer?"

The son has a good response for that, too. The father has a few tips of his own on how to handle the situation. Together they continue sharing possible replies and actions to similar situations.

Here's another example in which a mother and a daughter role-play the sexual advances of the daughter's boyfriend:

Mother: "You and Roy [the boyfriend] are sitting in his car one evening and he reaches over and kisses you. You're enjoying the kiss when he suddenly begins to fondle your breasts. What do you do?"

Daughter: "I grab his hand and tell him to stop."

Mother: "But he says, 'Come on, everyone does it. I promise I won't do anything else.' "

Daughter: "I'd tell him that I'm not comfortable with that kind of touching; I'm just not ready for it yet."

Mother: "But what if he says, 'If you really love me, you would at least let me touch you.' He also tells you that all his friends do this with their girlfriends, so why do you have to be so different?"

Daughter: "I'd tell him that if he really loved me, he would respect my feelings. I'd let him know that this is something that I feel very strongly about. I would tell him that I know for a fact that many of my girlfriends do not let their boyfriends touch them there. And I would also let him know that I don't do things just because other people do them!"

The mother praised her daughter for her responses to such a difficult situation. Then they switched roles, and in doing so the mother offers the daughter some other strategies that could work in that situation.

Although role-playing may seem awkward to you at first, you and your teenager will begin to see how helpful this exercise can be. Parents who role-play possible dangerous scenarios with their teen have reported good success. Teenagers realize its value after they encounter a real-life situation that they have already rehearsed.

FOLLOW YOUR OWN DICTATES ◇ Beginning in middle childhood and continuing through the teen years, my husband and I have always reiterated the importance for our children to think for themselves and not to follow the lead of a peer if it's a behavior or idea that they don't agree with or believe is right. We also told them that if they get into trouble, we will never accept the excuse that someone else made them do it. We taught them the value

---

TEEN TALK

Sometimes you just give in, just to fit in. (Anonymous, Colorado)

◇

Peer pressure can be good, too. I have made some positive changes, due to the encouragement of my friends. (Lenny, California)

---

of following their own dictates about right and wrong and the importance of always being their own person. Teaching individual thinking has to be encouraged and reinforced on a regular basis. *M.J.W., El Sobrante, California*

✕◆◆✕

PHONE CALLS

✕◆◆✕

Is your phone constantly in use by your teenager? If it is, join the crowd; it's part of the ritual of adolescence. Here are some suggestions for coping with the motto of all teens: Have phone, will talk!

CALL WAITING WAS MADE FOR PARENTS ◇
Most phone companies offer a service called "call waiting." This service allows you to know if someone is trying to get through to your phone line when you're on the phone. I'm convinced that this service was made for parents of teens, because our phone lines are frequently tied up by our children. We have a courtesy rule in our family: if you're on a lengthy phone call while another call comes in, you must wrap up your phone call and allow the other family member to return their call. *F.E.S., San Jose, California*

AUTHOR'S NOTE: *I have heard that some teens ignore the incoming call signal and keep right on talking. Advise your teen that some sort of phone restriction will be imposed if they are caught not responding to the call waiting signal.*

CALLS LIMITED TO TEN MINUTES ◇ Whenever anyone in the family is expecting a phone call, everyone else has to limit their phone conversations to ten minutes. *Anonymous, Brantford, Ontario*

CLOCK DETERMINES PHONE TIME ◇ When a family has more than one teenager living at home and only one phone line, I suggest dividing up small blocks of time to designate who can use the phone. Otherwise, one teen will tie up the phone while others in the house need to use it. In our house, I assign one teen the top of each hour to fifteen minutes after (O–15), the next teen fifteen minutes after until the half-hour (15–30), and so on every hour. This rule has cut down on the number of arguments about the phone. If one of the teens is caught using the phone at a time not designated for them (including incoming calls), they can't use the phone the rest of the day. *Joyce Small, San Jose, California*

EXTRA PHONE LINE ◇ We gave in to our daughter's request for an extra phone line, but it wasn't hers exclusively. My husband and I used it for our computer and our daughter used it to call friends. She wasn't allowed to give out the new number, though; our other number rings enough for her already. The extra line has been a real convenience for all of us. *Anonymous, Allentown, Pennsylvania*

TEEN PAYS FOR OWN PHONE ◇ When our daughter turned fourteen, my wife and I decided that she needed her own phone. It worked great for us, too! We paid the installation charge, but our daughter pays the monthly bill with her baby-sitting money. *Mike Horrocks, Fairport, New York*

TEEN PAYS FOR CALLS LONGER THAN TWENTY MINUTES ◇ After paying for too many lengthy long-distance phone calls placed by our teens, my wife and I established a new rule: talk over twenty minutes and you pay for the entire call. We stuck this rule on the phone with a Post-it note. It was amazing how quickly our phone bill dropped—and our teens learned how to get their message across in record time. *Julius Frei, Mission San Jose, California*

PHONE SERVICE FOR FAMILIES ◇ Many local phone companies offer a service that was made for families of teenagers. Called "ring mate" by some companies, it provides up to three separate phone numbers for a single phone line. Each phone number has its own distinctive ring, allowing the family members to know who the call is for. My husband and I answer our ring and our children answer theirs. Even call waiting provides a signal to let me know if the call coming in is for me or my children. If I'm on a business call and the call waiting signal is for my children, I don't have to interrupt my important phone call. This service is much less expensive than installing an extra phone line for your children. *Barb Kennedy, Shelburne, Vermont*

A PHONE FOR DISCIPLINE ◇ Our daughter begged my husband and me to install a private phone line in her bedroom. After much debate and with great reluctance, we finally did. It turned out to be one of the best things we ever did—both for her and us. First of all, our own phone line became ours to use when we needed it, instead of always being tied up with lengthy phone calls by our daughter. Second, the new phone line became one of my daughter's most valued possessions and, therefore, something we could use as a means of discipline. We explained to her that this phone was a privilege, not a right. I would unplug her phone if she did not follow through with her household responsibilities. To deprive a teenage girl of a phone is devastating. After a few "unpluggings," a mere threat of it would get her immediate attention. *Glinda Goodwin, Fremont, California*

THIS PHONE DOESN'T RING AFTER 10:30 P.M. ◇ After hearing my son's phone ring one night at 1:30 A.M., I decided to do something about it. Being an electrical engineer, I decided to rig up a timer system that automatically turns his phone off at any time I decide to set it, and then back on in the morning. I have it set for about 10:30 P.M. to turn off, and back on at about 6:30 A.M. I told my son that the telephone company provides this service and I just call them to make it happen. This way, he does not go looking for my secret device that I have hidden in the basement. *Mike Horrocks, Fairport, New York*

AUTHOR'S NOTE: *If you're not an electrical engineer, let your teen know what the consequence will be for late-night calls. Then let him communicate that message to his friends.*

TEEN PARTIES

From beach parties to slumber parties, whether it's just a few friends getting together or a bash involving many, parties are an important part of the teen scene. Parties are fun, they give teens something to do, and they provide an opportunity in which to socialize—the number one rated activity from a teen's perspective. Some teen parties can also be dangerous. Unsupervised parties and those involving drugs and alcohol can lead to many problems.

Here's a list of party tips from experienced parents, followed by a parent skill builder, A Parent's Guide to Teen Parties.

OLD-FASHIONED PARTY FOR TEENS ◇ I turned back the clock for my twins' sixteenth birthday party. We invited twenty of their friends to an old-fashioned afternoon birthday celebration, the kind young kids have, with apple bobbing and other games usually only enjoyed by young children. My husband and I barbecued hot dogs as the teens played games. They had the time of their life being kids again. Even to this day, some of the kids (they're twenty-six years old now) claim that it was one of the best birthday parties they had ever been to. *Candace Marteski, Costa Mesa, California*

ALL-DAY PARTIES—WITHOUT ALCOHOL ◇

Throughout our sons' teenage years, we threw at least two big all-day parties a year for their friends: a winter snow football party and a summer cottage water-skiing party. Usual attendance was thirty to thirty-five, coed. We worked hard to make sure there were lots of opportunities for fun and plentiful munchies, but were also clear at all times that the "package" included constant parental presence and absolutely no alcohol. After one winter party, which featured three video game setups, two computers, two VCRs running constantly, home-cooked custom-made pizza, and a new hot snack circulated once every forty-five minutes, two guests asked if we would consider adopting them. In the summer, we towed water skiers for miles and miles, rigged small sailboats, hung volleyball nets, and spent time getting to know our sons' friends over charcoal grills and bonfires. It became very clear to our sons and their friends that events could be so much fun that alcohol was irrelevent. *Bob and Jeanne Grace, Fairport, New York*

TEEN BIRTHDAY PARTY ◇

A great way to celebrate your teenager's birthday is to take her and two or three of her friends to the local hot spot (such as the Hard Rock Cafe) for lunch or dinner, followed by a movie. Depending on their age, let them go by themselves. *D.C., Poway, California*

INTERACTIVE PARTIES ◇

Instead of renting the current hot video or setting up video games for your teen's party, encourage more interactive activities such as games and activities. Social interaction is an important skill to learn during adolescence, especially now when television, video games, and computers seem to dominate the time of most teenagers. *Bob Wadley, Spanish Fork, Utah*

AUTHOR'S NOTE: *Here are some other ideas to promote interaction: Rent or borrow a karaoke machine and have a talent contest, play Twister, have a food party (you supply the ice cream and each guest brings a topping, or make spaghetti or pizza from scratch), make your own movie with a video camera, or have a scavenger hunt.*

MAKEOVER PARTY ◇

My daughter invited six of her friends to our house for a sleepover. We wanted to have an activity, so we invited a Mary Kay consultant to come over in the evening. The consultant gave each girl a facial, taught them some makeup tips, then let them practice applying the (age-appropriate) makeup she brought. It was a hit! *Connie Tenn, West Linn, Oregon*

BEACH PARTIES ARE ALWAYS A HIT ◇ If you live near a beach, a guaranteed hit for a teen's birthday party is an all-day beach party. Go with a tropical theme such as Caribbean Beach Party or Luau for the invitations, food, drink (but, of course, no alcohol), and entertainment (how about a steel drum or reggae band if you want to go all-out). Activities can include limbo, volleyball, clam dig and bake, and sand castle building. *Suzanne James, Fort Pierce, Florida*

PIZZA PARTY ◇ A pizza party followed by a movie or roller skating is always a hit with teenage girls. Or decorate a room in nightclub decor and have one of her friends be a guest DJ. *Julie Ormen, Randolph, New Jersey*

HOPE CHEST FOR NEW TEEN ◇ My husband made a beautiful, large wooden chest for my stepdaughter's thirteenth birthday. I painted it in her favorite colors and we both filled it with special things, some pertaining to becoming a teen and others that were mostly memorabilia. We enclosed a scrapbook of clippings from magazines about makeup, health tips, fashion ideas, and fun recipes; a video of some of her favorite shows; a book about being a teenager, and a copy of *Money Doesn't Grow on Trees. B.C. Lange, Grafton, Wisconsin*

SUPERVISION AT SLEEPOVERS ◇ Always check on the supervision for overnight trips and sleepovers. Talk to the parents who will be in charge. You may be surprised at what you discover. *B.B., Bountiful, Utah*

NO OVERNIGHTS WITHOUT ADVANCE NOTICE ◇ Slumber parties and overnight stays at friends' houses should always be prearranged between parents. I never give permission for spur-of-the-moment overnight plans such as when my son calls me from a friend's home and asks if it's OK to spend the night. I only approve overnight stays that are planned in advance and approved by the host's parents. *B.C., Dublin, Ohio*

PARENT SKILL BUILDER

A Parent's Guide to Teen Parties

The following are some suggestions to follow when your teenager hosts a party in your home or at another location under your supervision:

1. Be actively involved in the planning of the party.
   - Share your concerns about potential problems with your teenager and his or her friends who are helping organize the party.
   - Carefully decide what part of the house will be used for the party.
   - Plan to have plenty of food and nonalcoholic drinks available.
   - Be sure that your teen understands the type of activities that you consider unacceptable and knows that you will step in if these activities occur.
2. A parent should be at home during the entire party.
3. Alcohol and other drugs should not be served or allowed.
   - Your teenager and his or her friends may pressure you to allow or provide beer and other alcoholic beverages for the party because "everyone else is doing it." Under no circumstances should you submit to this pressure.
   - Be alert to signs of alcohol and drug use.
   - You may be liable for monetary damages in a civil lawsuit and/or to criminal charges if you furnish alcohol or other drugs to minors.
   - Guests who attempt to bring in alcohol or other drugs should be promptly told to leave.
   - If anyone arrives at the party under the influence of alcohol or other drugs, call the teen's parents to ensure his/her safe transportation home. Nobody should drive under the influence.
4. Teenagers who leave the party should not be allowed to return.

- This rule will discourage those who hope to drink or use drugs elsewhere and return to the party.
5. Limit party attendance and time.
    - Set time limits which will enable teens to be home at a reasonable hour.
    - If possible, make a guest list and send out invitations to discourage crashers.
    - Avoid open house parties. It is difficult for parents and teens to control this type of party.
6. Notify your neighbors before the party.
    - Encourage your teen to call or send a note to close neighbors to let them know the date of the party and that it is being properly planned and supervised. Ask that they inform you if there is too much noise.
7. Make sure your home does not become a party site when you are away.
    - Teenagers often seek out homes with no adults present for parties. Notify close neighbors of your travel plans and, if possible, arrange for an adult friend or relative to live in while you are away.

Printed with permission of the Santa Clara County Medical Association Alliance. Special thanks also to the Roane-Anderson Medical Society Auxiliary in Tennessee.

For Further Information

Boys and Girls Club of America, 771 First Avenue, New York, NY 10017, 212-351-5900. Promotes the health and social, vocational, and moral development of boys and girls from the ages of six to eighteen.

Boys and Girls Club of Canada, 7030 Woodbine Avenue, Suite 703, Markham, Ontario L3R 6G2, 416-477-7272. Offers children and teens opportunities to develop skills, knowledge, and values to become fulfilled individuals.

YMCA of the USA, 101 N. Wacker Drive, Chicago, IL 60606.

YWCA of Canada, 80 Gerrard Street East, Toronto, Ontario M5B 1E6, 416-593-9886.

YWCA of the USA, 726 Broadway, New York, NY 10003.

Recommended Reading for Parents and Teens

Philip Zimbardo, *Shyness* (Reading, MA: Addison-Wesley, 1987). Offers advice about how to overcome shyness and be more gregarious. Geared for adults, but adaptable for teens.

Recommended Reading for Teens

Lynda Madaras, *My Feelings, My Self* (New York: Newmarket Press, 1993). Includes a large section on friendships, including information about popularity, crowds, peer pressure, and crushes. Recommended for teen girls.

6

SCHOOL AND LEARNING

If a child is to keep alive his inborn sense of wonder,
he needs the companionship of at least one adult
who can share it, rediscovering with him the joy,
excitement and mystery of the world we live in.
— RACHEL CARSON, *The Sense of Wonder*

One morning many years ago, my wife and I were awakened by our oldest daughter at 6:00 A.M. She was fully dressed and was jumping around our bedroom half singing and half yelling, "I get to go to school today," over and over. It was the first day of kindergarten; she was five years old. Later that morning, after watching my daughter bounce into her kindergarten room, I walked into a classroom at the college where I teach. It was brimming with students, mostly freshmen, on this first day of a new academic year. Looking out into the sea of faces, I saw no signs of excitement like that I had witnessed earlier in the day with my daughter and her peers. I didn't expect my students to be jumping up and down, but I know excitement when I see it—and I wasn't seeing it. Most of these freshmen would come alive later in the semester, I reminded myself, but for most of that day and many other days as well, I thought about how drastically different my two morning experiences had been. I wondered at what point along the education highway those freshmen had made a wrong turn. Or maybe they just got dropped off.

Although a number of teens maintain the zest for knowledge they had in the elementary school years, there are many who don't. Somewhere between the beginning of middle school and the end of high school, they lose their enthusiasm for learning. Some claim that school is boring, others blame their lack of enthusiasm on not having any goals to shoot for, or not being interested in the curriculum, or feeling lost in the education shuffle.

Many experts believe that a child's natural inquisitiveness must be nurtured throughout the school years. Parents, as well as educators, must play a key role in developing and sustaining a child's love of learning and success in school.

Many educators believe that parental involvement in a child's education is one of the best ways to keep the spark of learning alive. New research solidly backs that claim. A recent study conducted by the research organization Child Trends confirms that children whose parents are active at school are more likely to thrive academically and participate in extracurricular activities. The researchers also discovered that "As children move from elementary school into junior high and high school, their parents become less and less involved in their school activities. By the time they reach high school, nearly half of the nation's students have parents who stay away from class plays, PTA meetings, football games, volunteer activities, back-to-school nights, science fairs and virtually every other school function."[13] Coincidentally or not, this is about the same time that many teenagers begin to lose their enthusiasm for learning.

Parents can actively demonstrate to their teens the value they place on learning and school by being interested and enthusiastic about learning, by reading themselves, by showing interest in and offering assistance with homework, and by attending school functions. Many parents of teenagers don't attend school functions because they don't want to appear to be inappropriately interfering in their son's or daughter's life. Sometimes their teenager asks them not to go. It's understandable that your teen may not want you to chaperone the junior prom, but you should not be swayed by your teen's desire to keep you from parent conferences or events such as back-to-school night. In fact, that should be a red flag for you to attend.

The following parenting tips are divided into three sections: Learning, School, and Homework. The tips include great advice on promoting a love of learning, the importance of progress reports from teachers, and how to survive the dreaded homework battles. The advice here will help you launch your teen on a lifelong quest for knowledge.

◇

✗✗✗✗✗✗✗✗✗✗✗✗✗✗✗✗✗✗✗✗✗✗✗✗✗✗✗✗✗✗✗✗✗

LEARNING

✗✗✗✗✗✗✗✗✗✗✗✗✗✗✗✗✗✗✗✗✗✗✗✗✗✗✗✗✗✗✗✗✗

THE VALUE OF BEING A WELL-ROUNDED PERSON ◇ My husband and I stress the importance of being a well-rounded person to our children, and we encourage them to not only do well in their academic work at school but also to have a knowledge of sports, music, and other areas of personal interest to them. We teach them that in today's world, many employers look for individuals who are flexible and have many talents. *A.B., Bountiful, Utah*

MUSIC LESSONS—DAUGHTER PAYS IF NOT PREPARED ◇ The more I nagged my daughter to practice for her music lessons, the more we got into a power struggle. Even though I felt as if I was throwing money away, I didn't want to give up on her music because she has a real gift for it. I finally told her that I would pay for the lessons she had practiced for, but she would have to pay for the lessons she was not prepared for. Luckily, she has long-term plans for her money and values what it takes for her to earn it. It's been a month now and she hasn't missed practicing yet. *Donna J. Carlyle, Austin Texas*

THOUGHTFUL CONVERSATION PROMOTES LEARNING ◇ Engage your children in thoughtful conversation and don't put down their thinking, even if their conclusions don't match your own. It takes time to develop a good brain. *Linda Sanderson, Garland, Texas*

TEACH TEENS TO BE SOLUTION ORIENTED ◇ Many teens arrive at the doorstep of adulthood with limited experience at making decisions. Well-meaning parents often rob their children of this experience by making many of their decisions for them. I have learned the value of not immediately answering my children's questions before I ask them, "What do you think?" For some questions I'll ask, "What are your alternatives?" If they answer correctly, I reinforce their decision making with praise. Otherwise, I offer an answer or add an alternative or two to their list—and praise them for their effort in answering. I'm amazed at how often they know the answer, and when they don't they at least exercised their brains. This solution-oriented approach gives them confidence, improves their thinking skills, and prepares them for adulthood. *E.M., Los Angeles, California*

THE BENEFITS AND FUN OF HOSTING AN EX-CHANGE STUDENT ◇ Our family hosts an international exchange student every year. Each year we look forward to inviting a different culture into our home. All of us, but especially our teenage son, who is host to our guest, have learned a myriad of things about other countries, cultures, and lifestyles—things that you could never learn from a class or book. My son enjoys teaching his counterpart the ropes of making it as a teen in America. The bonding between my family and our exchange students happens almost immediately and can last for a lifetime. My son also enjoys always having someone to do things with and introducing his new buddy to his own friends. My son's friends think that it's really cool to host an exchange student. I highly recommend this experience to other families. It's been one of the most rewarding programs I or my family have ever been involved in. *Ted Bennett, Matthews, North Carolina*

FOR MORE INFORMATION

For information about international exchange student programs and a listing of reputable companies, ask your middle school or high school principal to lend you the latest "Advisory List of International Educational Travel and Exchange Programs." Or write to CSIET, 3 Loudoun St. S.E., Leeburg, VA 22075 for your own copy.

LET'S MAKE A DEAL—TO LEARN ◇ To keep our two teens in the swing of learning during the long summer vacation, we make a deal with them about something they would like to learn or accomplish by summer's end. They pick a goal such as reading one book each week for two months, enrolling in a summer class, mastering a tough musical piece on the piano, or writing a lengthy report on some topic of interest to them. Then we negotiate a reasonable "reward" (money, gift, or special experience such as a hot air balloon ride) if they accomplish their goal. The deal and some method to keep track of their progress is put in writing. It's a great summer motivator. *A.M., San Diego, California*

TEACHING THE LOVE OF BOOKS ⋄ The best way to teach a love of books and reading is to be a good role model. Let your kids see you read. And don't hide your enthusiasm for a good book; let them see you chuckle out loud or share a special passage with anyone who will listen. Enthusiasm is contagious. If teens haven't yet discovered the value of books, they will think that they're missing something. Sometimes, it's just a matter of finding that special title or subject that sparks their interest. *M.J.W., El Sobrante, California*

✖✖✖✖✖✖✖✖✖✖✖✖✖✖✖✖✖✖✖✖✖✖✖✖✖✖✖✖✖✖✖✖✖✖✖✖✖✖

SCHOOL

✖✖✖✖✖✖✖✖✖✖✖✖✖✖✖✖✖✖✖✖✖✖✖✖✖✖✖✖✖✖✖✖✖✖✖✖✖✖

School plays a major force in your teen's cognitive and social development as well as the shaping of his or her identity. Approximately 30 percent (thirty-eight hours a week) of their waking moments are spent at school or in school-related activities.

(If after-school care is an issue for you and your teen, the next chapter ("Leisure Activities and Curfews") has some great suggestions in the section After School (page 105).

⋄

GET INVOLVED AT YOUR CHILD'S SCHOOL ⋄ Develop a good rapport with your children's teachers and school administrators. One of the best ways to do this is to volunteer or be an active member of the PTA. And, of course, always attend back-to-school night and parent-teacher conferences. Then, if you have a special request for a certain teacher or class, or if your child gets into a jam at school, you'll already have a good rapport with the individuals involved with the situation. *A.R., Bakersfield, California*

BE A GUIDE INSTEAD OF A TEACHER ◇ As a middle school teacher, I have had an opportunity to ask many parents of successful children what their secrets were. Many of them replied that they would review their child's homework before it was turned in at school. By doing so, many of them claimed, they were able to set a certain standard of quality that their children knew to expect— before it ever reached the teacher. A few of the parents added that they tried to be more of a guide than a teacher, they did not want to duplicate the role of the teacher. *Jane Lafay, Oviedo, Florida*

NOT COOL TO BE SMART ◇ Beginning in middle school, one of our sons started to slack off in his schoolwork. My husband and I learned that our son was getting hassled by his peer group for being smart. Peer pressure can be a strong force for a teenager, so it's especially important for parents to offset this negative peer pressure. Besides complimenting our son for his intelligence and encouraging his academics, we also explained that jealousy is often one of the reasons why people tease. Although my son already seemed to know this, our conversation was confirming and helped him get back on track. *Mary Hopkins, Sacramento, California*

EXPECTED TO DO THEIR BEST ◇ My husband and I never expected our children to get all A's in school, but we made it clear that we expected them to do their best. Their best might be A's or it might be B's and C's. We always told them that their job was school and they should do the best job they could do. It's also important for parents to stay involved in their teen's academic work. Stay in touch with teachers and counselors and, when possible, volunteer to participate in field trips and other school-related activities. The relationships you establish at their school could be invaluable in the future if any problems arise. *Holly McLay, Miami, Florida*

REAL-LIFE WAKE-UP CALL ◇ My son had great aspirations for college, but didn't take high school seriously. I tried everything to motivate him, but to no avail. Then one day he learned that universities are very selective for freshman admission. That was his wake-up call. He had thought that college was like regular school—if you show up, you're in. His studies improved almost instantly. Now he even enjoys walking around the local university campus and watching the myriad of activities. He can't wait to participate in campus life. For teens, it's just a matter of getting something to ring their bell. *Max Hamm, Lawton, Oklahoma*

N O T E: Don't miss the parent skill builder, Planning for College Begins in Junior High, in chapter 16 (page 221).

THEIR INTERESTS MAY BE DIFFERENT FROM YOURS ◇ Encourage your children's interests and talents, not yours or those you wish you had. *Linda Sanderson, Garland, Texas*

HOME SCHOOLING ◇ One of the best decisions that I ever made as a parent was to home school my two younger daughters. We began home schooling as an experiment for one semester when they were in the seventh and ninth grades, but we all enjoyed it so much that we continued throughout the high school years. We concentrated on those subjects that my daughters had a passion for, but covered all the basics too. Unlike the traditional public schools that have to cope with discipline problems and a plethora of learning levels and styles, we had the whole day to have fun and learn. We frequently met with other home schoolers and planned weekly field trips. My

---

FOR MORE INFORMATION

If you would like more information about home schooling, write to: National Home Study Council, 1601 18th St. NW, Washington, DC 20009; or the National Association of Home Educators, Route 3, Box 324-B, Gallatin, MO 64640. Also, many computer on-line services have home schooling forums.

TEEN TALK

My dad never appreciated my drama class because it wasn't academic enough. But at the time it was the most important class to me. I remember really wanting him to understand that. (A.S., California)

◇

I was a straight A student until I lost interest in high school. My grades plummeted. What got me back on track was learning from others how tough it is to be successful if you don't have at least a high school diploma. I also talked to people in the career field that I was interested in, and I learned how hard they had to work to get there. They told me that I better get in gear or I'd never make it. (Josh, Missouri)

◇

I didn't appreciate the value of an education until I had to work in a warehouse for low wages. I quickly realized that I didn't want to do this for the rest of my life. This experience motivated me to take school more seriously. It was more effective than any pep talk about school that I had heard from my teachers and parents. (Brian, Arizona)

◇

I'm thankful that my parents didn't push me into things that I didn't want to do. Some of my friends were always forced into advanced courses at school and summer school, even though they personally had no interest in them. They weren't happy because of it. (Anonymous)

◇

Parents should keep their minds open. Just because it's something you never did or experienced doesn't mean that it's wrong. (Anonymous)

◇

My senior year in high school was a real eye-opener. The closer I got to graduation, the more I started to notice the real world out there. It was scary. I told myself, I need to get my life together. I need to move on. I seemed to mature overnight. (Aileen, California) daughters are in college now and have done exceptionally well in their academics and their social life. My only regret is not home schooling my two older daughters. Home schooling is not for everyone, but it was wonderful for my family. _Edith Gutierrez, Fremont, California_

SCHOOL PROGRESS REPORT ◇ One of the most effective discipline approaches for poor schoolwork or failing grades in junior or senior high school is to base the discipline on the weekly progress report from the school. Students have more incentive to improve on a short-term basis compared to being disciplined for the entire school quarter or semester. Teachers are more than happy to provide a weekly _signed_ progress report to concerned parents. It's your child's responsibility to bring the report home. If a weekly report isn't brought home, you should assume there was poor progress and discipline should be based accordingly. _Susie Anderson, Mission San Jose, California_

"I'LL GO TO SCHOOL WITH YOU" ◇ When my children entered junior high school I told them, "If your teacher or principal ever calls me because you are not behaving or keeping up with your work, I'll go to school with you—from class to class—to help you focus on your schoolwork. We'll be like best friends!" Needless to say, I never had to follow through with this potentially embarrassing situation. Just the thought of it helped my children behave like angels in school. _G.G., Reedley, California_

✖✖✖

HOMEWORK

✖✖✖

DEMONSTRATING THAT HOMEWORK IS IMPORTANT ◇ Whenever my son asked me for help with his homework, I would respond, "Do you need help understanding it or do you just want the answer?" If the latter,

I was usually too busy to help. If the former, I would immediately drop anything I was doing and devote my full attention to my son's homework. By doing so, I made the point that homework was very important. *Vern Smith, Tustin, California*

ENCOURAGE GOOD STUDY HABITS ◇ Work with your teen to develop a comfortable and quiet place to study. Good lighting, a comfortable chair and desk, and other necessary supplies are prerequisites for good study time. Encourage a set time to study every day. *Patricia Stahler, Niles, California*

TEEN OFFICE ◇ To stimulate my son to do well in school, I helped him create a positive environment in which to study in his own room. Starting with his own desk and adequate lighting, we gradually added all the amenities necessary for an office: personal computer; stapler; hole punch; tape; assortment of pens, pencils, and paper; dictionary; thesaurus; handbook on grammar; etc. He enjoys this new setup and now spends more time on homework and studying. The more comfortable a study area is, the more time a teenager will spend there. And if they have the tools to create, they will be more creative. *Bennett Oppenheim, Mission San Jose, California*

HOMEWORK AND FAMILY—SUNDAY THROUGH THURSDAY ◇ Our children could not go out in the evenings from Sunday through Thursday except for school functions. This was a time for homework and family. Friday through Sunday afternoon was their free time to do whatever they chose. *Mary Hopkins, Sacramento, California*

HOMEWORK TIME ◇ Even well-intentioned teenagers are easily distracted from their homework, especially by phone calls from their friends and the lure of the television. So my wife and I have implemented a new rule: no television or phone calls from 7 to 10 P.M. on Monday through Thursday evenings. The once countless number of phone calls quickly diminished to only a few, and those are answered by my wife or me. We politely explain that our sons cannot accept phone calls at this time. Only homework-related phone calls to or from classmates are allowed. *Sterling Sakai, San Mateo, California*

AN HOUR OF TELEVISION FOR AN HOUR OF READING ◇ I allow my children to watch television for the same number of hours per week that they read books. And I keep track! Since beginning this new practice, my children read more and watch television less. It works. *Danni Vilas, Oakland, California*

HOMEWORK TALES ◇ As a high school counselor for many years, I learned that many students don't tell the truth about their homework to their parents. When asked about their homework, many students respond that they don't have any or have already completed it. A countless number of parents have sat in my office totally surprised to learn that their children were falling behind in school because they weren't completing their homework. If you have reason to believe that homework isn't being completed, check with your child's teachers. It doesn't take long for students to get behind in a class if their homework is lagging. *Georgia Lou, Flagstaff, Arizona*

"I DON'T HAVE ANY HOMEWORK" ◇ A quick way to cure the "I don't have any homework" or "I forgot my homework" comments from your child is to make her sit at her desk anyway for the same amount of time she usually spends doing her homework. She can read or study topics that you provide. This takes away the incentive for "forgetting" to bring her work home. *Patricia Carlson, Sandwich, Illinois*

ASSIGNMENT BOOK ◇ My son attends a private school that requires every student to have an assignment book for homework. The student writes down the daily assignments and the teachers initial it. At home, a parent initials the assignment book verifying that the homework was completed. This book has been a godsend to our son. He is assured of receiving and writing down his assignments every day, and I know what needs to be completed every night. *Stephanie Smaldone, LaPlata, Maryland*

AUTHOR'S NOTE: *Teenagers, especially those in middle school, are often very disorganized. A nice gift, and one that will help them get organized, is an appointment book. They will have a place to keep track of their homework, phone numbers, and calendar. Some appointment books have optional inserts for photo pages, a calculator, and memo pads.*

HOMEWORK CHART ◇ To help my teenagers keep track of their homework assignments, especially the big projects like term papers and reports, I created a homework chart. On a standard piece of paper I drew a seven-column (horizontally) by seven-column (vertically) grid. Above the first column on the left side I wrote "Subjects." Above the other columns I listed each subject (Spanish, Geometry, English, etc.) my son was studying. Inside the top left box I wrote "Monday," followed by "Tuesday" below it, and continued until "Friday." Inside the box below "Friday" I wrote "Date of Next Test," and in the box below that "Next Report Due." I made many copies of this form, which can be used for the entire semester. With a quick glance, my son and I can tell what his daily homework is in each subject, when his next test will be, and when his big projects are due. *D.H., Fremont, California*

HOMEWORK SHEET ◇ Getting my teenage son to do his homework was a real battle until I started a new system. I made up a "homework sheet" that my son had to take to school every day. The form had spaces to list his classes, what his homework was for that day, and a place for his teachers to sign. If he didn't have homework for a specific subject, he wrote in "no homework," and had his teacher sign it. He had to bring home the completed form every day, whether or not he had homework. If he didn't bring the form home, or if it was incomplete, he was put on restriction. When he came home, he was required to complete all of his homework before he did anything else. Within a short time he realized the importance of homework, as well as the fact that the sooner he completes it, the sooner he can do the activities of his choice. *Doug Harwood, Camarillo, California*

NO MORE HOMEWORK COP ◇ My husband and I used to quiz our daughter nightly regarding the completion of her homework. It was like playing cops and robbers. So now, instead of hounding her about her homework each evening, we review a semiweekly progress report from each of her teachers. Since her privileges depend on a good progress report, she is now motivated to complete her homework and get good grades—without our pestering. *Teresa Dulberg, Hayward, California*

BEWARE OF THIS TEEN SCHEME

Some teens are very slick about getting out of homework, even if you play homework cop. One trick is to avoid putting dates on any of their homework so they can show you the same paper over and over throughout the school year. Look at each paper carefully and make sure there is a date on each one. (Anonymous, Chicago, Illinois)

HOMEWORK TROUBLES ◇ The best advice about homework and teenagers is to back off and make them responsible. The more parents nag their teen about homework, the more it escalates into a big game between the two of you. Let your teen know that the ball is in his court. Advise him that you will help him anytime he needs it, but otherwise you will not be discussing homework with him. The worst thing that can happen is that he will flunk out and will have to repeat the class. It sounds harsh, but I learned the hard way that it really works. I was always rescuing my son because I didn't want him to fail. I realized that this approach was not teaching him responsibility and independence. It took awhile for him to turn things around, but he did and he now has A's and B's to show for it. *Diane Ranoldo, Tabernacle, New Jersey*

LEARNING ABOUT SCHOOL ACADEMICS ◇ I frequently ask my teenage son about his homework; not only to check up on his progress, but to see what he is being taught in school. Other than the semiannual parent-teacher conferences, the only way for parents to keep track of the level and quality of their child's academics is to periodically review their homework. It's an eye-opener! *B.O., Ventura, California*

EARNING AN EXTRA PRIVILEGE ◇ Every two weeks I read my daughter's progress report from her teachers and review the quality and timeliness of her household chore responsibilities. From this evaluation she can earn additional privileges or lose ones she already has. For example, for an excellent evaluation she can earn thirty more minutes each day for "phone talk" (her normal limit is one hour per day) or the privilege of having her weekend curfew extended by thirty minutes. It's her choice. On the other hand, for poor evaluations, she can lose daily "phone talk" time and/or weekend curfew time. It's been a wonderful motivator for her—chores get completed without constant reminders, and her schoolwork has improved. *Paul Dulberg, Hayward, California*

A REWARD FOR READING ◇ My husband and I love to read and we wanted to instill this value in our children. So during the early teen years we paid them five dollars for every book they read beyond what was required at school. Within a few years they had acquired a real appreciation for books and were motivated to read on their own, without a reward from us. *Shelley McKinzie, Fremont, California*

LEARNING CAN BE A FAMILY AFFAIR ◇ When our teenage daughter allows her mother and me to get involved in her studies, we enjoy discussing things together and debating points of view. My daughter especially enjoys it when we show an interest in areas that are important and interesting to her. Learning is a wonderful thing, and goes on throughout life, so there is much to share between parent and child. *John Cornett, High Rolls, New Mexico*

READING QUIZ ◇ To make sure that my son was comprehending his reading assignments, I read them myself and then quizzed him. He couldn't answer many of my questions the first few times that I did this, but he quickly improved as he learned the difference between skimming a story and reading carefully. *Cathy Hairup, Magna, Utah*

HOMEWORK HELPER ◇ I gave up nagging my teenage daughter about her homework long ago, but I do remind her that I'm available to quiz her with flash cards or offer suggestions for conducting research. Parents can offer support, encouragement, and their own expertise and knowledge without crossing the line of actually doing the homework for their child. *T.D., Mariposa, California*

"HOW ARE YOU GOING TO APPROACH THIS RESEARCH PAPER?" ◇ Parents can offer a variety of helpful hints and tips to their children about their homework without actually doing the work. For example, my son recently told me that he has to write a term paper, so I offered him my assistance. I told him that researching topics in the library used to be one of my favorite assignments when I was in high school, and if he needed help or advice to let me know. We ended up at the library, where he learned much more about using the library than he ever learned at school. And we had fun together. Sometimes I'll offer advice on study skills such as note or test taking. I have learned that as long as I don't preach or lecture to him, and I keep my comments brief, my son is open to listening to me. Another key is to constantly compliment him on his school progress and accomplishments. *Bennett Oppenheim, Mission San Jose, California*

PARENT SKILL BUILDER

Teaching Good Study Habits

Although middle and high school students are expected to know how to study, chances are that no one, including their teachers, has ever taken the time to actually teach effective study skills. I know this is true because I teach a study skills course at a college where the majority of freshmen have never learned good study habits. Here are a few proven study strategies that get results:

1. *Develop a homework routine* and stick to it as much as you can. Having a regular time and place to study is important and will lead to good homework habits.
2. *Study at least a few hours every day.* This will vary more or less depending on the subjects and amount of homework. Studies show that most students who study one hour or less each day consistently earn grades of C or lower. Students who study three or more hours per day usually earn B's or better.
3. *Family members need to be supportive and respectful of the study time.* Your teen should have a quiet place to study where he or she is not bothered by siblings or parents.

4. *Study boring or difficult subjects first.* Otherwise the student will find some reason (too tired, subject is too boring, etc.) to skip or shorten the study time for that subject. Always study the most challenging subjects first, when you're freshest and not tired.
5. *Unplug the phone!*
6. Practice being disciplined. *Say no to friends* if an activity interferes with your study time.
7. *Discover the many uses of 3×5 cards:* use as flash cards; and write out new vocabulary words, formulas, definitions, and information that need to be memorized before a test. Keep in a pocket or purse so you can review them frequently, which will help with memorization. Use waiting time (waiting for a friend, for a doctor's appointment, or between classes) for a quick review.
8. *Make a daily "To Do" list* on a 3×5 card. Prioritize each item and cross off when completed.
9. *Read each textbook chapter two or three times,* not just once. Highlight important information and facts. Review the highlighted material frequently.
10. *Use a dictionary.*

Recommended Reading for Parents

Colleen Alexander-Roberts, *The ADHD Parenting Handbook: Practical Advice from Parents to Parents*, (Dallas: Taylor).

Thomas Armstrong, *In Their Own Way: Discover and Encourage Your Child's Personal Learning*, (New York: J. P. Tarcher, 1988). This book explores various ways in which children learn. The author addresses the question, Is my child learning disabled or does he just learn differently?

Barbara Ingersoll, *Your Hyperactive Child: A Parent's Guide to Coping with Attention Deficit Disorder*, (New York: Doubleday, 1988).

Recommended Reading for Teens

Michael Gordon, *I Would If I Could: A Teenager's Guide to ADHD/Hyperactivity* (New York: GSI, 1993). With illustrations.

Marian Salzman and Teresa Reisgies, *Greetings from High School*, (Princeton: Peterson's Guides, 1991). A book by, for, and about adolescents with good suggestions about high school, college, and careers.

7

LEISURE ACTIVITIES AND CURFEWS

Children need time to practice life, and they do that when they are on their own or with each other.
— B R I A N   S U T T O N - S M I T H   Professor Emeritus at the
University of Pennsylvania, as quoted in *Parents*, Dec., 1993

LEISURE ACTIVITIES

Adolescents spend more time in leisure activities than in productive activities such as attending class and studying. That was the finding in a fascinating study in which teenagers were monitored by a beeper for one week. Forty percent of their time was spent in leisure activities such as socializing, sports and games, and watching television; 31 percent of their time was spent in maintenance activities such as eating, personal care, chores, and errands; and 29 percent of their time was spent in productive activities such as part-time jobs and school.[14]

Many parents are concerned about the large amount of leisure time their teenagers have. It drives some parents crazy to watch their teens "waste" time or hang out around the house doing nothing. But some solitude is good for teens; they need time to reflect on their life, to think, and just to daydream. Teens can also be too busy. If your teen

never has any down time between school, work, and a myriad of activities, it is a good idea to reevaluate her schedule
with her. The goal, say parenting experts and experienced
parents, is for a teenager to achieve a balance between the
two ends of the spectrum.

◇

SOME IDLE TIME IS NEEDED ◇ I have a rule of
thumb for deciding if my teenagers have too many activities and commitments in their life: If they can keep up
their schoolwork and get enough sleep so that they're
healthy, they're probably not too busy. I can also tell if
they are too busy or not busy enough by their actions and
comments. For example, if they get into trouble in their
free time, they need to be busier. On the other hand, if
they're stressed out from all their demands and commitments, they need to be less busy. I limit their part-time
jobs to a maximum of twenty hours per week. I want them
to have time to enjoy themselves, and to be bored occasionally. Too much idle time is not good at this age, but a
bit of it can be a time for introspection and creativity. *Lee
Margulies, Los Angeles, California*

LIMIT ON ACTIVITIES ◇ So as not to have our teenagers overburdened by too many organized activities such
as sports and lessons, we limited each child to two activities at any one time. Whatever they started, they had to
finish. *Edith Schuette, Ukiah, California*

ACTIVITIES—ON A SCALE OF ONE TO TEN
◇ My teenage daughters often had a difficult time trying
to decide between two or more activities to participate in.
To help them decide, I would ask them, "On a scale of one
to ten, how badly do you want to do each activity?" In
putting a point value on each separate activity, they were
able to decide which one they really wanted to do the
most. They also used this scale when purchasing items of
clothing. My daughters are young adults now, and they
use this system on their own now. It really works! *Edith
Gutierrez, Fremont, California*

BALANCING ACT FOR TEENS ◇ Teenagers need to
keep busy with school and activities, but they also need
free time for other needs and responsibilities. Parents

need to help them find a good balance between being active and being too active. Help your kids weigh out the pros and cons of adding another obligation, whether it be a job or an extracurricular activity, to their schedule. It's easy for teens to get overextended to the point where school or family gets neglected. Without making the decision for them, parents can gently ask them to consider the pros and cons of adding another activity to an already busy schedule. If they give it some thought, they usually will make the right decision. *David Hopkins, Sacramento, California*

COMMITMENTS ◇ We always encouraged our children to follow through on whatever commitments they make. *Dolly Hickey, Clearwater, Florida*

TEAM COMMITMENTS ◇ If our children wanted to participate on a sports team such as Little League or high school athletics, they had to make the commitment to play for the entire season unless there were unforeseen circumstances. This taught them commitment and teamwork. It also taught them not to be self-centered. *Susie Anderson, Mission San Jose, California*

ENCOURAGE EXTRACURRICULAR ACTIVITIES
◇ If you have a teen who is not involved in school activities, has few friends, or seems to be often bored, insist that he select one extracurricular activity (band, clubs, sports, etc.). After he selects one that he is interested in, ask him if he would like you to help his club or team by volunteering in some way (coaching, selling tickets, driving, etc.) Extracurricular activities are a good way to find new friends who have things in common with your son or daughter. It's also been proven that teens who get involved in these kinds of activities at school do better in their academics and enjoy school more. *Allan Heckel, Salem, Oregon*

REQUIRED ACTIVITIES ◇ My husband and I require our teens participate in at least one extracurricular activity (sports, music, scouting, etc.) of their choosing, and they must stick with it for at least one year. It keeps them busy, encourages new friendships with common interest, and helps them discover some of their hidden talents. Our teens also learned important adult lessons in time management as they balanced school, family, and social activities. *Shelley McKinzie, Fremont, California*

3.0 GPA TO PARTICIPATE IN SPORTS ◇ Since high school sports can be very time consuming and can cut into studying time and other activities, we told our boys that if their grades drop below a certain point (3.0 for our boys), they will have to quit their sports. They enjoy their sports so this rule has been a good motivator for their academics. *R.P.H., San Leandro, California*

ALTERNATIVES IN ATHLETICS ◇ Everyone can participate in athletics, even if they're not big enough, strong enough, or talented enough to play a specific sport. Many teenagers enjoy managing, keeping score, or assisting the coaches. It makes them feel like part of the team — and the chances of injuries are almost nil. *David Hopkins, Sacramento, California*

GET INVOLVED IN SCOUTING ◇ Scouting is a great activity for teenagers. It teaches leadership, encourages learning new skills, and promotes good values. Scouting encourages parent involvement also. It offers an opportunity for parents and teens to share high adventure, outdoor activities, and time together. My oldest son has achieved the highest level of scouting, the Eagle Scout, which will be of benefit to him throughout his adult life. Employers and scholarship committees are impressed to see this listed on a résumé. I credit the Boy Scouts of America for many of the positive characteristics that my sons have developed. I recommend scouting to all parents. *D.C., Dublin, California*

POOL TABLE CREATED SOCIAL CENTER AT HOME ◇ As I look back to my teen years many years ago I realize now how clever my parents were during my tough adolescent years. One thing I remember is our family pool table, a top-of-the-line Brunswick. It was definitely a splurge for my middle-income family, but this pool table was enjoyed by my entire family. And it was the envy of my teen friends. My house became the social hangout for my friends. My buddies still talk about the good times shooting pool at my house. Often, at my friends' request, my mom or dad would join us for a game. I remember great times and good conversations around that table, both with family and friends. It probably helped to keep my buddies and me out of trouble. *Thomas Leslie, San Diego, California*

ACT RESPONSIBLY AT THEIR ACTIVITIES ◇ Go to your children's activities regularly, and behave like a responsible adult: don't harass the umpire; don't talk during the performance; and praise the sponsors (their willingness if you can't praise their talent). Keep all comments on their performance positive and helpful, but don't lie either. Teens have a good idea how their performance went, and if you say it was wonderful when it clearly wasn't, your honesty and integrity will come into question. And don't undermine the coach or director! *Linda Sanderson, Garland, Texas*

CHEERING FROM THE SIDELINES ◇ As parents, it's important for us to attend the events our children participate in. Our kids appreciate our support and cheers. But be careful not to embarrass your children or take the spotlight off their success. *J.G., Reedley, California*

GET LOST SOMETIMES ◇ All kids want to know that their parents are in the stands when they score the winning touchdown. But they don't always want you chaperoning the school dance afterward. Ask your child if it's OK if you chaperone one of his activities before you volunteer. *Allan Heckel, Salem, Oregon*

PARENTS AS CHEERLEADERS ◇ My wife and I attend every school, sport, and musical event in which our children participate. We strongly encourage their brothers and sisters to attend too. This is one way to let your kids know how important they are to you and to their siblings. *B.B., Bountiful, Utah*

MOM AND DAD AS TAXI DRIVERS

Many parents spend so much of their time transporting their children to and from various activities that they begin to think of themselves as personal chauffeurs or taxi drivers. However, as you are about to learn from the parenting tips in this section, there are many secondary gains from driving your children and their friends around town.

THE VALUE OF CAR TIME ◇ I used to dread driving my daughter across town to the myriad of activities she was involved in, especially the thirty-minute drive to gymnastics practice. But I soon learned how valuable this car time was for us. It was usually in the car when a conversation would develop on a topic that otherwise would have been difficult to talk about. We talked openly and without interruption about sex, drugs, and other difficult topics. Maybe it was because I had to keep my eyes on the road, instead of our looking into each other's eyes. It's tough to find thirty minutes of alone time with anyone these days, so we just took advantage of the opportunity. *N.L. Colvin, Chapel Hill, North Carolina*

DRIVING TIME—MORE THAN REACHING A DESTINATION ◇ I spent many an hour driving my teenagers to school, soccer, dance, Boy Scouts, Girl Scouts, gymnastics, friends' houses, etc. I used this time to talk to them, but more importantly, to listen. For some reason, having me all to themselves in the privacy of the car gave them courage to ask questions about sex and other concerns they have. In fact, most of their sex education was done during our drives. I guess they figured that I couldn't bail out and would have to answer their tough questions. *Deborah Burt, Clovis, California*

"I NEED ONE DAY'S NOTICE" ◇ Teenagers should let their parents know of their requests of them one day in advance whenever possible. I implemented this rule after I tired of last-minute requests such as, "Can Johnny have dinner with us and sleep over tonight?" or "Can you drive me to the mall right now?" These demands put a lot of pressure on me and prohibited me from completing many of my own tasks and responsibilities. After starting this rule, I had to make very few exceptions to the rule. My kids learned to respect my time and need for planning ahead. *M.R., Orlando, Florida*

BEEP, BEEP, "I'M READY TO BE PICKED UP" (AND OTHER PRACTICAL USES OF BEEPERS) ◇ Even though they were the rage with teenagers,

I was very reluctant to allow my sixteen-year-old son to buy a beeper. Everything I had heard about them was negative: the schools had prohibited them on campus and the newspapers had reported their use in teen drug sales. My son convinced me that we could use one to stay in touch with each other, so we bought one. Now we own two, and my husband and I are very impressed with their many practical applications.

To notify someone by beeper, you call the beeper number and dial in the phone number where you can be reached. In our family, we then type in an ID code (my husband is 1, I am 2, my sixteen-year-old is 3, and my thirteen-year-old is 4) after the phone number so the person will know who is beeping them. Sometimes we also use other family codes after our ID number. For example, 333 means "I'm ready to be picked up," 311 means "come home, don't call back," 111 means "I'll be home by dinnertime," 000 means "have to work overtime," and 911 means "emergency, call me immediately." Here are a few ways we use beepers with our teens:

- *After school:* My husband and I can always be reached at our workplace by beeper, even if our phone lines are busy or we're away from our desks. We feel more secure and connected to our sons knowing that they can reach us immediately if they need to get in touch with us.
- *Pick me up:* Instead of having an agreed-upon time (which often changes) to be picked up after a sporting event, movie, or meeting, my sons beep me with their code when it's time to be picked up. I don't have to be home waiting for a phone call; I can be anywhere— shopping, at a neighbor's house, or on the road.

- *I'll be late:* My sons beep me with a specific code to let me know they will be coming home from school later than expected so I won't worry.
- *Need assistance:* Both boys recently went to a large amusement park with their friends. I felt a sense of security knowing that my younger son could beep his older brother if he and his friends encountered a problem. A simple, agreed-upon code could be used to locate each other.

D.H., Fremont, California

AUTHOR'S NOTE: *A number of parents have told me that beepers are also useful in keeping track of their teens or contacting them no matter where they are—at work, out with friends, or on a date.*

EVENING ACTIVITIES

MUST HAVE A DESTINATION IN MIND ◇ Our teenagers always had to have a destination in mind when they went out with friends or on a date. The comment "We're just going out" was not adequate. We wanted to know where they were going and with whom. We also expected a phone call if their plans changed. *Bob Wadley, Spanish Fork, Utah*

FAMILY RULE—DON'T MAKE OTHERS WORRY ◇ From a very early age my husband and I taught our children that they should never make another family member worry about them. It was a family courtesy that we acted on too. We gave them examples, such as calling home when they were going to be late or when they had a change of plans. This training became especially valuable during their adolescent years. On many occasions they called home more than once in one night to update their father and me to their plans and time expected home. *Alice Cross, Deltona, Florida*

EMERGENCY MONEY ◇ Before our girls went out for the evening with their friends or on a date, I always asked them if they had enough money for a cab ride home if it became necessary. I wanted to make sure that they always had alternatives of getting into a car if they were in an unpleasant or dangerous situation and they needed another ride home. They also kept a quarter in their shoes for an emergency phone call. *R. Merrill, Orem, Utah*

ADDRESS BOOK FOR TEENS' FRIENDS ◇ We kept a separate address book that contained all of our children's friends' names and telephone numbers. It came in handy whenever we needed to contact our children when they were at a friend's house. It was especially useful on those few occasions when we were pacing the floor worrying because one of our teenagers stayed out way past his curfew. I would start calling his friends, and usually one of them had seen him and knew what he was doing. Sometimes our teenagers even asked us for one of their friend's phone numbers, which they had lost. *Francis and Nadine Kleinschmit, Omaha, Nebraska*

CURFEWS

"It's ten o'clock. Do you know where your children are?" There are so many parents who cannot answer that question—the same one that flashed on our television screens in the 60s—that communities across the country are imposing their own curfews for children. Most community curfews are aimed at children under the age of sixteen who are "just hanging out" after ten o'clock. For teens sixteen and seventeen, the curfew is often a bit later. Community leaders are hoping to cut down on juvenile crime and victimization, which has become rampant in many parts of the country.

Teenagers need limits, and this is especially true for their evening activities. Regardless of whether your community has curfew laws, parents should impose their own reasonable deadlines for their teens to return home in the evening. For ideas on what has worked for other parents, here are some great tips for teen curfews.

◇

THE ALARM ENFORCES CURFEW ◇ Before our two teens went out with friends for the evening or on a date, my husband and I would negotiate a reasonable curfew for their return. Instead of waiting up for them past our own bedtime, my husband and I would set our alarm to ring at their curfew time. Then my husband and I would retire to bed at our normal time. If our children came home before their curfew, they would tiptoe into our bedroom and shut off the alarm before it went off. If, however, they were late and the alarm woke us up, we would know that they missed their curfew. We always encouraged them to call us if they were going to be late. We preferred waking up to their voice on the phone rather than being startled by the alarm going off and not knowing where they were. *Patty McMillan, Long Beach, California*

ALARM OUTSIDE DOOR ◇ We set the wind-up alarm clock outside our bedroom door. Our daughter would turn if off when she returned home from a date or other evening activity. *Terry Lister, Galloway, Ohio*

THE LIGHTS ARE ON ◇ It was always comforting to know that my daughters had returned home safely from an evening outing. Instead of trying to stay up until they returned home, I would always leave a light on in the living room, which they would turn out when they came home. If I woke up during the night, I could see out through my slightly open bedroom door whether the light was off or not. If it was, I could go right back to sleep knowing that my daughters were home. *Anna E. Johnston, East Haven, Connecticut*

WATCH OUT FOR THIS TEEN SCHEME

When I was a teen, my mother told me always to turn off the hall light when I got home so she would know that I had gotten home safely from a date. Well, I did turn out the light, but I turned right around and left again, staying out as long as I wanted. *A.P., Carson City, Nevada*

"SAY GOOD NIGHT TO YOUR PARENTS" ◇ My wife and I usually wait up for our teenagers when they go out in the evening with friends or on a date. We believe that they are less inclined to get into trouble if they have to face their parents when they get home. So far, we think it's working. *B.W., Tacoma, Washington*

THE BEST ALCOHOL DETECTOR ◇ My husband and I never slept well until our two teenagers came home safely after an evening outing. If we did fall asleep, we asked them to wake us up and give us a quick good night kiss when they arrived home. Our teens knew that they couldn't get away with alcohol on their breath with this loving bit of scrutiny. *Susie Anderson, Mission San Jose, California*

"WHAT TIME WILL YOU BE HOME?" ◇ Instead of setting a specific curfew for my daughter to return home from a date, I would ask, "What time do you expect to be home tonight?" If the time was unacceptable to me, we would discuss it until we reached a time that we both could live with. This seemed to work better than having the parent immediately dictate a curfew. *Lois Ulrich, Fremont, California*

CALL HOME IF PLANS CHANGE ◇ My husband and I always encouraged our children to call home if they had a change in their itinerary while they were out with friends or on a date. In turn, my husband and I would extend the same courtesy for our children if there was a change in our plans, or if we would be coming home later than what we had told them. *Georgia Lou, Flagstaff, Arizona*

NO SET CURFEW ◇ We have no set curfew for our teenagers; it is decided individually, based on where they are going and with whom. *B.B., Bountiful, Utah*

REASONABLE CURFEWS ◇ Instead of having a rigid curfew, be willing to judge each activity separately, keeping in mind the teen's schedule for the next day. Usually, if the activity is one that I approve of, so is the time frame. I try to be reasonable, not rigid, when deciding curfews. *Linda Sanderson, Garland, Texas*

ENFORCING CURFEWS ◇ If you have a set curfew for your teenagers, you need to be home to enforce it. If my husband and I are out for an evening, we always come home before the curfew we have set for our teens. A rule that is not enforced will cease being a rule. *Maureen Powell, Gahanna, Ohio*

GROUNDED FOR BEING LATE ◇ If you have a curfew, you should be consistent in enforcing it. If you let a curfew slip by once, even for a few minutes, your children will continue stretching the time until the curfew you originally set has no meaning. If our teens missed a curfew, they could not go out the next night no matter how inconvenient it might have been for them. No exceptions. It's never a good time to be grounded. *Karen Dombek, San Diego, California*

"HEY, IS THAT BRAD ON A DATE WITH HIS GIRLFRIEND—AND MOM?" ◇ My teenagers have always known exactly what the consequence would be for disobeying certain rules. The consequence for coming home past their curfew was for me to accompany them on their next outing or date so I could make sure that they would be home on time. And they knew that I would do it! Once my son cut school, so I accompanied him to school the next day. I bet that you can guess that he never cut his classes again. *Deborah Burt, Clovis, California*

PENALTY FOR MISSED CURFEW ◇ For every half hour your teen is late for his curfew, reduce the curfew for the next evening he goes out by thirty to sixty minutes. He will get the message quickly. *Anonymous, Toronto, Ontario*

EARLY BEDTIME ◇ When my son was eleven or twelve years old, he had a habit of coming home late from his friend's house. To correct this, I started a new policy: for every minute that he was late in coming home, he would have to go to bed the same number of minutes earlier than his regular bedtime. I only had to enforce this rule once or twice before he started getting home on time. It really worked! *Lynn Richey, Detroit, Michigan*

✖◆◆✖

TELEVISION

✖◆◆✖

When used judiciously, television can be a relaxing and, at times, even educational activity for your teen. When used excessively, however, television can have many negative consequences. According to many parenting and educational experts, our youth spend too much time watching television. In a study of how teens use their leisure time, television viewing was second on a list of eight favorite teen leisure activities (socializing was first).[15]

When asked about television and its impact on their lives, most children ages ten to sixteen say that what they see on television encourages them to take part in sexual activity too soon, to show disrespect for their parents, to lie, and to engage in aggressive behavior.[16] Aggressive behavior alone is modeled in a big way on television, reports the American Psychological Association. The APA estimates that a typical child (who averages twenty-seven hours of viewing a week) will watch 8,000 murders and 100,000 acts of violence on TV before finishing elementary school.

Many educators and critics of television also argue that heavy television use is at least partially to blame for lower achievement test scores. Others claim that it teaches a young person to be a passive learner and to live a passive lifestyle. Research confirms some of these serious accusations. In a study of over 400 adolescent boys, those who watched a lot of television were less physically active and fit than those who watched a little television. Infrequent viewers were also more imaginative and outgoing.[17] Even the nation's education secretary, Richard Riley, suggests that "The teenager who is perpetually glued to the tube is well on the way to having a very dull mind and a very dull—and perhaps risky—future."[18]

CREATIVITY BEGINS WHEN THE TV IS TURNED OFF ◊ It's amazing how creative kids can be when the options of television and video games are taken away. *G.D., Des Moines, Iowa*

TELEVISION COP ◊ I recently decided to embrace technology to help me cure my son of his wicked TV habit: I purchased a TV allowance box. It lets me decide how much time to allow my son to watch television or play video games. I simply code the time in. When the chosen amount of time is up, the machine shuts down the screen. I told my son that I would buy back any unused hours at the end of the week for $1 per hour. This has been so successful with my capitalist son that he has watched exactly one hour of television in three months since we started. Many of his old familiar but forgotten activities now fill in the hours. In an interesting twist, my son suggested we start a new family "game." Each week I select an extra chore for him to do. If he does that chore without complaining (his suggestion), he gets to watch without TV allowance cost, one show of his own choosing. *Joann Scherrer, Cupertino, California*

DISCOURAGE WEEKDAY TELEVISION ◊ My husband and I discourage weeknight television viewing for our teenagers and absolutely never allow it unless all homework is completed first. We encourage our sons to tape weekday programs they want to watch in order to save them for weekend viewing. *D.H., Fremont, California*

NO TV FOR A MONTH ◊ There was a period in our household when television was not used judiciously by our children. So we unplugged it for one month—and oh what a lovely month it was: we interacted more, talked to each other more, and played games together. Each of us learned how time-consuming television can be and how it distracts us from more important things. Although it wasn't practical to remove our television permanently, this monthlong experiment helped to teach our children better self-control in watching television. *JoAnn Wadley, Spanish Fork, Utah*

PARENTS AS ROLE MODELS ◇ As parents we sometimes forget that our actions become standards for our children. Television is a good example. For instance, we may not want our children to watch an excessive amount of television, but we do ourselves. Sometimes the message we give to our children is "You go do your homework—I'll watch TV." Parents need to set an example for their children by not watching television. *B.D., Fort Meyers, Florida*

TELEVISION OFTEN WORKS AGAINST FAMILY TEACHINGS ◇ Unfortunately, television often models the negative behavior of our society more than the positive. Before long, children tend to believe incorrectly that this is the norm of our society. *B.W., Tacoma, Washington*

✕◆◆◆✕

AFTER SCHOOL

✕◆◆◆✕

One of the biggest concerns of parents who work outside the home is the issue of what to do with their teens in the afternoon when they return home from school. This concern is confirmed by the recent findings of a survey involving 4,000 fourteen- and fifteen-year-olds. Published in the medical journal *Pediatrics*, the study reports that children left unsupervised after school are more likely than others to be depressed; use alcohol, marijuana, or cigarettes; take risks;

and get bad grades. Girls were more at risk than boys.[19] The research also pointed out that working parents who set firm limits and kept tab on their children's whereabouts—even from a distance—had fewer problems with their latchkey teens. Parents who were authoritative in their parenting style (see Chapter 14, "Teen-Family Relationships") had the best outcomes.

Researchers also have the following recommendations for parents: (1) Arrange for some sort of structured activity with adult supervision such as community centers, church groups, athletics, and after-school clubs. (2) On a regular basis, let your child know how much you care about them. (3) Keeping individual differences and needs in mind, have specific rules and enforce them. One such rule should be for the teen to seek your permission to go somewhere and that an adult must be in attendance at that location.

CALL ME WHEN YOU GET HOME FROM SCHOOL ◇ My daughter has to call me at work as soon as she gets home. She tells me where and when she is going someplace and with whom, and gives me a description of what she is wearing. She also has to leave this information in writing at the house. If her plans change, she must call again. *Judi Grace, Chicago, Illinois*

"I'M HOME" ◇ As often as possible, be there when your teenagers come home from school, work, or dates. Your presence at these times is very important to them. *Linda Sanderson, Garland, Texas*

TEEN TALK

My mother was always there to greet me when I returned home from school in the afternoon. I never knew how much I really appreciated this until I noticed how off-base I felt the few times she wasn't there when I came home. (Becky, Utah)

LET ME KNOW WHAT YOU ARE DOING ◇ If I wasn't home when my daughter went out after school or in the evening, I always asked her to leave me a note telling me where she was going, the phone number of the location, who she was with, what she was doing, and what time she expected to be home. *Anonymous*

AFTERNOON PLEASURES ◇ My teenagers and their friends told me that the backseat of a car is not where most teen sex occurs—it's in their own bed during the afternoon when their parents are at work. *Anonymous, Reno, Nevada*

"PAGE HIM" ◇ When our children want to get in touch with me or their dad, they page us at work. No matter where we are, in the office or on the road, we can call them back in a few minutes. A code of 911 at the end of the phone number will speed up our response time. We don't even discourage the trivial calls like "Sissy's eating all of the ice cream," "It's my turn to have the remote control," etc. We want them to be comfortable with using the pager. *Dolly Hickey, Clearwater, Florida*

CHECKING IN WITH MOM BY BEEPER ◇ My twelve-year-old daughter is obviously too old for a babysitter, but I still like to keep track of her activities when she gets home from school. Every afternoon, as soon as she gets home from school, she has to call my beeper at work every hour to let me know where she is and what she's doing. We have a code for most of her usual activities. For example, the code 777 tells me she's riding her bike around the neighborhood. If she's at a friend's house, she uses their phone number so I can call her if I need to talk to her. My beeper holds up to five numbers and messages so it's easy to track her afternoon activities. I call her back occasionally just to check in. This system helps us stay in touch with each other and my daughter knows that she can always contact me, even when I'm away from my desk at work. *K.G., Lake Forest, California*

ERASABLE MESSAGE BOARD ◇ Our family uses a magnetic erasable message board and an attached marking pen to leave messages for each other. We keep ours on the refrigerator door—a place guaranteed to be the first stop when our teens return home. We use it to let each other know our whereabouts and to list possible agenda topics for our weekly family meeting. *R.H., Fremont, California*

IN CASE OF EMERGENCY ◇ Teenagers who are home alone after school or who baby-sit for younger siblings after school should be well versed in how to handle any potential emergency. Review emergency procedures with your teen, then role-play some possible scenarios (e.g., "What if . . .). Keep emergency and neighbors' numbers by the phone. Make sure all home safety appliances (smoke detectors, etc.) are installed correctly and in good operating condition. These precautions could save a life. *T.L., Arcata, California*

8

DISCIPLINE: SETTING LIMITS

The thing that impresses me most about America is the way parents obey their children.

— DUKE OF WINDSOR, quoted in *Look*, Mar. 5, 1957

FAMILY RULES

Here's a secret about teenagers: they want rules. It's a well-kept secret—something teens will never tell you directly—and one that they will deny if you ever confront them with it. But it's true. They need rules and limits. Without parameters by which to live, teenagers, like all of us, will not have a sense of security and will not know what is expected of them. Without clear rules, teenagers will eventually act out in inappropriate ways, exhibit behavior problems, and maybe even get into trouble with the law. A teenager without behavioral parameters will also not accomplish all the important developmental tasks of adolescence. He will surely not accomplish his full potential, and he will be lacking in maturity and good judgment.

Setting limits and establishing family rules is the first step of any effective discipline program. It's a proven fact that teenagers are less likely to engage in inappropriate behavior that they have previously discussed with their parents and for which there are clear consequences. For example, if you have clearly communicated a family rule that has very strict consequences pertaining to driving in a car with someone who has been drinking alcohol, there is a much better chance that your teen will abide by that rule. Curfews, dating, drugs and alcohol, school, and family responsibilities are just a few of the topics you can discuss. Explain to your children that we all live by rules; there are rules for almost everything, from traffic rules to societal rules. Similarly, families must have rules in which to live by. Most parenting experts agree that it's best to involve the children in establishing rules, but it is the parents' responsibility to make the final decisions. After the rules are set, the consequences for not obeying a rule should also be established. The most important part of this whole procedure is to make sure that you and your children know what to expect from each other. *Clearly define what is acceptable and what is not.*

Most important is that the rules be age appropriate and not too oppressive. They should also be reviewed occasionally and renegotiated if needed. Here are some suggestions from other parents.

WRITTEN AGREEMENT ◇ When I make an agreement with my daughter or establish new rules, I often put it in writing and we both sign it. Both the rule and the consequence for disobeying that rule is clearly written out. The formality of a written agreement means more to a teen and they take it more seriously. *Christy Giroux, Indianapolis, Indiana*

PRESENT A UNITED FRONT ◇ Teenagers can be worthy opponents in an argument, just ask any parent. Teens have a knack for finding a crack in your logic or using one parent against another. However, if parents present a united front to their teenager regarding rules and requests, there will be less chance of being divided and conquered and ultimately losing the argument. When possible, parents should confer and agree on rules, requests, and discipline before talking with their teenager. Presenting a united front to your child is one surefire way to cut down on the length and frequency of arguments. *M.J.W., El Sobrante, California*

HONESTY—THE MOST IMPORTANT RULE ◊
Honesty is the most important rule in our family. My teens know not to lie to my husband or me. The consequence of lying is worse than anything they could possibly do, because we will have lost our trust in them. *K.S.D., Pittsburgh, Pennsylvania*

ONLY TWO FAMILY RULES ARE NECESSARY
◊ We don't believe in having too many family rules, but the few we do have are taken very seriously. Rule number one is to have mutual respect for each and every other family member. Rule number two is to be responsible for your own actions. So far, these rules have worked very well for us and our three teenagers. *Anonymous, Nash Creek, New Brunswick*

"I DON'T CARE WHAT MARY CAN DO!" ◊ My
teens were always comparing our family rules (curfew, school expectations, bedtime, etc.) to what their friends could do. My reply would always be the same, "I don't care what goes on in someone else's house, I only care about what goes on in our house." Parents should never feel pressured to conform to others' values and rules if they truly believe in their heart that what they are doing is right. *Karen Dombek, San Diego, California*

AUTHOR'S NOTE: *More often than not, your teenager's friends do not have the freedom and relaxed rules that they brag about. A quick chat with other parents will usually confirm standards similar to your own.*

THESE BEHAVIORS ARE ACCEPTABLE, THESE ARE NOT ◊ When my son became a teenager, we sat
down and had a long talk. I made it very clear to him which behaviors were acceptable and which were not. I told him, "Your teenage years will be whatever you make of them. If you choose to make it hell, it will be hell for both of us. If you choose to make it fun, it will be fun for both of us." Luckily, he chose the latter; they were good years for both of us. They key is to let them know early what the parameters are and that they are in control of their own destiny during adolescence. *Gladys Wallace, Columbus, Ohio*

FOLLOW-THROUGH IS MOST IMPORTANT ◇ If you give instructions to your children, it is important for you to follow through and see that they do them. Don't threaten consequences that you don't really intend to enforce. Otherwise children won't respect your directives or take them seriously. *JoAnn Wadley, Spanish Fork, Utah*

✕✖✖✖✖✖✖✖✖✖✖✖✖✖✖✖✖✖✖✖✖✖✖✖✖✖✖✖✖✖✖✖✖✖✖✖✖✖✖✖✕

DISCIPLINE STRATEGIES

✕✖✖✖✖✖✖✖✖✖✖✖✖✖✖✖✖✖✖✖✖✖✖✖✖✖✖✖✖✖✖✖✖✖✖✖✖✖✖✖✕

According to many parents, discipline is one of the most challenging and frustrating aspects of parenting adolescents. It's also one of the most important.

Although many people equate the word *punishment* with discipline, I prefer the word *guiding*. I also equate discipline with love. For it takes a loving parent to discipline a child or teenager. Through a system that includes both preventive and corrective methods, we guide our children through the peaks and valleys of adolescence with the hope that they will soon become self-disciplined in preparation for adulthood.

Conflict between teens and their parents is normal and should be expected. Most of the conflict is a result of a teen's growing need for independence and autonomy. During periods of conflict, it's important to separate your dissatisfaction with a teen's behavior from your love for him. In other words, communicate to your teen that you are upset by what *he did,* but you still *love him.*

Teenagers need clear, firm, and age-appropriate guidelines for their behavior. And, of course, the most critical aspect of discipline is consistency and follow-through. The quickest way to lose credibility with your children is to make a threat and not follow through.

Discipline should always fit the crime. Too harsh a discipline can backfire and cause even more rebellion and problems. Try to keep your cool and be patient, but stand your ground for what you firmly believe in. Always remember that you are the parent and that you are in charge.

Although the implementation of discipline is challenging for many parents, the rules of discipline are rather simple. Three of the most frequently used approaches by parents of teenagers are listed below. Keep in mind that each teenager is unique and will respond differently to different approaches. Even children within the same family may need to be disciplined in very different ways. Therefore, all three approaches are good to have in a parents' repertoire.

1.   *Three-step approach:* This is a very simple but effective discipline strategy for teens. *Step one* is to explain the rule or rules to your teenager. The Family Rules section (page 109) at the beginning of this chapter explains this step. *Step two* is to explain what the consequences will be for disobeying this rule. (Recommended consequences for teens include grounding, taking away privileges, or extra chores.) *Step three* is to always follow through with step two if the rule is broken.

EXAMPLE: You tell your sixteen-year-old son what his curfew is for the evening. You and your son have previously agreed that the consequence for missing a curfew is to be grounded (he can't go out) the next day or evening. Your son comes home fifteen minutes later than his curfew. You enforce the consequence (being grounded) the next day. No exceptions. You must be consistent in following through to make this discipline strategy work. It's as easy as 1-2-3.

---

2.   *Natural (or logical) consequence:* This discipline strategy allows the natural consequences of a situation to take place without parental interference. Natural consequences are directly related to a behavior. Natural consequences always offer a choice and promote self-discipline. For example, a natural consequence for constantly being late for work is the possibility of being fired. This discipline strategy is not

recommended for potentially dangerous activities like reckless driving or drug use.

> EXAMPLE: A parent tires of nagging her daughter to do her homework each evening, so she stops nagging and allows natural consequences to take over. Her daughter doesn't turn in her English homework for two weeks, at which time she shows her mother a note from her teacher. The note informs the daughter that she may have to repeat sophomore English next year. The mother tells her daughter that the issue is between her and her teacher. "Remember," says her mother, "I'm not involved in homework battles anymore." Not wanting to miss graduating with her peers, the daughter begins catching up with her homework without any nagging from anyone.

3.   *Positive reinforcement:* Many households are negatively oriented: parents are quick to find fault with their teens and criticize them frequently but seldom notice or acknowledge their teens' good or positive behaviors. Think back to the past twelve or twenty-four hours and try to remember all of the negative comments you made to your teenager ("When are you going to clean your room?" "Why do you dress so sloppy?" "You're never going to amount to anything if you don't study."). Then try to remember the positive comments you made to him ("Thanks for mowing the lawn, it looks great." "Your mother and I appreciated that you came home before your curfew last night." "You used good judgment last night when you took your friend's keys away from him after he had been drinking.").

Most parenting experts believe that if parents catch teens being good more often, that is, reinforce their positive behavior, there will be much less negative behavior to criticize or punish. The premise of this discipline approach is that positively reinforcing a behavior will increase the likelihood of that behavior's occurring again.

EXAMPLE: Your daughter has been quite lax about completing her chores on time, which has caused a few arguments. One afternoon you notice that she finished one of her chores early, and you comment, "Thanks for unloading the dishwasher so early. It's nice to have that done before dinner." You make a similar comment each time she completes a chore on time. In a few days all of her chores are being completed on time.

The following tips cover a wide range of discipline issues and strategies. They are followed by even more tips in sections on: Natural Consequences, Positive Reinforcement, Disagreements, When Communication Breaks Down, and Dealing With a Crisis. There are two parent skill builders in this chapter: The Art of Successful Confrontation (page 123) and The Toughlove Program (page 128). In addition, chapter 14 ("Teen-Family Relationships") covers topics related to discipline, including the most effective parenting styles (page 183) and the importance of family meetings (page 189).

SELF-DISCIPLINE ◇ We discipline our children with the hope that they will eventually become self-disciplined. I talk frequently to my teenagers about the importance of this. When their behavior suggests a lack of self-discipline, I tell them, "Since you obviously haven't learned self-discipline, I will help you by giving you some of my discipline." Gradually, they get the message that self-discipline is better than receiving someone else's discipline later. *B.W., Tacoma, Washington*

TWO PRINCIPLES OF DISCIPLINE ◇ Whenever I have to discipline one of my teens, I try to remember two rules: 1) The punishment should be fair and fit the crime, and 2) Never discipline in the heat of anger. *Anonymous*

UNCONDITIONAL LOVE DOES NOT INCLUDE ALL BEHAVIORS ◇ My children know that I love them, no matter what they do. But that doesn't mean that I always approve of their behavior. *K.S.D., Pittsburgh, Pennsylvania*

FIRST OFFENSES ◇ The teen years are a time for test-ing boundaries and behaviors, so my wife and I believe in going lightly on disciplining our daughter for most first offenses that don't put her personal safety in jeopardy. We try to turn it into a learning experience by saying something like, "OK, you blew it. Let's talk about what we can learn from this." During these discussions, we also inform her—in very clear language—what the conse-quences will be for a second offense. So far, it's worked for us. *Anonymous, Queens, New York*

TEENS NEED STRICT BORDERS ◇ Teenagers need to have borders (things that you feel strongly about them not doing) communicated clearly to them and enforced consistently by their parents. It's also important for a par-ent to listen carefully to their teenager about those areas of disagreement. Teens need to at least feel as though you are listening to them, even though you don't agree with them. One strategy that has helped my teens understand me is the question, "How would you feel if you were me?" *Debbie, Cape Corral, Florida*

BE THE PARENT, NOT THE BUDDY ◇ Let your teens know that you won't tolerate dangerous situations like drugs, drinking, sex, etc. Be the parent, don't be a buddy. Provide boundaries for them to bounce against. Let them know that you are not afraid to take control of them if they get out of control. Teens want to test the world, but their security and safety should be paramount to the parents. *Anonymous, Toronto, Ontario*

CREATIVE DISCIPLINE ◇ I always tried to come up with creative methods of disciplining that were directly associated with the infraction. For example, if one of my teens broke a window (and not just accidentally), he must not only pay for the damaged window out of his savings or work it off, but he also had to make the arrangements to have it repaired. This method of discipline teaches him to take responsibility for his own actions as well as learn-ing how things get done. *Anonymous*

PUNISHMENT FITS CRIME ◇ Whenever our teenage daughter got mad, she would go to her room and slam her door as hard as she could. We repeatedly asked her to stop this annoying practice, but she didn't. So, after one slam, my husband went in and calmly took her door off the hinges. Our daughter did without a door for a week, and since we rehung it, she hasn't slammed it one time. *Terry Lister, Galloway, Ohio*

LOUD MUSIC ◇ My two teenage daughters share a bedroom where they love to play their music loud. Occasionally it would be so loud that you could hear it from every room in the house, even with their door closed. I got tired of yelling for them to lower the music; they couldn't hear me over the noise anyway. So one day, I walked over to the electrical breaker box and cut the power to their room. Instant results! I only had to do this on two other occasions before my daughters got the message to keep their music at a reasonable level. *Judy Voelker, Palmer Lake, Colorado*

"BUT DAD, I DIDN'T KNOW IT WAS AGAINST THE LAW!" ◇ After hearing this comment from my son after he got in trouble with the law, part of his discipline was to write a lengthy essay on the law, which had to include one or more of the ten commandments, the California criminal code, and, in this case, the city's curfew law. *Vern Smith, Tustin, California*

TEENS DECIDE OWN PUNISHMENT ◇ We frequently ask our two adolescent sons to suggest their own punishment for bad behavior. Their suggestions are often harsher than what we had planned, but the best part is that there is no complaining about the punishment (like they do when we give it!). They think it's fair because it was their idea. *Lauren Kramer, Houston, Texas*

"WE'LL TRY IT YOUR WAY" ◇ It's important to recognize that our children often have better solutions to certain situations, including their own discipline, than we do. So my husband and I will say to our daughter something like, "You have a good point. We'll try it your way for two weeks and then evaluate it. It will be an experiment." We've discovered that it promotes respect between us and it encourages our daughter's critical thinking skills. *Anonymous, Hayward, California*

TEENS SET OWN CONSEQUENCES ◇ When explaining new rules (curfew, driving, etc.) to your teenager, ask him to recommend a fair consequence for disobeying that rule. I'll ask him, "If you were a parent, how would you handle this?" Make sure you agree with his recommendation, although my teens frequently set harsher consequences than I do. If the rule is broken, there is not much that your teen can complain about, since he, himself, set the punishment. *JoAnn Wadley, Spanish Fork, Utah*

FINED FOR SWEARING ◇ When my son started swearing in middle school, we fined him one dollar off his allowance for every swear word. He doesn't swear at home anymore, at least not around me. *K.V., Bellingham, Washington*

"YOU'RE GROUNDED" ◇ The discipline that worked best for my two young teens was to prohibit them from leaving the house for a certain number of days. Except for school-related activities, they couldn't go out with their friends or invite them to the house. A few days for minor infractions, or one full week for extraordinary discipline problems, seemed to instill a new importance of house rules to our teens. *F.E.S., San Jose, California*

CREATIVE SOLUTIONS OR COMPROMISE ◇ If you and your teen are at loggerheads about something, try thinking of creative solutions together. For example, if he plays his music too loud for your taste but he doesn't want to lower the volume, suggest that he buy some headphones. There's usually a creative solution to most problems. If that doesn't work, try compromising. *Anonymous, Portland, Oregon*

SOME WORDS CREATE DEFENSIVENESS ◇ Teenagers, like all of us, respond more positively to words that inspire empathy instead of defensiveness. For example, if I tell my kids how "angry" I am because they were late coming home, they will usually get very defensive. However, if I tell them how "worried" and "frightened" I was when they were an hour past the time they had promised to be home, they seem genuinely more understanding of my feelings and more apologetic for their actions. "Angry" is often an overused word to describe our deeper feelings of being scared, worried, threatened, or frightened. The more often we are able to select words that promote communication instead of destroying it—even when we're upset—the better our chance of getting the point across to our children. *R. Merrill, Orem, Utah*

TAKE AWAY PRIVILEGE ◇ The most effective form of discipline for our teens has been to take away a privilege for one to two weeks, depending on the misdeed. The withdrawn privilege could be something like television or video games or, for more serious offenses, being grounded (not being able to leave the house except for school). Once the misdeed is discussed with the child and the discipline explained, I would drop the subject and not berate them any more. Our family activities and relationships would continue as they always had, but the lost privilege would be strictly enforced. Holding a grudge for a long time only destroys relationships. *Susie Anderson, Mission San Jose, California*

"NOW YOU HAVE TO REBUILD OUR TRUST" ◇ My husband and I felt that it was important for our teenagers to realize that they would have more freedom and opportunities if they maintained a relationship with us based on trust. If they violated our family rules, we restricted their freedoms until their trust could be rebuilt. *J.R., Kimberly, Idaho*

ENDED ON A POSITIVE NOTE ◇ Whenever my husband and I had to discipline our teenagers, we always tried to end the conversation on a positive note. This demonstrated to them that we also recognized the positive aspects of their behavior and it helped to get our relationship back on track. *Karen Dombek, San Diego, California*

✕✕✕✕✕✕✕✕✕✕✕✕✕✕✕✕✕✕✕✕✕✕✕✕✕✕✕✕✕✕✕✕✕✕✕✕✕✕✕

NATURAL CONSEQUENCES

✕✕✕✕✕✕✕✕✕✕✕✕✕✕✕✕✕✕✕✕✕✕✕✕✕✕✕✕✕✕✕✕✕✕✕✕✕✕✕

HERE ARE THE RULES—HERE ARE THE CONSEQUENCES ◇ In our family we have a list of rules and the consequences for disobeying them. Teenagers need a clear understanding of what's expected of them by their parents, as well as knowing what the discipline will be if they don't adhere to the rules. Knowing what the discipline will be—with no exceptions—is a deterrent in itself. *Joyce Small, San Jose, California*

LET NATURAL CONSEQUENCES PREVAIL ◇ Don't always bail your teens out of circumstances that they get themselves into. They need to learn that there are consequences for their behavior. If you always rescue them, chances are they will continue with the same poor choices of behavior. *Bob Wadley, Spanish Fork, Utah*

LOGICAL CONSEQUENCES CAN BE LETHAL ◇ Everybody learns best by being in control of their decisions and experiencing the consequences of those decisions. To the extent possible, structuring logical consequences to behavior and allowing teens to experience them avoids unnecessary confrontation. If you miss the school bus, you'll have to walk to school and deal with being late. If you don't do your laundry, you won't have a clean shirt to wear to work. BUT . . . adolescents as an age group are particularly prone to sudden contagious attacks of the "stupids," and some behaviors (reckless or drunken driving, sexual activity, etc.) have logical consequences that can be lethal. That's when clear family rules to avoid dangerous situations, confrontations about transgressions, and activity-restricting penalties should be applied. *Bob and Jeanne Grace, Fairport, New York*

IT'S YOUR FUTURE, NOT MINE ◇ I tried many different tactics to convince my daughter that unhappy and long-term consequences could result in her behavior regarding sexuality, school, and other topics. None seemed to work as well as my comment to her: "You get to live with your future, not me. What you carve out for yourself is the piece of pie you will have to live with." *F.E.S., San Jose, California*

TWO KINDS OF MISTAKES ◇ Share with your teenagers that there are two kinds of mistakes in life: those that make you feel silly for a while and those that change your life forever. Do not be afraid to commit the first kind; that's what helps you learn. Be extremely cautious of committing the second kind; they don't let you go back. *Linda Sanderson, Garland, Texas*

POSITIVE REINFORCEMENT: CATCH THEM BEING GOOD

NOTICE AND ACKNOWLEDGE THE POSITIVE ◇ Catch your children in the act of doing something right or helpful, even if it's something as trivial as clearing their plate from the table. Tell them you appreciate it! Make a conscious effort to notice the positive things they do and focus in on those. *Phyllis Ahlman, Papillion, Nebraska*

GUIDE, DON'T FORCE ◇ There is a difference between guiding and forcing your teen to do something. Guiding is being a role model, offering information, and supporting good choices. Forcing is telling them what to do. Guiding works with teens, forcing doesn't. *Michael Stahler, Niles, California*

POSITIVE OVER NEGATIVE ◇ While there are times for negative reinforcement (punishments, grounding, etc.), a good rule of thumb is to use positive reinforcement over negative on a ratio of four to one. Positive reinforcement is the key! *John Cornett, High Rolls, New Mexico*

TEEN TALK

We get sick of being yelled at for every little thing. (Kelly, New Jersey)

◇

Take the time to notice when we do something right, too. (Amy, Arizona)

◆◆

DISAGREEMENTS

◆◆

RULES FOR DISAGREEMENTS ◇ We have two rules for dealing with disagreements: 1) no name calling, and 2) no interrupting when the other person is talking. Although simple, these rules have really made a difference in our family. *Judy Harris, Seffner, Florida*

THE TONE OF THE CONVERSATION ◇ If I have to confront one of my teenagers or discuss a touchy subject with them, I always try to remember that it's not what you say, but how you say it. A friend said it better: If you bounce a ball against the wall it will bounce back right at you with the same velocity that you threw it. *Glinda Goodwin, Fremont, California*

DON'T DRAG UP PAST ISSUES ◇ As tensions rise during a disagreement or reprimanding, focus only on the precise issue at hand. Don't drag up past issues with a comment like, "And another thing that I'm angry about is . . ." I've learned that when I do that, nothing gets resolved. *W.C., Spokane, Washington*

CALM, CLEAR, AND QUICK DISCIPLINE ◇ Most teens learn that if they argue long enough they'll eventually get their way by wearing you down. The best discipline is explained clearly and administered calmly. This strategy has worked well with my teens. *Leith Harris, Windsor, California*

AUTHOR'S NOTE: *Teenagers can sometimes carry on and argue long after a decision has been made by a parent. The longer the argument goes on, the greater the chance that one of you will make a comment that could burn bridges. When an argument goes on too long, politely disengage from the situation.*

"IT'S HARD BEING A PARENT" ◇ Sometimes, usually during a disagreement with my sixteen-year-old daughter, I say, "It's hard being a parent and I know it's hard being a teenager. Let's help each other." This simple comment brings out empathy in both of us and helps us toward a resolution of our problem or disagreement. *Teresa Dulberg, Hayward, California*

PARENT SKILL BUILDER

The Art of Successful Confrontation

A confrontation does not have to create more anger and defensive behavior. Follow these simple guidelines for a responsible and caring approach to confrontation:

1. *Timing is everything* when it comes to confronting someone. Time the confrontation so that the individual will be open to hearing your feedback. If the individual is in a bad mood, tired, or angry, wait for another time to confront him.
2. Be *courteous.*
3. Make your point *clear and concise.*
4. Communicate a *genuine and sincere* interest in the individual.
5. *Express your appreciation* whenever you have gained a minor concession.

✖✖✖✖✖✖✖✖✖✖✖✖✖✖✖✖✖✖✖✖✖✖✖✖✖✖✖✖✖✖✖✖✖✖✖✖✖✖

WHEN COMMUNICATION
BREAKS DOWN

✖✖✖✖✖✖✖✖✖✖✖✖✖✖✖✖✖✖✖✖✖✖✖✖✖✖✖✖✖✖✖✖✖✖✖✖✖✖

KEEP COMMUNICATION CHANNELS OPEN ◇
One of the worst things that can happen to a family is
when two or more family members stop talking to each
other. As a parent, always try to keep the communication
channels open. Keep talking and trying to understand
each other. Don't fall into the trap of "It's his turn to talk
or apologize." No one wins these kinds of battles, and
they can go on for days, months, and even years. As long
as you keep the communication channels open, there is a
chance that the issue will be resolved. *Thomas Leslie, San
Diego, California*

"TIME OUT, I'M FEELING TERRIBLE" ◇ When the
going gets rough between me and my daughter, I simply
say, "Time out, I'm feeling terrible about how we're getting along. How about you?" That gives my daughter permission to express her feelings about our relationship.
We usually end up in a deep conversation and a better
appreciation of each other. *S.J., Detroit, Michigan*

SEND A LETTER ◇ When feelings are volatile, write
your child a note instead of talking. This gives you both
space to take your own time in digesting information on
your own terms and in your own space. *T.D., Mariposa,
California*

WRITE A "LOVING LETTER" ◇ Sometimes, when
the tensions are high, and we're having a difficult time
communicating with one of our four daughters, we will
write what we call a "loving letter" to them. In the letter,
we first reiterate how much we love them, then we explain to them why we think or feel the way we do about a
certain issue. When one of our daughters started a phase
of not being very nice to us, including walking right by me

after coming home from school and not even saying, "Hi, Mom," I wrote her a short note and told her how hurt I felt when she did this. Teens respond better to letters because they have time to absorb the message before they have to reply. I strongly suggest that you don't write letters just to gripe. They need to be loving letters, or you won't get the response you are looking for. We've saved many of the replies that we have received from our daughters—many of them are precious and heartwarming. *Rita and Mike Miltner, Corning, Iowa*

DEALING WITH A CRISIS

For the purpose of this section, a crisis is defined as a serious problem with your teenager that needs immediate action. It could be an arrest for a crime, the discovery of drug abuse, running away, expulsion from school, reckless driving, unwanted pregnancy, an individual who is out of control and defiant to parents, or a variety of other problems that you consider serious.

If a crisis is brewing with your teen but has not yet erupted, act now. Remember that prevention through intervention can prevent a full-blown crisis. Talk to school officials, law enforcement authorities, or other professionals who have expertise with the particular problem. Just being better educated about a situation can relieve much of the stress. There are also many crisis hotlines you can call toll free that offer immediate assistance and guidance. Your local directory assistance or the 800 directory can help you locate these services.

During a crisis, provide immediate and unconditional support to your teen. Try to stay focused on the immediate problem. If there is a series of problems, deal with one at a time. Remember, a teen in crisis at one time or another is very common. Many other parents have been in your shoes, and together with their teen, have successfully resolved the crisis.

The emotional reaction of a parent can actually compound an already serious situation. A crisis is not the time to yell, lecture, attack, criticize, or moralize. If you need to let off steam (and you probably will), do it in a way that is not directed at your child. A crisis is a time to be as calm and steady as possible. It's also a time to brainstorm solutions to the problem. Do not hestitate to seek professional assistance if needed. Individual or family counseling often helps a family regain their equilibrium during and after a crisis.

The following parenting tips offer some sage advice. Also included in this section is a parent skill builder about the Toughlove Program, an organization that has helped thousands of parents.

◇

DON'T IGNORE PROBLEMS ◇ All families have problems, even those that don't appear to. If your teenager encounters a problem, whether it's drugs or alcohol, trouble with the law, or poor performance at school, don't think that you are the only parent to experience this. You aren't. The worst thing that you can do is to ignore it and hope that it will go away. It probably won't. Confront it now before it gets worse. And never be afraid to seek outside help if you feel that you can't handle it yourself. *JoAnn Wadley, Spanish Fork, Utah*

"I WANT TO BE THE FIRST TO KNOW" ◇ I told my three children that if they ever get into trouble, no matter how serious it is, I want to be the first to know about it. I promised to react civilly and in a helpful manner. I would use any resources I had available to help them resolve their problem. I may get angry later, I conceded, but my first concern would be for them. *Anonymous, Portland, Oregon*

FOR THE GOOD TIMES AND BAD ◇ I have found the statement, "Love the child, not the behavior," to be true. My son had some problems that got us involved with the justice system. He was guilty and I disapproved of what he had done (and he knew it!), but I stood by him throughout the process. I didn't bail him out, but was

---

TEEN TALK

I can't believe how naive parents can be sometimes.
(Brian, Arizona)

---

there to support him through whatever the consequence.
Parental support should be there for the good and bad.
Anonymous, Clovis, California

**TROUBLED TEENS CAN DISRUPT THE ENTIRE
FAMILY** ◇ I have raised five children, one of whom had
serious discipline problems and many run-ins with the police. A troubled teen takes a lot of time and energy. When
dealing with troubled teens, always remember that you
are in charge. Also, never forget to think of the family as
a whole, and to consider the innocence and safety of other
individual members. Do not destroy everyone's home life
while you devote all of your time and energy to one troubled teen. *Anonymous*

YOU NEED A BABY-SITTER ◇ As a last resort to get
the attention of a teen who's out of control and not trustworthy, threaten to hire someone (a baby-sitter of sorts)
to watch when you go out. If the behavior doesn't improve, you may have to follow through with your threat—
but probably not for long. Just the thought of someone
being hired to keep an eye on them is enough to improve
their behavior. When they begin showing signs of being
trustworthy again, they can have their privileges back.
Rebecca Smith, Boise, Idaho

CURE FOR TRUANCY ◇ When my foster child was
truant at school, I tried many different discipline strategies, but none worked. He continued skipping classes or
didn't attend school at all. At a friend's suggestion, one
day I removed all of his personal belongings from his
room except for a few essentials, including a week's
worth of clothes, toiletry items, a few books, and his
school supplies. He received one item back for every day
he attended all of his classes. He got the message in no
time and soon had recovered all of his personal belongings. *Teresa Norris, San Diego, California*

WHEN TEENS NEED US MOST ◇ Sometimes teens need our love most when they are most unlovable—that is, at times when they act out and get into trouble. *F.D.W., Omaha, Nebraska*

PARENT SKILL BUILDER

The Toughlove Program

The Toughlove Program is a nonprofit educational organization offering assistance to parents for out-of-control children. Toughlove is a network of parents helping other parents bring change into the lives of their young people who are incorrigible, uncontrollable, addicted, physically or verbally abusive, in trouble at school, in trouble with the law, and/or destroying a family. Toughlove uses a combination of philosophy and action to help families. They do not advocate or support physical or verbal abuse, nor do they advocate kicking kids out.

Toughlove is a crisis-intervention program, structuring group meetings to support parents and spouses in demanding responsible cooperation from out-of-control family members. One of the goals of the program is to empower parents with skills and knowledge. There are over 500 registered groups for parents and kids.

Toughlove either refers toubled people to groups in their area or assists them in starting their own community support group. For further information, write to:

Toughlove International, P.O. Box 1069, Doylestown, PA 18901 or call 1-800-333-1069.

For Further Information

National Runaway Switchboard 1-800-621-4000 (TDD for the Hearing Impaired 1-800-621-0394) for parents and runaways

National Center for Missing and Exploited Children 1-800-843-5678

National Child Abuse Hotline 1-800-532-3208

Recommended Reading

Phyllis York and David York, *Toughlove* (New York: Bantam, 1982).

Phyllis York, David York, and Ted Wachtel, *Toughlove Solutions* (New York: Bantam, 1985).

Gregory Bodenhamer, *Back in Control: How to Get Your Children to Behave* (New York: Fireside, 1983).

Stanley Turecki, *The Difficult Child* (New York: Bantam, 1989). Understanding and managing hard-to-raise children.

Katherine Gordy Levine, *When Good Kids Do Bad Things: A Survival Guide for Parents of Teenagers* (New York: Pocket Books, 1991).

Jane Nelsen and Lynn Lott, *Positive Discipline for Teenagers* (New York: Prima, 1991).

Joy Oryfoos, *Adolescents at Risk* (New York: Oxford University Press, 1990).

9

VALUES

You are the bows from which your children as living
arrows are sent forth.

KAHLIL GIBRAN, *The Prophet*

TEACHING VALUES

Values are like stars—they help guide us through life. Our values are the foundation of our character and influence our thoughts, feelings, and actions. We teach our children values with the hope that those values will help guide them through the many negative influences of our society.

Let your teen know your beliefs and values. Share them at a time and in a way that she will be open to listening. In turn, find out how she feels about certain issues. Chances are, she may have different ideas and beliefs than you do. Try to appreciate these differences instead of being threatened by them. Remember that she is in the process of forming her own identity, and she wants to be recognized as a unique person with her own thoughts, feelings, and beliefs. Like anyone, teens appreciate being allowed to come to their own conclusions about important issues. They dislike having ideas imposed on them and attitudes with the message "I know what's best for you."

Research sheds some interesting light on the values of adolescents. In regard to spiritual matters, adolescents show a strong interest. A national survey indicates that almost 90 percent of adolescents pray and more than 90 percent believe in God or a universal spirit. Only one in a hundred had no religious preference or affiliation, but only 25 percent had a high degree of confidence in organized religion.[20]

Some researchers have compared the values of adolescents today with their contemporaries in different time periods. There have been two striking findings. One is that there has been a steady increase over the last twenty years in teenagers' concern for their personal well-being. The other is that during the same twenty-year period there has been a steady decrease in concern for the well-being of others, especially the disadvantaged.[21] These findings suggest the importance of teaching our teens to accept people who are different from them and to be tolerant of lifestyles different from their own. We also need to teach them the value of forgiveness. But above all, we need to teach them that any value is meaningless unless it is acted upon.

The tips that follow represent many that I received from parents across the country. This section is followed by two other related sections: Parents as Role Models and Volunteering and Helping Others.

INFORMAL VALUE LESSONS ARE BEST ◇ Values are best taught to teens during informal times and in a way that doesn't appear to be a lesson. For example, family discussions about current events, television shows, radio talk shows, movies, books, or situations at school often provide entrees to sharing your views and values with your children. Use real-life examples they can relate to. It's also important for them to understand that their values will determine how they react to things, what kind of friends they will choose, and many other aspects of their life. If values are not taught by parents, children will acquire their values from other external forces such as the media and their friends. *Paul Dulberg, Hayward, California*

TALK ABOUT IMPORTANT ISSUES WELL BEFORE TEENS HAVE TO FACE THEM ◇ If you have an important rule or value that you would like to teach your children, don't wait until he is an adolescent to talk about it. Start mentioning these issues as soon as he can understand them. For example, if you fear that your son may start smoking when he becomes a teenager, talk about the dangers of smoking throughout his childhood. Don't wait until he is thirteen, when he may have already made up his own mind about smoking. If you don't want him to date until he is sixteen, mention this rule when he is a preteen or even sooner. The sooner and more frequently you discuss important issues with a child, the better chance that he will accept your beliefs well before he has to deal with or confront them. *Pat Loontjer, Omaha, Nebraska*

FOCUS ON A VISION ◇ Think of the qualities you hope your child will have when she enters adulthood. If you focus on this vision as you make decisions pertaining to your child, the vision will probably come true. I call it "tunnel vision," and I have found it to be a gift in raising my three children. *Barbara Browe, Clinton Township, Michigan*

OUTSIDE SOURCES REINFORCE FAMILY VALUES ◇ When family values are reinforced by other sources outside of the home, teenagers are more likely to believe and act upon them. For example, both our church and scouting have taught our boys many of the same values that we teach at home. *R.H., Fremont, California*

LIVE YOUR VALUES ◇ The best way to teach values to children is to live them yourself. *David Hopkins, Sacramento, California*

FINE-TUNING VALUES ◇ Teaching values to children should begin at an early age, but the fine-tuning of those values should continue through the teen years and possibly beyond. Fine-tuning is best done on a one-to-one basis (never in front of their friends) and during a moment when a real-life situation arises. For instance, during a recent driving lesson with my son I noticed that a pedestrian wanted to cross the street. I explained to my son that when you see someone trying to cross the street, it's a nice courtesy to stop (if it's safe to do so) and let them cross. On another occasion, my son was getting ready to go to a basketball game with a friend whose father had bought the tickets. I explained that, in turn for the kind-

ness offered by his friend, he should offer to buy the re-
freshments during halftime. Gradually, over time, the
fine-tuning has paid off and I now witness my son sponta-
neously responding in a courteous and gentlemanly manner. *Bennett Oppenheim, Mission San Jose, California*

**OUR SOCIETY IS MORE PERMISSIVE THAN WE
ARE** ◊ As television, movies, advertisers, and other
forms of media target the teenage market with more violence, sex, drugs and alcohol, and foul language, it becomes even more difficult to teach our children good
values and manners. As parents, we cannot shield them
entirely from this barrage of high-tech media, but we can
offset some of its impact with a short comment or talk.
For example, my husband and I let our children know that
our society is much more permissive than we are, and
through our own life experiences and values we strongly
disagree with much of what we see. In addition, if teenagers hear this message from at least one other source, such
as their church, a friend, another parent, or even a
teacher, they will be more likely to believe their parents.
A.B., Bountiful, Utah

AUTHOR'S NOTE: *Comments from your teen such as "But
Billy can go!" or "All my friends watch R-rated movies," can lead to
an important talk about family values.*

YOUTH PROGRAMS ◊ Be actively involved in a
church with a good youth program that promotes the values you are trying to instill in your child. Children need
a support group and so do parents. *Virginia Bourgeous,
Syracuse, Utah*

THE CHOICE IS YOURS ◊ When discussing values
and morals with my teens, I always made it clear that
these were my feelings and beliefs, but they would have
to make up their own mind about these same issues. This
showed respect for their individuality, which they appreciated. They are both adults now, with morals and values that any parent would be proud of. *Jim Goodwin,
Fremont, California*

PROMOTING THE VALUE OF COURAGE ◊ Our
teenage daughter often has points of view outside of the
mainstream of thinking. For example, she recently

wanted to give a speech to her high school student body about the failures of some of Martin Luther King's ideas. As an African-American herself, she knew that she would receive criticism from her teachers and fellow students, but she still chose to proceed with her speech. My husband and I applauded her courage and individuality and supported her right to promote ideas that she believes in. We also used this situation to teach her some skills in presenting her ideas so people will be more open-minded in hearing them. We taught her to always present her views in a respectful and mature manner, and we shared with her the importance of attacking ideas, not individuals or groups. We also warned her to expect a variety of comments after her speech, ranging from praise for her courage to angry comments about her beliefs. We explained that there can be pain, agony, and occasional bouts of loneliness when a person goes outside of the mainstream of thinking. But above all, we reaffirmed our appreciation for her individuality and told her that we would always be there for her. *Anonymous, El Sobrante, California*

"THIS IS WHAT CAN HAPPEN" ◇ A fourteen-year-old acquaintance of our family recently became a father. We used this unfortunate situation as an example to show our teenage boys how a young person's life changes when a baby is born out of wedlock. There's nothing like a real-life experience to open up a teenager's eyes. *Anonymous, California*

RESPECT THE DIFFERENCE OF VALUES ◇ Treat your teen as you would an adult when listening to his beliefs and values. Respect him for the person he is—not for the person you want him to be. *Lynn and Nancy Meyer, Omaha, Nebraska*

TEEN TALK

Realize that your child is not an extension of yourself like an arm or leg. Your child is a separate person complete with his or her own soul, talents, passions, thoughts, and dreams. (Monica, California)

SHOWS SHOULD BE AGE APPROPRIATE ◇ Parents should allow their children to watch only age-appropriate movies, videos, and television programs. Young children and teenagers tend to mimic their heroes and what they see in the media. If they see a certain behavior (sex, drinking, drugs, foul language, violence, etc.) on television or in a movie, the chance of their repeating that same behavior is more likely to occur. *Penny Cole, Scotia, New York*

AUTHOR'S NOTE: *I believe parents also have the right to prohibit music having lyrics and messages that clash with family values.*

RETURN WITH HONOR ◇ Some friends of ours have a plaque hanging near their front door with the words, "Return with Honor." It was a simple way to remind each family member to be honorable in his interactions with the world and to be true to his own values and those of their family. *R. Merrill, Orem, Utah*

DON'T BE DISCOURAGED—VALUES DO SINK IN ◇ Sometimes, after I finish an important conversation with one of my teenagers, I get the feeling that nothing I have said has sunk in. It's so frustrating. Then, sometimes months later, that same child will make a comment that indicates that he did hear what I said months earlier. So even though it sometimes appears that your teen isn't listening, chances are he or she hears more than we parents think. *Debbie Lincavage, Fremont, California*

PARENTS AS ROLE MODELS

Our example as parents will influence our children more than any other. We need to remind ourselves of this every day of our lives.

◇

"DO AS I SAY, NOT AS I DO" ◇ Don't expect standards of behavior from your teens that you don't practice yourself: obeying the speed limits; giving priority to family time; using drugs, tobacco, or alcohol; cheating; or lying. For example, if you cheat on expense reports, your teens may think that it's no problem to cheat on tests. Your attitude about alcohol will probably decide theirs. *Linda Sanderson, Garland, Texas*

ROLE MODEL FOR FUTURE RELATIONSHIPS ◇ As parents, we are the most influential role models for our children, both as parents and as a husband or wife. Chances are that our children will become parents someday based on our own example. They also learn the role of husband and wife by our example. By showing respect, love, and caring for your spouse, you are setting a positive role model for a future husband or wife. It's important to remember that we are setting the foundation from which our children will launch themselves into the same roles that we are acting in today. *R. Merrill, Orem, Utah*

COMPLIMENT YOUR SPOUSE ◇ I asked some friends who have grown children to give me some tips on raising our two boys. I expected some advice on always knowing where your kids are and who they're with, or don't forget to tell your kids how much you love them. The advice I got was just as important, but something my husband and I rarely remember to do. And that was, "Don't forget to compliment your spouse in front of the children." *K.T. Hom, San Jose, California*

TEACH BY EXAMPLE ◇ Teach your teens by your own attitude and actions to respect all people and cultures. *Linda Sanderson, Garland, Texas*

✖◆◆✖

VOLUNTEERING AND HELPING OTHERS

✖◆◆✖

The value of helping others is an important one to teach our teens. Encourage your teenager to volunteer in your community. Helping others in need will enrich your teen even more than the people he will help. The spirit of volunteerism needs to be rekindled in our country, and it begins with each of us.

◇

COMMUNITY SERVICE ◇ As a form of discipline for getting into trouble at school, my wife and I required our son to work at least four hours of community service. We offered him a list of community service projects from which to choose. He picked one that was interesting to him. He enjoyed it so much that he worked there way beyond the required four hours. There are many positive byproducts for teens working at a community agency, organization, or church: they gain valuable work experience, they're exposed to a potential career, and they feel good about themselves for helping others. *Anonymous, Utah*

THE VALUE OF HELPING OTHERS ◇ My wife and I taught our children that many other people have less than we do and that we should always be thankful for what we have. To impress this point, we invited our children to help us with a volunteer program for the homeless. It was a real eye-opener for them and a lesson that they all still remember. *David Hopkins, Sacramento, California*

REINFORCING ACTS OF KINDNESS ◇ To motivate my four children to do kind deeds for one another and others, I began rewarding each of their acts of kindness. "Privilege points" are given for unsolicited and extra-special acts of kindness—ones that go above and beyond a child's own chores and family responsibilities. Examples include writing a letter to a grandparent, doing a family member's chore for them, or writing their birthday thank-you notes without being nagged. I record the points and good deeds on individual index cards that I keep for each child. After earning ten privilege points, the child gets a special family acknowledgment during dinner and a reward from me or my husband. The reward is usually a small gift (under $10) or a special outing with one or both parents. This family project has not only helped to get my children into the habit of doing kind deeds for others, it has also spread goodwill to one another in our family. *Beth Self, Aloha, Oregon*

THE VALUE OF VOLUNTEER SERVICE ◇ We encourage our children to volunteer their services to a community or church organization that helps people in need. Another option, which a few of our teens took us up on, is to volunteer their time for someone in our community who needs assistance. Volunteer service provides many dividends for teens: it increases their self-esteem, expands their outlook on the world, and helps to turn their focus from inward to outward. *Bob Wadley, Spanish Fork, Utah*

Recommended Reading

Linda Eyre and Richard Eyre, *Teaching Your Children Values* (New York: Fireside, 1993).
Linda Kavelin Popov, *The Virtues Guide: A Handbook for Parents Teaching Virtues*. The Virtues Project (604-537-4647), 1993.

10

SEXUALITY AND DATING

Would you be more careful if it was you that got pregnant?
—Advertisement in *Time*, April 28, 1986, urging birth control by men

TEEN SEXUALITY

Sexuality is a beautiful thing, one of the most natural aspects of life. And adolescence is when we become acquainted with it—when we discover its mysteries.

As natural as it is, sexuality is also one of the most complex and emotion-filled subjects confronting parents and teenagers. Adolescent sexuality is not just about sex, it's about physical and emotional needs, moral and ethical guidelines, values, and religious doctrines. It's about behavior, consequences, and responsibility. And it's about love.

Guiding your teen through the issues, information, and experiences of sexuality is no easy task. Although teenage sexuality has been of concern to every generation of parents before us, the closing years of the twentieth century pose new and frightening challenges for both parents and teenagers: sexually transmitted diseases that may be incurable or even deadly, an adolescent pregnancy rate in the United States that is the highest in the Western world, and a society whose media and entertainment industry presents a blatant and exploitive view of sexuality to our teens.

By the time a child reaches adolescence today, he or she already knows a great deal about sexuality. It's a hot topic among friends, on television, in movies, in music and rock videos, in advertising, and in books and magazines. Sex permeates almost every aspect of teenagers' lives. Even if your teen has never mentioned the subject of sex to you, chances are that he or she spends a great deal of time thinking about it, fantasizing about it, and talking to his or her friends about it. Teens may also be sexually active; a large number are. The older a teen becomes, the more likely it is that he or she will become sexually active.

Never before has the need been greater to talk to our children about sexuality. Every year in the United States approximately one million teenagers become pregnant and three million teenagers contract a sexually transmitted disease. Study after study confirms that the risk of unwanted pregnancies and sexually transmitted diseases are much greater for individuals who are uneducated about sex. A recent study by the Alan Guttmacher Institute suggested that "the most effective pregnancy prevention programs are those that include sex education, skills for decision-making and communicating with partners, and access to family planning."[22]

Parents should not rely on the schools to teach sexuality to our children. Although most schools provide some sex education, it varies widely both in content and effectiveness. Many teens have personally told me that the sex education program in their school was a joke.

The American Social Health Association strongly believes that sexuality education begins at home and that a parent is a child's most important sexuality educator. But according to research, teens still learn more from their friends than their parents. A study on sources for sex education among early adolescents found that peers top the list, followed by literature, mothers, school, experience, and fathers.[23] It's a sad commentary when more teens learn by "doing it" than by talking to their fathers.

Let's face it; coming to grips with the fact that your child is becoming sexually aware is difficult enough, let alone having to talk to him or her about it. And, for many parents, it's awkward and embarrassing to talk so openly about sexuality. If you feel uncomfortable, share your discomfort with your child; chances are, he or she will be feeling the same way. Some parents believe that talking about sexual issues will encourage sexual activities, but this has been disproved many times. Although these are all real concerns for many parents, the risks of not talking to your child are far greater than the discomfort you will experience doing it. Without guidance from parents, sex education for our teenagers will be taught on television, at the movies, and in the locker room.

Talking to teens about sexuality is actually just a continuation of the dialogue that began years ago when your child asked about the difference between boys and girls and was curious about where babies came from. As a child gets older, the answers to these questions becomes more and more detailed. Puberty is a developmental milestone—the beginning of sexual maturity—and a time when profound changes take place in your child's body. Since children begin puberty at varying ages, with girls usually ahead of boys by as much as two years, many parents begin talking to their child about puberty around age nine or ten. This enables their children to know in advance about changes before they happen. This is also the age that usually coincides with the beginning of sex education at school.

Continuing the dialogue about sexuality with your child through the preadolescent and teen years is important. Keep in mind that the best sex education includes both information and values. In a pamphlet called *Becoming an Askable Parent,* the American Health Association states that children need "a clear set of values, accurate information, a strong sense of self-worth, and decision-making and communication skills."[24] A parent's own views about teenage sexuality in the context of his or own personal beliefs, morals, and, if applicable, religious convictions can offer guidance to the teen. Many parents recommend buying a book about teenage sexuality that you can read yourself before talking to your child, then give to your child as a supplement to your talk. A list of recommended books is at the end of this chapter.

No matter how good the dialogue is between you and your teen, there is always a chance that your son or daughter will make sexual choices that you disagree with. Teenagers do become pregnant, they do contract sexually transmitted diseases, and they do announce their homosexuality. If any of these situations happens in your home, your teen will need your love, understanding, and support more than ever. Families need to stick together in good times and in bad. Remember that you may not approve of their behavior, but you love your son or daughter.

The following tips are a sampling of ones I received from parents across the country. They cover a wide range of views on many different topics of teenage sexuality.

◇

YOU CAN EXPLAIN SEX MORE ACCURATELY THAN THEIR FRIENDS ◇ Remember, even if you do a horrible job in explaining sex to your children, it will still be a much better job than your children's friends will do. *JoAnn Wadley, Spanish Fork, Utah*

READ ALL ABOUT IT ◇ To help educate my teens about sexuality, I collected reading material that I thought was appropriate for their age and left it around the house for them to read. Some good sources were magazine articles, pamphlets, and library books. The schools often have free informative pamphlets too. *Mary Hopkins, Sacramento, California*

BOOKS FOR SEX ED ◇ I highly recommend buying one of the many books written for teenagers on the topic of sexuality. I found one that I thought was appropriate for my preteen daughter. I read it first, then we read some of it together. It prompted some great questions and discussions. My daughter commented that she liked the illustrations (some have real pictures but I thought that was a bit too much to begin with) about how the body grows during puberty. Although we usually keep it on our family bookshelf, I find it in my daughter's room occasionally. That's a good sign. *Anonymous*

KNOW THE CONSEQUENCES ◇ When discussing sexuality with teens, always make sure they know the responsibilities and possible consequences of sex. If they choose to have sex, they will at least know that there are responsibilities and consequences that go beyond the sexual act. *Glinda Goodwin, Fremont, California*

POSSIBLE SCENARIOS AND ROLE-PLAYING FOR SEX ED ◇ One of the most powerful ways to get the message across to your teen about sexuality is to use role-playing or "what if" scenarios. Questions that confront the teen with real-life and very possible situations are best. Here are a few examples: "How would you feel and what would you do if you became pregnant?" or "How would you feel and what would you do if you contracted a sexually transmitted disease?" or "How would you feel if your boyfriend broke up with you the day after you had sex with him for the first time?" These types of real-life scenarios, plus the teachings of your own values about sexuality, will do more to educate your teen about possible negative consequences than any other method. *Anonymous, El Sobrante, California*

AUTHOR'S NOTE: *Please refer to the parent skill builder "Role-Playing" (page 63) for a detailed explanation of how role-playing can be used to help your teen make wise choices about sexuality.*

A MOTHER'S WORRY ◇ I worried about my daughter's promiscuity, but nothing I said to her seemed to sink in. Then one day in total frustration I said, "I can cry with you and feel bad for you, but I can't die for you. If you get AIDS, you have to die yourself. No one, not even a mother, can do that for you." I'm still not sure if my daughter got the message, but I think it helped. And I know these words helped me, because from that point on I was able to pull back from these worries and truly realize that I could not be responsible for my daughter's actions. *Anonymous, San Jose, California*

"SAVE SEX" OR "SAFE SEX" ◇ There seems to be a growing trend among young people to believe in "save sex" instead of "safe sex." I applaud them for their restraint and wisdom. *J.R., Kimberly, Idaho*

AUTHOR'S NOTE: *One of the largest organizations promoting sexual abstinence for teens is "True Love Waits." For further information, call 1-800-LUV-WAIT.*

AIDS TEST ◇ One of the most frightening experiences of my life, and I'm sure of my daughter's too, was accompanying her to a clinic to receive the results of the AIDS test that she had taken more than a week before. I'll never forget sitting in the waiting room of the clinic with my daughter, both of us dealing head-on with the fear of receiving the worst possible news. The results were negative and we rejoiced quietly and separately, but my daughter had just learned a lesson about unprotected sex that couldn't be duplicated in any pamphlet or sex education class. An AIDS test makes you reflect about the past and be more careful in the future. *Anonymous, Queens, New York*

TEEN TALK

Make sure you talk to your kids about sex, because the sex ed programs at school are often a joke. (Anonymous)

◇

What teens don't know can hurt them! (Vanessa, California)

◇

My parents never once talked to me about sex, drugs, or alcohol. I guess they assumed that if they didn't mention it, I wouldn't do it. I thought that if they didn't want to talk with me about it, I shouldn't talk to them about it. So I learned things from my friends and television. (Anna, South Carolina)

◇

There's a lot of pressure to be sexually active when you're a teenager, but I'm glad that I'm not. Many of my friends are frequently afraid that they're pregnant and some of them have confided in me that they have a sexually transmitted disease. One of the pay-offs for not being sexually active is that you don't have to worry about all of that. (Anonymous, California)

◇

All my mother did to teach me about sex was to give me a book by a doctor and say, "If you have any questions after you read it, let me know." I thought her approach was kind of cold. (Y.V.E., Charlotte, North Carolina)

A CONDOM DEMO ◇ Around the time my daughters began dating, I became extremely concerned about many of the issues surrounding their sexuality, especially sexually transmitted diseases and pregnancy. So one day I came home and plopped a few condoms on the table and announced, "We need to talk." I shared my concerns with them and even brought out a cucumber, which I used to demonstrate the correct procedure for using a condom. Even though one of my daughters said, "This is gross," from that point on they knew that they could talk to me about anything. And they did! *Anonymous, Miami, Florida*

ESSENTIALS FOR HER FIRST PERIOD ◇ When our granddaughter was about twelve and a half, it was obvious to me that she would start her first period any day. She and her family were in the process of moving to another city, so I made up something I called the "Happy Package." I gave it to her mother along with instructions to keep it with the luggage so she could get to it quickly if needed. Sure enough, their first night at a motel, it was needed. Her mother gave her the package and said, "Jenny, Grandma sent something special for you on this special occasion." Besides the basic essentials, I included personal grooming products, bath powder, cologne, and a red heart necklace. I also enclosed a note saying,

> *Dear Jenny:*
>
> *Congratulations! You have now begun your new life as a woman. You may have some turbulent days, but these will pass when your body becomes accustomed to the new you. Remember, we all love you very much. Welcome to our world.*
>
> *Grandma*

I found out later that she was very pleased with her package and was proud to have been treated so specially. *Mary Ann Hyde, Omaha, Nebraska*

CRITERIA FOR INTIMACY ◇ My daughter and I sat down one day and had a heart-to-heart talk about sex. I told her that I didn't think it was necessary to be a virgin when she got married, because in all honesty most people aren't, including her dad and me. I told her that the minimum criterion for sharing this very intimate part of your-self with someone is that you should care deeply for the person. Each person should have his or her own well-thought-out criteria for becoming sexually involved with someone. It should never be taken lightly. *Anonymous, San Diego, California*

GAY TEENS ◇ When a teen comes out and announces to his parents that he is gay, it's understandably a trying time for parents as they try to deal with and understand the situation. There are many groups, including parenting groups, that can help. Please don't hesitate to contact one of these support groups to talk to other parents who have been through this before. Keep in mind that your child needs to be reassured that you love him. His willingness to talk to you about being gay shows he has a trust in you that most parents would envy. Too many teens think their parents will hate them, so they isolate themselves and often resort to drugs and alcohol and, all too often, sui-cide. Above all, don't let anyone try to make you ashamed of who your children are. *R.D.F., Kansas City, Missouri*

FOR FURTHER INFORMATION

A helpful organization for parents is Parents and Friends of Lesbians and Gays (P-FLAG). For infor-mation, support, and a listing of local chapters, con-tact them at 1101 14th St. NW, Suite 1030, Washington, D.C. 20005 (202-638-4200).

HER FIRST GYN APPOINTMENT ◇ After my daughter established her first serious relationship with a boyfriend during her late teens, I asked her if she was considering becoming sexually active. She said, "Not yet." I asked her to tell me when she was, so I could make sure that she was prepared, and took all the necessary precau-tions. Five months later, she told me that she wanted to go on birth control. Since I was due for an exam myself, I made back-to-back appointments for my daughter and me with my own gynecologist, whom I trusted completely. To lower my daughter's anxiety about her first exam, I explained what to expect: First the doctor will talk to you, then he will give you a gown to put on, etc. Both of our exams went smoothly and we felt that we had shared something very special together. It helped us both get through a difficult event in our lives. This experience was much preferable to having my daughter go to a birth control clinic by herself. *Anonymous, San Diego, California*

A WOMAN'S PERSPECTIVE ◇ My husband is an excellent father to our two teenage daughters, but occasionally he didn't understand some of their needs or behaviors to the same degree that I did. Occasionally, when we were alone, I would offer a woman's perspective to his thinking. He seemed to appreciate that and I know it helped him understand our daughters better. And I know that my daughters appreciated it, too. Similarly, I can see how important a male perspective would be for a mother to understand her sons. *F.E.S., San Jose, California*

SEXUAL STANDARDS ◇ I believe that it is wrong to give mixed messages to teenagers regarding sexual morals. Many parents tell their children that sex is something for mature consenting adults or for marriage, then they say, "Here's some condoms in case you need them." This is not only confusing for teens; it opens the door for sexual behavior. We should give them one clear message that we believe in, followed by a confirmation of our love and an offer of our support. *Edith Schuette, Ukiah, California*

ALTERNATIVES TO INTERCOURSE ◇ I explained to my two teen boys that having sexual intercourse is a very serious decision to make and one that can lead to many negative consequences, which I described in detail. I told them that although I do not condone teenage sex— and I gave my reasons—I did offer them an alternative to intercourse if they became sexually active. I explained that couples could give each other a great deal of sexual pleasure by using their hands in a sensual way, and I offered some explicit examples. I also told them that when they limit their activities to hand touching—and only hand touching—they also limit their chances of dealing with one of the negative consequences that I talked about earlier. *Anonymous, Ventura, California*

"NOT IN MY HOUSE!" ◇ My own mother was very clever in handling teenage problems. One day my older brother stuck up pictures of naked ladies on the walls of his room. While he was at school, our mother painted clothes on all his "pinups." After school that day they both had a good laugh. He had declared his manhood and she had made it very clear that her message was, "Not in my house!" I think of this incident often when I hear parents struggling with moral issues with their teenagers. *Sandra Pavick, Milpitas, California*

ADVANCE PLAN FOR "IN THE HEAT OF THE MOMENT" ◇ When your teenagers begin dating, don't be afraid or embarrassed to talk about potential situations that could happen on a date. If you do, there is a greater chance that your teenager will handle the situation in a positive way because they are prepared for it. There isn't one person who can always be intelligent and do the right thing in the heat of the moment. *A.B., Bountiful, Utah*

◆◆◆◆◆◆◆◆◆◆◆◆◆◆◆◆◆◆◆◆◆◆◆◆◆◆◆◆◆◆◆◆◆◆◆◆◆◆

DATING

◆◆◆◆◆◆◆◆◆◆◆◆◆◆◆◆◆◆◆◆◆◆◆◆◆◆◆◆◆◆◆◆◆◆◆◆◆◆

Every parent has an opinion about teenage dating—at least, all the parents I interviewed for this book. About the only thing that parents could agree on was the need for family rules about dating. But they couldn't agree on the rules. Although most agreed that age sixteen was a good minimum age for real one-on-one dating, some parents had strong arguments against imposing any minimum age. Many parents promote group dates for the early adolescent years. Here's a sampling of their tips.

◇

JUST LIKE YOUR SISTER ◇ When I began dating, my mom told me to "always treat your girlfriend the same way that you would want your sister treated by her boyfriend." Without moralizing or going into great detail, my mother was able to communicate some important standards with this statement. *Mike Gunn, San Francisco, California*

GROUP DATES ARE BEST ◇ During the early dating years, we always encouraged our teens to go on their dates with a group instead of going out solo with their boyfriends or girlfriends. Groups are usually safer, and they offer alternative choices if one or more individuals in the group choose to do something illegal or unsafe. *Mary Hopkins, Sacramento, California*

NO DATING UNTIL SIXTEEN ◇ My wife and I have a rule for our five children: No dating until they are sixteen years old. They can participate in group activities and outings with members of the opposite sex before sixteen, but no couples dating until they are sixteen. We believe that there is a natural progression of intimacy when dating begins; therefore, if a teen begins dating at a young age such as fourteen, he or she will be more likely to reach a more advanced level of intimacy before having the maturity to make wise judgments and understand the consequences of his or her choices. *Bob Wadley, Spanish Fork, Utah*

AUTHOR'S NOTE: *Research backs up this wisdom. The earlier teens begin to date, the earlier they are likely to have sexual relations.*

DATING DEPENDS ON THE MATURITY OF THE TEEN ◇ We always shoot for the age of sixteen to be the minimum age for our four daughters to begin dating, but we also took each girl's level of maturity into consideration. Although we wanted our four daughters to wait until they were sixteen to begin dating, we also took into account each girl's level of maturity when we decided if they could begin dating. *Rita and Mike Miltner, Corning, Iowa*

MINIMUM AGE FOR DATING ◇ My husband and I would not allow our four daughters to go on a date until they were sixteen years old. Although sixteen was a minimum age, there was no pressure, encouragement, or expectation for them to begin then. Each of our daughters began dating at very different ages. *Edith Gutierrez, Fremont, California*

NO AGE LIMIT FOR DATING ◇ When my daughters were in their early teens, they began asking me when they could start dating. Instead of giving them a specific age, I always answered, "When you're ready." I explained that there is no magical age to start dating. Some teens begin parental supervised dates when they're fifteen, other teens don't start dating until late in high school. If I had given them an exact age, they would have either wanted to begin dating then or felt pressure to date because the time had arrived. By being nonspecific, the dating process followed a natural course. Each of my daughters started dating at a different age. *Holly Frei, Mission San Jose, California*

HOUSE RULES ◇ Our teen daughters were not allowed to have guys in the house when no parents were home. And guys were never allowed in any of the bedrooms, whether we were home or not. *Edith Schuette, Ukiah, California*

BEDROOM DOOR MUST REMAIN OPEN ◇ When our daughter's boyfriend comes over, he can go into her room but the door always has to remain open. *Carolyn Denise Friend, Fontana, California*

PUPPY LOVE ◇ Adolescent romantic love, sometimes called puppy love or infatuation, should be taken seriously by parents, because it's quite serious for the smitten teenagers. Although it is usually short-lived, it's a real feeling for teenagers, and one that should be validated by parents. Teens hate to have their feeling downplayed and not taken seriously. We can all look back to our own teenage years and remember how we felt about our own romances, however fleeting they usually were. *D.S.C., Escondido, California*

PARENT SKILL BUILDER

Preventing Date Rape

Every parent needs to talk to their teenage son or daughter about rape—what it is, how to avoid it, and what to do if it happens. It should also be made clear that it is a serious and punishable crime. Rape is when someone forces you to have sex against your will. In other words, if someone continues a sex act, whether it's sexual touching or some other sexual activity, after the other person says no, a rape or sexual assault has occurred. The frequency with which rape happens to teenagers, especially in situations that began as an innocent date or a party, has reached alarming numbers. It's estimated that one in five teenage girls and young women will be raped on a date and, sadly, only a small fraction of them will ever report it.

The topic of date rape should be discussed with teens (both boys and girls) as part of a more general topic about dating—guidelines, appropriate behaviors, curfews, etc.—well before they begin dating or attending mixed-gender parties. They should be encouraged to go on double dates or group dates whenever possible. Explain how alcohol and other drugs can impair one's judgment and lead to date rape or other negative consequences. Many teenage girls report being taken advantage of after they became intoxicated by alcohol or high on drugs. Both boys and girls should be taught to clearly communicate their feelings and limits and to respect their partner's feelings and limits. Girls need to learn the importance of expressing themselves forcibly so that their words and their nonverbal behavior convey the true force of their opposition. Role-playing a possible scenario can be very helpful (see page 63). *Boys should be taught to believe what girls are saying.*

Another preventive strategy is to let your daughter's date or group of friends know that your daughter has given you the itinerary for their outing and appropriate phone numbers (when possible) where she can be reached in case of an emergency. Knowing that a parent is monitoring the date can be a deterrent against date rape.

If your daughter becomes a victim of date rape, she will need your love and support (see "Dealing with a Crisis," page 125). Guilt and confusion are often common feelings after a date rape. She will need to be assured that the rape or sexual assault was not her fault. She should also seek immediate medical attention. For information, guidance, and support, call your local rape crisis center.

For Further Information

National HIV/AIDS Hotline (English) 1-800-342-AIDS; (Spanish) 1-800-344-7432; (TTY for hearing impaired) 1-800-243-7889; for information, education, and referrals.
National AIDS Hotline for Teenagers 1-800-234-8336
V.D. National Hotline—Herpes Hotline 1-800-227-8922
American Social Health Association/Herpes Resources Center 1-800-230-6039; or write: ASHA/HRC, Dept. PR45, PO Box 13827, Research Triangle Park, NC 27709.

Recommended Reading for Parents

The American Social Health Association, *Becoming an Askable Parent: How to Talk with Your Child about Sexuality, 1994. To receive a copy of the booklet, send $2 (price subject to change) to The American Social Health Association, Dept. PR, PO Box 13827, Research Triangle Park, NC 27709.*
Judy Blume, Are You There God? It's Me, Margaret (New York: Dell, 1970). Recommended for both early adolescent girls and their parents, especially fathers. Offers a glimpse into the world of early adolescent girls, their friends, and their experience of puberty.

Recommended Reading for Teens

Judy Blume, *Are You There God? It's Me, Margaret* (New York: Dell, 1970). See above.

Paulette Bourgeois, *Changes in You and Me: A Book about Puberty* (Kansas City: Andrews & McMeel, 1994). Recommended for girls. Features beautiful transparent overlays.

Robie H. Harris, *It's Perfectly Normal: Changing Bodies, Growing Up, Sex and Sexual Health* (Candlewick Press, 1994). Color illustrations.

JoAnn Gardner-Loulan, *Period* (Volcano, CA: Volcano Press, 1979). Revised and updated. Includes a removable parent's guide. A teenage girl's guide to menstruation.

Kathy McCoy and Charles Wibbelsman, *The New Teenage Body Book: Honest Answers to the Hundreds of Questions You Have about These Vital Years* (New York: The Body Press/Perigee Books, 1992).

Lynda Madaras, *What's Happening to My Body? Book for Girls* (New York: Newmarket Press, 1988). Illustrated with drawings.

Lynda Madaras, *What's Happening to My Body? Book for Boys* (New York: Newmarket Press, 1988). Illustrated with drawings.

Wardell Pomeroy, *Boys and Sex* (Delacorte: New York, 1991). This book covers many issues and topics related to adolescent male sexuality.

Wardell Pomeroy, *Girls and Sex* (Delacorte: New York, 1991). A comprehensive book on female sexuality in adolescence.

Gail B. Slap, *Teenage Health Care* (New York: Pocket Books, 1994).

11

DRIVING

He made fuzz come out of my bald patch.
— CHARLES A. LINDBERGH, discussing the first time he
took a drive with one of his teenagers

LEARNING TO DRIVE

Other than high school graduation, there is no more important milestone from a teenager's perspective than getting a driver's license. Getting their "wheels," as teens call it, represents freedom and status. Although a teen's newfound mobility may help to ease up on Mom and Dad's role as the family taxi drivers, this teenage milestone isn't one that many parents look forward to. Parents know there will be new expenses and concerns that come with this new territory.

It is now common knowledge that teen drivers receive more citations and are injured and killed in greater numbers than any other group of drivers. The National Highway Safety Administration has reported that traffic crashes are the number one killer of teenagers in the United States.[25] A report by the Insurance Institute for Highway Safety states that "teenagers as a group are more willing to take risks and less likely to use safety belts. Teenagers are also more likely than older drivers to underestimate the dangers in hazard-

154

ous situations, and they're less able to cope with such dangers."[26]

Researchers say parents can help lower the risks. A Georgia-based research group stated that "parents need to provide longer periods of supervised driving in low risk settings and serve as role models by driving safely themselves."[27] The National Highway Safety Administration agrees that young people need to practice their driving skills more. The administration's recommending that states go to a three-tier licensing that includes a learner's permit, provisional license, and a full license.

Parents cringe when they see the cost for insuring their young drivers. Insurance rates can soar up to 250 percent when a young man is added to a policy in some states, and by 50 percent or more for young women. Parents recommend shopping around for insurance policies. Good student discounts are available from most insurers, and some offer substantial discounts if teens and parents attend a company-sponsored workshop.

The following section includes some creative tips you can use with your teen driver and a parent skill builder, Is Your Teenager Ready for a License? Later in this chapter there are some potentially lifesaving tips in the section Drinking and Driving.

◇

SAFETY FEATURES FOR OLDER CARS ◇ Many of the older models of cars—the ones that many teens are attracted to because of the low price—are not equipped with even the basic safety features, such as shoulder harnesses. I told my son that any car he considers buying must have a headrest and shoulder harnesses. If they don't have these features, he must install them before he gets behind the wheel. *Bennett Oppenheim, Mission San Jose, California*

DRIVING CONTRACT ◇ Soon after my son received his driver's license, I gave him a written contract to sign which listed his responsibilities for using the family car. He was responsible for all tickets, paying for his own gas, washing the car weekly, checking the fluid levels weekly, and returning the car on time for the rest of the family to use. If my son failed on any of these responsibilities, his car privileges could be taken away (this was also included in the contract). Teens take written contracts more seriously than verbal agreements. *M.I., Minneapolis, Minnesota*

LOG 1,000 MILES BEFORE GETTING LICENSE
◇ After receiving their learner's permits to drive, our three teens had to log 1,000 miles driving with my husband or me before they could apply for their license. It usually took them less than a year to accumulate the mileage because we would let them do much of the driving on our vacations and they would frequently drive from our country home to town. They kept track of their miles in a little book that was kept in the car. By the time they had logged 1,000 miles, they had driven at night, in winter road conditions, and had encountered most other driving conditions. *Shirley Yungclas, Webster City, Iowa*

DRIVING LICENSE FOR B AVERAGE
◇ I required my teens to achieve a B average in their schoolwork before they could apply for a driver's license. It was a great motivator to pick up the pace in school. The minimum grade point average should be tied to your child's ability. For example, if the child has been getting substandard grades, perhaps a C average would be a reasonable goal to achieve. *Susie Anderson, Mission San Jose, California*

B AVERAGE TO DRIVE
◇ Long before my son was old enough to apply for his driver's license, I explained the rules: He must have a B average in school before he can apply for his learner's permit, and he must pay for one-half of his car insurance. If he loses his B average, he loses his privilege to drive. If he maintains a B+ average, Dad pays for all of his car insurance. This rule turned out to be a better motivator for good grades than anything I had previously tried. *B.O., Ventura, California*

CAR OWNERSHIP AND RESPONSIBILITY
◇ I believe that teenagers who share in at least some of the financial responsibility (insurance, car payments, maintenance, etc.) for the vehicle they use tend to be more responsible drivers and take better care of the vehicle. After all, it's their investment, too. I also get my teens involved in some of the other more mundane aspects of car ownership: shopping for insurance, taking care of pa-

perwork at the Department of Motor Vehicles, and getting the car repaired and serviced. *B.M., Natchitoches, Louisiana*

CONSEQUENCES OF CAR OWNERSHIP ◇ Think twice before you decide that your newly licensed sixteen-year-old needs to have his or her own car. There are many long-term consequences of car ownership, including the financial burden of car and insurance payments, one or both of which may be the responsibility of your teenager. The added expenses of car ownership cause some teens to add more hours to their part-time job, leaving even less time for family and studying. *Georgia Lou, Flagstaff, Arizona*

"CAN I BORROW *YOUR* CAR?" ◇ When I was a teen, my parents let me drive their car, but they never gave me my own set of keys. I always had to ask for them. Looking back now, I think that was smart of my parents. I couldn't just take the car without asking, and it was always clear who owned it. Driving was a privilege, not a right, so it was something that I always valued. *Dave Moody, Livermore, California*

PAY FOR PARTIAL CAR INSURANCE ◇ My fifteen-year-old son is just learning to drive. My wife and I discovered that it's much less expensive to add him to our car insurance policy than for him to get his own policy. Before we allow him to get his license. he has to come up with one-half of the extra cost of adding him to our policy. We'll pay the other half. We also expect him to help with some of the driving chores. *W.G.W., New Paltz, New York*

CAR INSURANCE ◇ Our teens had to pay for their own car insurance before they could drive. They needed to save their allowance or have a part-time job to be able to afford insurance. They knew that speeding tickets and accidents would raise the insurance premiums, so they were responsible drivers from the beginning. *David Hopkins, Sacramento, California*

CHARGE BY THE MILE ◇ My father came up with a fair and equitable way for his teenagers to share the costs of operating the family car. He would check the odometer before we left and again when we returned, and he charged us a nominal fee per mile that we had driven. That covered the cost of gas, oil, maintenance, and insurance. We thought twice before driving someplace without a real purpose in mind, and cruising was out of the question. *B.B., Bountiful, Utah*

PARENT SKILL BUILDER

Is Your Teenager Ready for a License?

When your teenager drives well enough to pass the state driving test for a provisional license, ask yourself the questions below. You may have overlooked some practice or knowledge your youngster needs.

1. Have we discussed alcohol, drugs, and driving?
2. Does my son or daughter know what to do if he or she has been drinking and feels it's unsafe to drive?
3. Have we practiced in heavy city traffic?
4. Have we practiced on one-way streets and at intersections with three-way signals?
5. Have we practiced using a left-turn lane?
6. Have we practiced on small country roads, on graveled roads with potholes, and on hills?
7. Have we practiced in bad weather?
8. Have we practiced at night?
9. Have we practiced what to do if an emergency occurs?
10. Have we discussed what to do if a collision occurs?
11. Does my teenager know I can cancel his or her license at any time, for any reason I feel is valid? Does my young driver know I will cancel the license if he or she drives irresponsibly or violates traffic laws?

Reprinted from *Parent-Teen Training Aide,* published by the California Department of Motor Vehicles.

"TICKETS WILL COST YOU!" ◇ My husband and I paid for our teenagers' car insurance unless they got two moving violations in a period of three years. This was great incentive for them not to have a lead foot on the accelerator pedal. *Karen Dombek, San Diego, California*

PAY FOR TICKET AND INSURANCE ◇ If one of our children gets a ticket while driving, they have to pay for the ticket and the resulting increase in our car insurance policy premiums. *P.R., Billings, Montana*

REWARD FOR GOOD DRIVING ◇ When each of our four children turned sixteen and started to drive, we made them an offer. If our car insurance had not been increased by their twentieth birthday due to an accident of theirs or excessive tickets, we would write them a check for an agreed amount of money. I joyfully gave them the money on their twentieth birthday. This was great incentive for them to drive safely during their teen years. *Becky Beel, Johnstown, Nebraska*

DRIVING LESSONS ◇ All three of our sons went to driver education programs shortly after they acquired learner's permits, but we also supervised a lot of practice driving ourselves. After the first week or so, I stopped making "Look out for . . ." comments. Instead, I asked the learning driver to talk out loud about the things he was considering as he drove. When I knew he'd already seen the car at the stop sign two blocks up or was planning to downshift for the light that couldn't possibly stay green until he got there, I didn't have to behave like a nervous mother. *Jeanne Grace, Fairport, New York*

"NOW YOU HAVE TO PASS MY DRIVING TEST!" ◇ As soon as my son received his learner's permit to drive, I warned him that he had to pass two driving tests—mine and the state's—before he could drive on his own. My test involved safety, defensive driving, and responsiveness. I explained the importance of each safety feature in the car; how it works, and the possible consequences of being involved in an accident without one. Next, I had him bump into a stationary and solid object at 1 mile per hour to demonstrate what an impact feels like and point out, once again, how the safety features work. I then had him imagine what an impact would be like at 50 miles per hour. To teach defensive driving, I explained the importance of being aware of everything around him when he drives. To practice this awareness while he's driving, I occasionally asked him to tell me everything he observed such as, "I see a truck passing me on my left, I see the brake lights on the red car in front, I see a car on my right entering the freeway," etc. And finally, the last part of my test is responsiveness. Before driving on his own, I made sure that he had appropriate reactions and judgments to various driving situations. If not, I gave him more supervised experience. When it came time to take the state's driving test, he was confident and self-assured; after all, he had passed a much more difficult test—his dad's. *Bennett Oppenheim, Mission San Jose, California*

NO PASSENGERS WITHOUT OUR APPROVAL ◇
Our daughter had to get our permission first before having passengers with her during the first three months after receiving her driver's license. We implemented this rule for safety reasons and because we had heard that teens sometimes drive in an unsafe manner to show off for their peers. After three months, we dropped this rule because she had demonstrated responsible driving. *M.J.W., El Sobrante, California*

"SORRY, MOM, I JUST GAVE THE ACCELERATOR A LITTLE TAP" ◇ When your child is taking driving lessons, be sure he knows that a car is capable of moving under its own power, depending on how high the idle is set, and that an accelerator pedal can be very touchy. I didn't realize that my son didn't know that until he was driving my car into the garage one day. It needed to go a little farther, and instead of letting the car's idle inch it along, he gave the accelerator a little tap. It was just a little one but enough to propel the car into the wall of our town house. Luckily, no one was hurt. Needless to say, the next day we went down to the school parking lot to experiment with what a car is capable of doing on its own power or with a little tap on the accelerator. *L.K.K., Houston, Texas*

"YOU MUST NOT BE MATURE ENOUGH TO DRIVE" ◇ My husband and I confronted our sixteen-year-old daughter after we received a phone call from a neighbor who reported seeing her driving fast and dangerously in our neighborhood. We told our daughter that we were very concerned about her safety. We also told her that, if this report was true, she had not used good judgment in driving and we were now wondering if she was mature enough to drive. We explained that if we ever see or hear reports of this kind of driving again, we will automatically take away her license for three to six months. We reminded her of our parental responsibility to protect her from herself if we thought that she wasn't making safe and mature choices for herself. We also outlined a detailed scenario of the possible financial consequences to us if she was involved in an accident. All of this information—knowing that she was being watched by us and others, the negative consequences of poor driving, and our liability being at stake—had a profound effect on her and resulted in better judgment when she was behind the wheel. *Anonymous, Queens, New York*

CONSEQUENCE FOR CAR CRASH ◇ After our son crashed our family car at a location to which he had previously been told not to drive, I stapled his driver's license to the repair bill and made him responsible for the entire bill. It took him a few months to pay the bill and get his license back. *Anonymous*

A CLUTCH DRIVER ◇ I used a car with a clutch to teach both of my children how to drive. By doing so, they knew early on how to drive any car. I also taught them how to change a tire. *Julius Frei, Mission San Jose, California*

AUTHOR'S NOTE: *Although it's important for every driver to learn how to drive a clutch (stick) vehicle, most experts recommend beginning driving lessons with a vehicle equipped with an automatic transmission.*

✕✦✦✦✦✦✦✦✦✦✦✦✦✦✦✦✦✦✦✦✦✦✦✦✦✦✦✦✦✦✦✦✦✦✦✦✦✦✦✕

DRINKING AND DRIVING

✕✦✦✦✦✦✦✦✦✦✦✦✦✦✦✦✦✦✦✦✦✦✦✦✦✦✦✦✦✦✦✦✦✦✦✦✦✦✦✕

Drinking and driving is a deadly combination—especially for teenagers. Car crashes are the number one cause of death for teenagers, and alcohol is frequently a factor.

Talk to your teen about drinking and driving and about being a passenger with someone who has been using drugs or alcohol. Tell your teen never to make an exception for mixing drugs or alcohol and driving; there are *always* better alternatives. It takes only one incident to cause injury or death. Talk about realistic situations that could happen on a teen outing or date and offer alternatives to getting into a car with a driver who has been drinking (see parent's tip "No Second Chances" on page 163).

State legislators and local governments have experimented with a variety of plans to curtail the problem of teenage drinking and driving. The most effective policies are ones that include zero tolerance of driving under the influence of alcohol or drugs and, most importantly, involve the immediate suspension of the driver's license. The threat of losing his or her driver's license gets a teen's attention faster than anything, including trying to instill a fear of possible injury or death.

Many states have already adopted or are considering zero tolerance laws relating to teens. California adopted a law stating that anyone under twenty-one who is arrested for any alcohol or other drug offense will have their license suspended for at least one year. The alcohol or other drug offense need not be driving related. If the teen doesn't have a driver's license they must wait an additional year before one will be issued. If the teen is convicted of driving under the influence of alcohol, they could be sentenced to serve time in a juvenile correctional facility and/or be charged fines and schooling fees amounting to $1,000 or more. *Any measur-*

able amount of alcohol is enough to be arrested if the individual was driving. Other states have adopted similar laws.

There is also a growing trend for parents to adopt their own zero tolerance rules, including loss of license, for their teens in regards to drinking and driving. "A driver's license is sacred to teenagers. They will do almost anything to ensure their privilege to continue driving," said one mom who wrote out the rules for her teen and made him sign it before she even let him take out his learner's permit. Strict rules and tough consequences are in order for an infraction that has such frightening potential results.

The following tips represent the feelings and ideas of many parents I talked to during the course of preparing this book.

DRINKING AND DRIVING ◇ I lost my oldest teenage daughter at the hands of a drunk driver—her best friend. I have told my other children that if I ever hear of them getting into a vehicle with a driver who has been drinking or using drugs, or if they drive under the influence themselves, they will never again have access to the keys of my car. And they know that I mean business. I hope that no other mother has to go through the ordeal of losing a child. I beg you to open your eyes and not be in denial about the possibility of your teens using alcohol or drugs, and then driving. Talk to them and warn them before another tragedy happens. *Ann Salah, Fremont, California*

NO SECOND CHANCES ◇ I made my son promise that he would never—under any circumstances—drive a car after he had consumed ANY amount (even one sip) of alcohol. The same rule applied to any driver of a car in which he was a passenger. I explained that car accidents were the number one cause of death for teenagers and that many of these accidents were alcohol related. I also told him that this is one of those life and death situations where you may not be given a second chance. I explained that you may think you can drive a car after only one beer, but you can't. I reminded him that all of those teenagers who died in alcohol-related accidents thought the same thing when they got behind the wheel. Together we thought of scenarios that he might encounter and solutions to each one. We brainstormed options: call me, call a cab, go with another driver, stay at a friend's house, etc. Finally, I explained that if he ever disobeyed this rule, especially after this conversation, the consequences would be far worse than anything his imagination could think of. *B.O., Ventura, California*

AUTHOR'S NOTE: *Role-playing, as suggested in this tip, is one of the most effective strategies to convince teens that there are alternatives to getting into a car with a driver who has been drinking or using drugs. For a detailed example of how role-playing can be used by parents and teens, see page 63.*

EMERGENCY CAB FARE ◇ My daughter confessed to driving home one night with a driver who had been drinking. She claimed that she had no other way to get home. I explained emphatically that there are always better alternatives than riding home with a drunk driver or even someone who had consumed only one beer. I encouraged her to call a cab and I would gladly pay for it. I showed her where I had hidden $50 to cover any cab fare in case I wasn't home. She now feels less trapped in potentially dangerous situations. *R.R., Houston, Texas*

AN EYE-OPENING EXPERIENCE ◇ Upon learning that my teenage daughter drove our car after drinking some beer, I arranged for the two of us to spend a Saturday evening at the emergency room of our local hospital. Two alcohol-related car crashes that evening resulted in a number of individuals being treated at the emergency room. The lesson my daughter learned that night was better than fifty stern lectures. Teens have to see to believe! *B.J.J., Phoenix, Arizona*

**SEE CHAPTER 12 FOR MORE TIPS ON
DRUGS AND ALCOHOL.**

For Further Information

Students Against Drunk Driving (SADD) P.O. Box 800, Marlborough, MA 01752. Educates adolescents about the dangers of drinking and driving. SADD publishes a newsletter and guidelines for starting new groups.

12

DRUGS AND ALCOHOL

A new generation of young people is at risk of growing up and losing their way when it comes to drugs.

— D O N N A S H A L A L A , Secretary of Health & Human Services

Today, in the mid 1990s, drug use by teenagers is on the rise for the first time in ten years.[28] Use of marijuana, LSD, amphetamines, and inhalants (glues, aerosols, and solvents) is all on the increase, but these drugs are overshadowed by the real drug of choice among teenagers and even preadolescents—alcohol. Study after study confirms that alcohol should be the number one public enemy of parents:

The use of alcohol is often associated with the leading causes of death and injury (i.e., motor-vehicle crashes, homicides, and suicides) among teenagers and young adults.[29]

Two-thirds of eighth graders and nearly nine-tenths of seniors have tried alcohol.[30]

Approximately two-thirds of teenagers who drink report that they can buy their own alcoholic beverages.[31]

The first use of alcohol typically begins around the age of thirteen.[32]

Middle school and high school students consume 1.1 billion cans of beer each year.[33]

Many people blame the popularity of drug use by teens on their rebelliousness or curiosity. Perhaps, but these reasons only scratch the surface of the problem's explanation. We have to look deeper for the real answers:

First, we have to recognize that we live in a drug-oriented society. From the time we were babies, we learned that drugs can cure just about anything that ails

165

us: pain, anxiety, fatigue, or even boredom. Drugs can change our mood or relieve us—temporarily—from many unpleasant aspects of life. Entire aisles in supermarkets are devoted exclusively to over-the-counter drugs, and over two billion prescriptions are written every year in the United States alone.

Second, the increasing amount of stress reported by teenagers can also be partially to blame for the increase in teen drug use. Teens learn that drugs can help relieve the pain (once again, temporarily) of adolescent problems and issues.

Third, many parents use the same drugs that they tell their children not to use. Many teens have watched their parents drink alcohol, pop pills, and smoke cigarettes. Some parents even condone alcohol use for teens as long as they don't use other drugs (even though alcohol is even more addicting than many illicit drugs).

Fourth, teenagers can't watch television or listen to the radio without being barraged by advertisements for beer and other alcohol beverages, many of which are aimed at teens and young adults. Fifty-six percent of students in grades 5 to 12 say that alcohol advertising encourages them to drink.[34]

The most effective drug prevention programs are ones aimed at young children, as early as the kindergarten years. There is also some evidence that prevention programs work for teens as well, especially those that include training in life skills such as decision making and coping. Parents are encouraged to communicate clearly to their teens and strictly enforce family rules regarding the use of drugs. Promoting an open and ongoing dialogue with your teen about the dangers of drug use is also recommended, but be careful not to lecture or overstate the facts. There's a very good chance that your teenager knows more about drugs than you do, so don't pretend to have all the answers. Many parents recommend role-playing as one of the most effective strategies to combat peer pressure as it relates to drug use. (See page 63 on role-playing.)

If you discover that your teen is using drugs, don't panic

or confront him in a hostile manner. Most experts believe this will only make the matter worse. Instead, talk to him, listen to him, and try to determine the extent of his drug use. It's also helpful for a parent to know, if possible, why their son or daughter is involved in drugs. Is it because of peer pressure, was it to escape from something, or was he just experimenting? Depending on the extent of involvement, a parent may want to seek professional assistance such as counseling for the teen or to get more information from a community drug abuse program. Of most importance, parents should not bury their heads in the sand and pretend that there isn't a problem. Usually there is. Don't be embarrassed to reach out and ask for help. Early intervention is extremely important in dealing with drug abuse.

The following parenting tips offer some sage advice about teen drug use, from preventive measures to dealing with an abuse problem. Also included are phone numbers and addresses for many drug abuse organizations and a parent skill builder, "Possible Signs of Teen Drug Abuse."

For tips and information about drinking and driving, see Chapter 11, "Driving."

EARLY LESSONS ABOUT DRUGS ◇ From the time my children were in grammar school, I taught them that all drugs, even aspirin and cough medicine, had negative side effects. My children are adults now and I credit those early lessons to their being cautious about using any drug. *Mary Hopkins, Sacramento, California*

PAMPHLETS PLACED STRATEGICALLY ◇ Many well-done educational pamphlets about drug abuse are aimed at the adolescent audience. Most are available at no cost from schools, health clinics, and community agencies. I occasionally leave these and newspaper clippings about drug abuse around the family room where my teens will see them. I know they read them because I sometimes find a pamphlet in one of their rooms. *J.J., Austin, Texas*

SET AN EXAMPLE ◇ I wanted to set a good example for my son as he was growing up, so I quit using alcohol. It's been many years since, and my son is grown now. I still abstain. Setting a personal example is always better than telling someone not to do something, especially if you do it yourself. *U.C.S., Oakland, California*

"WE CAN'T PREVENT YOU FROM DOING DRUGS" ◇ I told my daughter that her mother and I can't prevent her from doing drugs, but we can explain the possible physical and emotional consequences of using drugs. I also explained to her—in no uncertain terms—the consequences that she would face from us if we ever found out that she was using drugs. *Anonymous, Queens, New York*

DRUG ABUSE CAN STRIKE ANY HOME ◇ I have learned the hard way that no one is immune from having a child turn to drugs. I used to think that something negative had to be going on in families—no love, a lack of standards, bad role modeling, etc.—for a child to get involved in drugs. As a mother who tried to do everything right in raising her kids, from enrolling in parenting classes to being involved in their lives and always knowing where they were and who they were with, I had to swallow a big dose of humility when my own daughter, at age thirteen, got involved with drugs and ran away from home. Sometimes, even when you do your best, drugs and other hazards of adolescence can strike your family. Don't blame yourself! *Kristi Vanselow, Bellingham, Washington*

"BUT HE'S NOT AN ALCOHOLIC" ◇ As a high school counselor, I frequently hear parents downplay their child's drinking problem by saying, "But he's not an alcoholic." My reply was to agree with them, but add, "You don't have to be an alcoholic to have an alcohol problem." That comment seemed to get their attention better than anything else I could say, and it often resulted in the parents getting professional assistance for their child. *Susie Anderson, Mission San Jose, California*

DRUG ABUSE MAY BE ONLY THE TIP OF THE ICEBERG ◇ As a high school principal, I have learned that most youngsters who get involved in drug or alcohol abuse have other serious problems lurking beneath the surface. Don't just focus on the symptoms of the drug or alcohol use; this is often an indicator of being out of balance in some other area of their life, which is usually fam ily or school related. Through understanding and active listening, you can often discover the deeper issue. Professional counseling may also be needed. *Bob Wadley, Spanish Fork, Utah*

TEEN TALK

If you find any evidence of drug involvement, chances are your son or daughter is NOT HOLDING IT FOR A FRIEND! Don't be in denial. (Anonymous, California)

⬦

Don't push your kids into being cool. I know of some parents who actually encourage their kids to drink because everyone does it. (Mike, Nevada)

PROFESSIONAL HELP FOR DRUGS ⬦ If you discover that your child is using drugs, talk to a professional who has experience with adolescent drug abuse. It could be a school counselor, therapist, or counselor from a community drug abuse agency. My husband and I were totally at a loss for what to do until we talked to a professional. We also joined a support group with other parents having similar problems. My husband and I were relieved to hear from the counselor and other parents that our child's drug use wasn't our fault. *Anonymous, San Jose, California*

PEER PRESSURE TO DRINK ⬦ I was so proud to learn that my son told his friends that he couldn't drink alcohol because he came from a family of alcoholics and was afraid of becoming one himself. It was a great (and real) excuse to use with his peers, and one that no one questioned. *Anonymous*

AUTHOR'S NOTE: *Susceptibility to alcohol dependence can be genetic. Teenagers who come from a family with a history of alcohol-related problems should be warned that this puts them in a high-risk group for addiction.*

NOT A FRIEND WORTH HAVING ⬦ Many teens think they will lose a friend or not be a part of a group if they decline to smoke, drink alcohol, or use drugs. They may lose that friend, but I tell my teenage son that if he does, his friend was probably not worth having. Over time, my son has learned to believe this is true. It just took time and some personal experiences for the lesson to sink in. *J.B., San Diego, California*

MAKE YOUR OWN NONALCOHOLIC DRINK ◇

My son came up with a clever way to avoid the peer pressure to drink alcohol at parties. When asked if he wants a drink, he says "Thanks, not right now. I'll grab one myself in a minute." He makes his own nonalcoholic drink later and even pops a cherry on top if one is available. He says it's less hassle this way because he doesn't have to explain to anyone why he doesn't drink alcohol. *Anonymous*

DON'T BE FOOLED BY THE ADS ◇ Teenagers get

bombarded by advertisers for tobacco and beer. The message is always the same: Drinking and smoking are cool. Unfortunately, these ads never show smokers in cancer wards or alcoholics retching in the gutter. Parents need to offset these ads by explaining the unglamorous and dangerous side of these products. *B.W., Tacoma, Washington*

WRITE A RESEARCH PAPER ABOUT SMOKING

◇ When I caught my daughter smoking, I told her that she was grounded until she wrote a ten-page research paper on the dangers of smoking. I don't know if it will work for good, but it was a real eye-opener for her. *J.A.C., Minneapolis, Minnesota*

AUTHOR'S NOTE: *The American Lung Association would be happy to send you or your teenager information about smoking, including brochures and graphic pictures of the effects smoking has on the lungs. Call your local chapter or write to: American Lung Association, 1740 Broadway, New York, NY 10019-4374.*

WRITE A REPORT ON DANGEROUS BEHAVIOR ◇ If you discover that your teen has been doing

something dangerous, such as smoking, drinking, taking drugs, engaging in unsafe sex, or driving under the influence, an effective and educational form of discipline is to have him write a lengthy report about the dangers of that specific behavior. A friend of mine made his daughter

---

PARENT SKILL BUILDER

Possible Signs of Teen Drug Abuse

1. Sudden change of habits and/or behavior.
2. Missing or watered-down alcoholic beverages in the home.
3. Sleeping at unusual times.
4. Diminished ambition and drive.
5. Extreme moodiness.
6. More secretive than usual.
7. Change in peer group.
8. Sudden carelessness of appearance.
9. Frequent use of breath mints or eye drops.
10. Items missing from the house.
11. Loss of interest in school.
12. Incoherent or slurred speech.
13. Drug paraphernalia found in house or car.
14. Sudden loss of weight.
15. Physical symptoms such as red eyes, dilated pupils, chronic runny nose, constricted pupils, scars, or needle marks.

Note: Numbers 3, 5, 7 and 11 listed above can be normal teen behaviors and not necessarily a symptom of drug abuse. However, if even one of the other behaviors noted above (such as incoherent or slurred speech) or a majority of those listed are observable in your teen's behavior, drug abuse could be a factor.

---

write a ten-page paper about the dangers of smoking as well as walk through a cancer ward at a local hospital. He claims that she has not touched another cigarette since. *Sabrina Burton, Wyoming, Michigan*

DO SOME RESEARCH ABOUT SMOKING BEFORE YOU BEGIN ◇ After announcing to his mother that he was old enough to begin smoking, a friend of mine told her son that it would be OK with her if he smoked, but only if he did one thing for her first. She asked him to do a little research about the hazards of smoking and write up a short report about his findings. She also requested that he interview someone with a serious smoking-related disease like cancer or emphysema. He did the report and interview—and never began smoking. *Teresa Norris, San Diego, California*

PAID FOR BEING A NONSMOKER ◇ To encourage my grandchildren not to smoke, I agreed to pay them the cost of a pack of cigarettes per day from their sixteenth birthday until they reach twenty-one, if they never smoke. So far, it's worked; neither of my teenage grandchildren smoke. I deposit $60 in each of their savings accounts each month, which will be used for education. The $60 is even a strong enough incentive to overcome the peer pressure to smoke. They tell their friends, "I would be crazy to give up $60 a month for this." I am currently offering the same deal to my twelve-year-old grandson with the hope that he will never even consider smoking. *J.E.D., Bellingham, Washington*

For Further Information

Canadian Centre on Substance Abuse, 613-235-4048.
National Institute on Drug Abuse Hotline 1-800-662-HELP
National Clearinghouse for Alcohol and Drug Information
    1-800-729-6686; information, education, and referral service.
National Cocaine Hotline 1-800-COCAINE: information about cocaine and other drugs; referral service.
NARANON (310) 547-5800; information and support for family and friends of narcotic abusers.

Recommended Reading for Parents

Marti Heuer, *Teen Addiction: A Book of Hope for the Parents, Teachers, and Counselors of Chemically Dependent Adolescents (New York: Ballantine, 1994).*

Recommended Reading for Teens

Charles Wetherall, *Quit for Teens,* (Kansas City: Andrews and McMeel, 1995). A humorous but realistic view of the causes and effects of cigarette smoking. Stresses the importance of a nonsmoking lifestyle.

13

PROMOTING A HEALTHY SELF-CONCEPT

If I talk, everyone thinks I'm showing off; when I'm silent they think I'm ridiculous; rude if I answer, sly if I get a good idea, lazy if I'm tired, selfish if I eat a mouthful more than I should, stupid, cowardly, crafty, etc., etc.

— ANNE FRANK, *The Diary of a Young Girl*

SELF-ESTEEM

Self-esteem, the appreciation of one's worth as a person, is a powerful force in many aspects of a teenager's life. It influences a teen's thoughts, actions, and choices. A high level of self-esteem can give her the courage to try new things, help her make the right decision at each crossroad, and allow her to reach her potential. It can also be a factor in her decisions: whether to raise her hand in class, to try out for the basketball team, or to resist the pressures from her boyfriend to have sex.

There is a wealth of research showing that parents have an especially powerful influence on an adolescent's self-esteem. Considering its many benefits, self-esteem is one of the greatest gifts a parent can give to a teen. It is usually given in little nudges—one at a time. Simple words of encouragement, noticing an accomplishment (even a small one), praise, listening, and comments of appreciation go far to instill a sense of self-worth and confidence in a teenager.

Praise for a teenager cannot be overdone as long as it is sincere and honest. Many parents make the mistake of only praising major accomplishments, but remember that teens need to be nudged and encouraged along the way. For example, instead of just praising a semester report card, offer encouragement and praise regularly for well-done homework assignments, completed projects, test scores, and for just trying her best.

Physical appearance, social acceptance, and achievement are also powerful contributors to an adolescent's self-esteem. Although parents may not have as strong an influence as peers do in some of these matters, there are still ways that we can help. Instead of downplaying the importance of physical appearance (because they won't believe you anyway), accentuate the importance of character, personality, and friendliness. Also, help them to establish reasonable role models to compare themselves to; most teens unrealistically compare themselves to teen idols, movie or rock stars, or glamour models.

Rejection by school classmates and other peers will usually lower self-esteem. When this happens, parents can help by listening, acknowledging feelings, and, if appropriate, gently offering suggestions on ways to improve peer relations. For many teens, social acceptance becomes less of a problem after they learn new social skills that can help promote friendships. For other suggestions, see Chapter 5, "Friendships."

A sense of achievement also contributes to an adolescent's self-esteem. Recognize and support special abilities, skills, or competencies that your teen has demonstrated. It doesn't have to be an academic ability; it can be a musical, artistic, athletic, or other talent. The key is to focus on their strengths.

The adolescent years appear to be tougher on girls' than on boys' self-image. *The New York Times* recently reported that "Girls emerge from adolescence with a poor self-image, relatively low expectations from life and much less confidence in themselves and their abilities than do boys, according to a study. A survey of 3,000 children found that at age nine a majority of girls were confident, assertive and felt good about themselves. But by the time they reached high school, fewer than a third felt that way." Boys lost some sense of self-worth too, but not nearly as much as girls. The article explained that "when elementary school boys were asked how often they felt 'happy the way I am,' 67 percent answered 'always.' By high school, 46 percent still felt that way. But with girls, the figures dropped from 60 percent to 29 percent."[35] Armed with the information from this study, parents should do everything possible to promote their daughters' self-esteem during preadolescence and the middle school years, when girls' self-image seems to falter the most.

Teenagers cannot develop self-esteem alone. They need you and other significant people in their life to nurture it for them. And for something that takes only a moment to do, the benefits for both you and your children are long-lasting. Always remember that you are your child's most important advocate.

◇

CELEBRATE THOSE LITTLE VICTORIES TOO ◇ When there is victory, people like to celebrate. That is especially true for teenagers. Celebrate those good test results, a project successfully completed, an award, or anything else that is cause for celebrating. It can be a simple toast at dinnertime, tickets to a show or concert, a banner in the family room, a weekend camping trip, or whatever. The important thing is to let them know we care and are proud. *John Cornett, High Rolls, New Mexico*

TALK ABOUT THE POSITIVE ◇ As parents of teens, we sometimes overemphasize the negative things they do and overlook some of the positive things. I have learned to not only tell my daughter how proud I am of her but also to talk about how she accomplished certain things that I am truly in awe of. For instance, I recently attended a reading by my daughter of her poems. As I sat there watching and listening, I was impressed by her composure and ease in performing before an audience. Afterward, I asked her how she prepared for the event, how it felt appearing before an audience, and how she felt after the performance. I wanted to emphasize all the positive things she did to pull off a great show. It was a wonderful talk and I could tell that she enjoyed knowing how impressed and interested I was in one of her activities. *Anonymous, Queens, New York*

DON'T POINT OUT THEIR FAULTS—THEY ARE PAINFULLY AWARE OF THEM ALREADY ◇ I believe that unconditional love and acceptance of teenagers as real people, with real problems, is perhaps the most important gift a parent can ever give. It does no good to constantly point out their faults—they are usually painfully aware of them already. It pays long- and short-term dividends to magnify any and every good trait, and to downplay the less desirable ones as much as you can. *Anonymous*

"LOOKS LIKE YOU NEED ONE OF MY FAMOUS HUGS" ◇ Whenever I sense that one of my teenage girls is hurting, I say, "Looks like you need one of my famous hugs!" Without trying to pry into her life, my hug has let her know that I sense her feelings and that I care. Sometimes it even initiates a heart-to-heart talk. *Rita Miltner, Corning, Iowa*

WHEN TEEN NEEDS AN EXTRA BOOST ◇ When I feel as if my daughter needs an extra boost emotionally, I buy flowers for her and write her a card reminding her how special she is to me and what a beautiful soul she is. *T.D., Mariposa, California*

TEEN TALK

Teens love to receive little messages or gifts from our parents that give us the message, "You're special." (Monica, California)

◇

I love to find notes in my lunch sack from my mom, especially ones that say, "I am so proud of you!" "I love you," and "You are special!" (Brittney, Oregon)

PARENT SKILL BUILDER

Recognizing Eating Disorders

Two common eating disorders seen in teens are *anorexia nervosa* and *bulimia*. Teenage girls are much more at risk for these disorders than boys. Symptoms usually begin between the ages of twelve and thirty, with late adolescence and early adulthood being the most common time of onset.

People with anorexia spend an enormous amount of time thinking about food and dieting. They have an obsessional fear of obesity coupled with a distorted body image. Even when they are severely underweight, they view themselves as being fat. Since anorexics fear gaining weight, they eat very little and many also exercise frequently. Some use diuretics and laxatives. Anorexics usually deny their symptoms and resist help and treatment.

People with bulimia eat large amounts of food in a short time (binge eating), followed by self-induced vomiting or use of laxatives. The bulimic is usually of normal weight and more willing than anorexics to seek help for the disorder. Tooth decay and other dental problems are common, due to the frequency of throwing up.

Through research, we now know that some teenage girls are more susceptible to anorexia and bulimia. Those who are perfectionists, have low self-esteem, are high achievers, and have a preoccupation with attractiveness and appearance are more likely to have an eating disorder. Other known causes are high stress and depression.

Both anorexics and bulimics should seek medical and psychological professionals who are specially trained in the treatment of eating disorders. Anorexia can be life threatening and should not be taken lightly by parents. A list of referral organizations are listed at the end of this chapter.

A third eating disorder, *compulsive overeating,* can affect teens of both sexes. Professional attention should also be sought for these individuals.

TEENS OFTEN BELIEVE WHAT THEY HEAR ◇
Don't use degrading names or nicknames when address-
ing your children. They probably get enough of this from
their friends and classmates. Home should be a loving
haven from humiliating name calling. Children often start
believing that they are an "idiot" or "stupid" when they
hear it regularly, even if a parent says it in a playful way.
Jennie Eccher, Crystal River, Florida

LET THEM OVERHEAR POSITIVE COMMENTS ◇
Occasionally, when my teenage son is in earshot while I'm
talking to a friend or relative on the phone, I'll say something positive about him. I can tell that he is proud of
hearing me talk so positively about him. This works especially well when he's down in the dumps or low in confidence. I believe every little comment helps. *S.E.,
Newark, California*

PASS ON COMPLIMENTS ◇ If someone compliments
you about your teen, share the positive feedback with
your teen. *Charly Kasal, St. Paul, Minnesota*

POSITIVE STATEMENT AT BEDTIME ◇ I always try
to make the last thing I say to my daughter before her
bedtime something positive. It's usually a quick compliment or expression of appreciation for something she did
that day. It's always nice to end the day on a positive note.
Nancy Lee, Chicago, Illinois

A LIST OF POSITIVE QUALITIES ◇ Teenagers can
really get down on themselves. At times, my daughter gets
in such a negative mood that she can't recognize anything
positive about herself: she's not pretty enough, smart
enough, or popular enough. That's when I usually step in
and give her an infusion of positive attributes that I see. It
seems to perk her up to the point where she begins to see
that things aren't really so bleak. *B.J., Pleasanton, California*

TEENS LIVE DOWN TO LOW EXPECTATIONS ◇ I
work as a cashier in a large department store. I'm frequently appalled by how many parents call their kids degrading names, tell them that they're worthless, and put
them down in countless different ways. It's sad because
many of these kids will live down to their parents' low

expectations of them. It's no wonder that so many children have such low self-esteem and low expectations of themselves. *Anonymous*

TRYING TO LIVE UP TO *VOGUE* STANDARDS ◇
Teens try to live up to the beauty standards set by the glamour and teen magazines and the rest of the media. Whenever my daughter fusses about her looks and compares herself to a media star, I ask her, "How many people do you know who look like that?" "None," she always replies. Case closed! *N.S.G., New York City, New York*

A LETTER FROM DAD ◇ I recently wrote a letter to my son telling him how proud I am to be his dad and acknowledging all his wonderful talents. I left it on his bed for him to find after school. Although it would have been awkward and difficult for me to speak the same words to him, the words flowed easily on paper. My son thanked me for the note. For those of us who have a difficult time expressing our feelings, this is a good way to begin. The method shouldn't count anyway, it's the message that's important. *R.P., San Diego, California*

✖◆◆◆◆◆◆◆◆◆◆◆◆◆◆◆◆◆◆◆◆◆◆◆◆◆◆◆◆◆◆◆◆◆◆◆◆◆◆◆✖

VALUING YOUR TEEN'S UNIQUENESS

✖◆◆◆◆◆◆◆◆◆◆◆◆◆◆◆◆◆◆◆◆◆◆◆◆◆◆◆◆◆◆◆◆◆◆◆◆◆◆◆✖

DON'T COMPARE TO SIBLINGS OR PEERS ◇
Teenagers hate for parents to compare them to siblings, friends, or norms. They each have a unique combination of strengths and weaknesses. Unfortunately, sometimes we parents tend to do more comparisons of weaknesses than strengths. *C.B., San Jose, California*

PRIZING TEENS' SPECIAL QUALITIES ◇ It's important to recognize and appreciate the uniqueness of each child in a family. They are not carbon copies of us parents; their personality and interests are often very different from our own. When I remember this simple fact, I find myself prizing these differences instead of being threatened by them. There are often two important by-products of this: the relationship between parent and child is strengthened and the child's self-esteem is increased. *Bob Wadley, Spanish Ford, Utah*

DIFFERENT THAN ME ◇ When I came to the frightening conclusion that my daughter was not a clone of me, but in fact her very own person with hopes, dreams, likes, and dislikes often very different from my own, our relationship improved dramatically. I began to appreciate her as she is instead of how I would like her to be. In turn, my daughter became more open with me and we talked more. I realized that I had subtly (and sometimes not so subtly) steered her in directions that were important to me, but not to her. I only wish that I had "discovered" my wonderful and unique daughter sooner. *F.E.S., San Jose, California*

TEEN TALK

I hate for my parents to compare me to my friends because it's usually negative. I'm tired of hearing, "Why don't you dress like that," or "Why don't you act like that." (Crystal, Connecticut)

"OUR CHILDREN TURNED OUT TO BE THE PEOPLE THEY ARE COMFORTABLE BEING" ◇ Parenting toddlers teaches you that you can't eat, sleep, or go to the bathroom for your kids. Parenting teens teaches you that you can't succeed for them or do their hurting for them, either. Be very clear about who owns what dreams, and whose problems are whose. Our sons are not turning out to be quite the people we expected, but they are turning out to be the people they are comfortable being. We've discovered that we like that—and them—a lot. *Bob and Jeanne Grace, Fairport, New York*

For Further Information

National Eating Disorders Organization, 445 E. Granville Rd., Worthington, OH 43085 (614-436-1112); for information and referral.

National Association of Anorexia Nervosa and Associated Disorders, Box 7, Highland Park, IL 60035 (708-433-4632); educational material in English and Spanish; provides list of support groups.

Anorexia Nervosa and Related Eating Disorders, Inc., P.O. Box 5102, Eugene, OR 97405 (503-344-1144); provides information on support groups and sponsors workshops.

Recommended Reading for Parents

Douglas Bloch, *Positive Self-Talk for Children: Teaching Self-Esteem Through Affirmations* (New York: Bantam, 1993). A guide for parents, teachers, and counselors.

Diane Loomans, *Full Esteem Ahead: 100 Ways to Build Self-Esteem* (Tiburon, CA: H. J. Kramer, 1994).

Michele Siegel, *Surviving an Eating Disorder: Strategies for Family and Friends* (New York: Harper Perennial, 1989).

Recommended Reading for Teens

Gershen Kaufman, *Stick Up for Yourself: Every Kid's Guide to Personal Power and Positive Self-Esteem* (Minneapolis: Free Spirit Publishing, 1990).

14

TEEN-FAMILY RELATIONSHIPS

When I was a boy of fourteen, my father was so ignorant I could hardly stand to have the man around. But when I got to be twenty-one, I was astonished at how much he had learnt in seven years.

—MARK TWAIN

Of all the forces affecting a teen's development, the family remains the most important by far. Laurence Steinberg, author of *Adolescence*, writes, "Regardless of the family's structure or composition—one parent or two, natural or reconstituted, employed mother or not—having positive and warm family relationships stands out as one of the most powerful predictors and correlates of healthy psychosocial growth during the adolescent years."[36] This chapter is devoted to helping you achieve such a relationship with your teenage son or daughter.

Over the years, parenting experts and researchers have learned that, overall, relationships between teens and their parents are much more positive and optimistic than most people realize. Although the teen years are often thought of as being full of conflict and problems, no substantial evidence indicates that there are any more family problems in adolescence than in other developmental stages in the life span. Study after study also reveals that the overwhelming majority of teenagers feel a mutual love and respect for their parents. Even the "generation gap" isn't as wide as once thought. Many teens share the same values and attitudes of their parents; the main gap seems to be centered on personal tastes, such as music and style of dress.

Parenting style has a significant impact on parent-teen relationships. Researchers have studied various parenting styles
and associated behaviors in order to determine if one style is
associated with healthy adolescent development more often
than others. Psychologist Diana Baumrind and many other
parenting experts believe that there are two elements of
the parents' behavior that are critical: responsiveness and
demandingness.[37]

Responsiveness refers to the degree to which the parent
responds to the child's needs in a supportive and accepting
manner. Demandingness refers to the extent to which the
parent demands and expects responsible and mature behavior from the child. Using various combinations of responsiveness and demandingness, researchers have labeled four
different classifications of parenting styles. A parent who is
equally responsive and demanding is labeled "authoritative,"
whereas one who is neither responsive nor demanding is
"indifferent." A parent who is responsive but not demanding
is "indulgent," and one who is demanding but not responsive
is "authoritarian."

The authoritative style—equally balanced between responsive and demanding—is the one most lauded by parenting experts for promoting healthy adolescent development.
Authoritative parents are warm and nurturing, yet they
place controls and limits on a teen's actions. They are ratio-
nal and issue-oriented. Authoritative parents also tailor their
demands to fit the needs and competencies of their teenager. In general, adolescents raised in authoritative homes
are more adaptive, self-assured, and responsible than teens
who have been raised in authoritarian, indifferent, or indulgent homes.

This chapter is divided into seven sections: Teens Need
Love and Support, Promoting Family Time, Parent-Teen
Dates, Mutual Respect, Parents are Real People Too, Siblings, and Family Vacations. There is also one parent skill
builder here: Family Meetings.

◇

TEENS NEED LOVE AND SUPPORT

A LETTER TO MY PRETEEN ◇ When my daughter turned twelve, I wrote her a letter welcoming her to the threshold of adolescence. I told her that I look forward to the adventure ahead. I also warned her that there will be times when we won't see eye-to-eye, but that I will always love her and always make decisions in her best interest. I signed off hoping that we would be best friends in her twenties and beyond. It was a nice way to begin a new era together. *Anonymous*

FOR GOOD TIMES AND BAD ◇ When our children entered adolescence, my husband and I told them that we would always be there for them and support them, both in good times and bad. We explained that we might initially be angry upon hearing of a misdeed or problem, but we would get over it. We let them know that we would never turn our backs on them. Families aren't just for the good times, they're for sharing the bad times, too, and kids need to know that—before problems occur. *Susie Anderson, Mission San Jose, California*

"JEEPERS, I LOVE YOU" ◇ Occasionally, when things are quiet around the house, and my teenage son is hanging out not doing much, I'll say something like, "You know what? I love you so much that it feels like my heart is bursting." I came from a family where feelings were not voiced or respected. I'm trying to change that in my own family. *S.S., Toronto, Ontario*

NO MAJOR REGRETS ◇ One of my goals in life is to have no major regrets about my job as a parent. I think about this occasionally and it helps me stay focused on what's really important. On my deathbed I don't want to think or say, "I wish I had . . ." or "I need to . . ." *K.S.D., Pittsburgh, Pennsylvania*

"I DO LOVE THIS CHILD—WHOEVER HE IS"
◇ Teenagers tend to go through stages when you don't feel that you know them. I keep telling myself, "I do love this child—whoever he is." I also try to remember what it was like to be thirteen. *Nicci Leamon, Casco, Maine*

ASK PERMISSION FOR HUGS AND KISSES ◇
When my boys reached that age where they hated to be hugged and kissed, I said, "I understand that you're grown up now and you may not need hugs and kisses like you used to, but mothers always need hugs and kisses, even when they're eighty years old. So when I need a kiss or hug, I'll ask you if I can have one." Only on rare occasions did they refuse me, saying something like, "No, you can't have a hug. I'm angry!" or "I don't feel like it." But even then they would often come up to me later and say, "Would you like that hug now?" Sometimes they would initiate a hug or kiss on their own by saying, "Mom, you look like you need a hug." How wonderful! *Jamie Conner Garcia, St. Petersburg, Florida*

TEEN TALK

I always knew, without a doubt, that my mom would always be there for me—no matter what happened. What a great, secure feeling that is! (Cynthia, California)

TEENS NEED AFFECTION, TOO ◇ They may not
be young kids anymore, but teenagers still need hugs or some form of affection from their parents. Don't embarrass them by being affectionate in public, but daily hugs or a kiss good night could be a welcome reminder that you love them. One of the many reasons that kids become sexually active is because they lack affection. People, not just teens, will get affection any way they can. *Anonymous, Flagstaff, Arizona*

"CAN I GIVE YOU A BIG HUG?" ◇ Even though
they will seldom admit it, teens still need at least occasional hugs from their parents. During moments when I'm

intensely proud of my teenage daughter or after a good heart-to-heart talk, I'll say to her, "Please indulge your mother and let me give you a big hug." Her sheepish grin tells me that she likes it too (but don't tell anyone!). *Anonymous, Mariposa, California*

TAKE ADVANTAGE OF THOSE SPECIAL MOMENTS ◇ Laugh together, get silly together, and play together. Grab those moments whenever you can! After the teen years have gone by, you will wish you had more of these moments. *Charly Kasal, St. Paul, Minnesota*

A PARENT'S REGRET ◇ My only regret in raising my children is that I didn't say "I love you" enough. If I had to do it over, I wouldn't let a day go by without saying this at least once. My children are all adults now and I find myself making up for lost time by frequently telling them "I love you." I'm sharing this with you now so you won't have to make up for lost time later—like I am. *Anonymous, Orlando, Florida*

XXXXXXXXXXXXXXXXXXXXXXXXXXXXXXXXXXXXXXXXXXXX

PROMOTING FAMILY TIME

XXXXXXXXXXXXXXXXXXXXXXXXXXXXXXXXXXXXXXXXXXXX

MEMORIES OF CHILDHOOD AND ADOLESCENCE ◇ My husband and I are in our sixties now and our three boys have families of their own. Our most vivid memories of our own childhood and of our own boys when they were younger were times spent together— parents and children—doing simple things like playing games and ball, fishing, and hunting. Our best memories don't involve activities that required money. So, you don't need money to enjoy the simple things in life with your children. They will remember most of all what you did *with* them. *Mrs. Karen Lindstrom, Holdrege, Nebraska*

QUALITY TIME IS A PREREQUISITE ◇ The more time you spend with your teen, the better chance your teen will turn out as you hope. If I had to do it over again, I would structure my time so I was with the kids more during their teen years. *Michael Stahler, Niles, California*

FAMILY HOME EVENING ◇ Our entire family reserves Monday evening for what we call "Family Home Evening," a time when we all stay home and spend time together. It's a time to focus on the family and have fun together. We try to participate in activities that promote interaction, such as parlor games. Watching television is not an option unless it's something very special. Each of us, including our teenagers, tries hard to schedule our work and other activities around Monday evenings. *Bob Wadley, Spanish Fork, Utah*

NO PHONE, TELEVISION, OR VIDEO GAMES IN BEDROOM ◇ My husband and I currently have four teenagers living in our home, ages twelve, fourteen, sixteen, and eighteen. One of the most successful rules we have ever implemented is not to allow a phone, television, or video game in any of the bedrooms. Teenagers tend to isolate themselves too much anyway, so parents should not give them the tools to spend more time in their bedrooms. Other positive outcomes of this rule is that we know who our kids are talking to on the phone, we have a better idea of what they do with their free time, and they have become more involved in family activities. *Susan Mitchell, Livelin, Texas*

INTELLECTUAL CONVERSATION TIME ◇ My wife and I strongly encouraged all of our children to be home in time for dinner. There were occasional exceptions due to various activities or part-time jobs, but everyone made an effort to have dinner together. We turned off the TV and talked to each other. I called this "intellectual conversation time." My wife and I promoted discussions and debate about school or current events. Only one of our eight children lives at home now, but the memories of our large family eating dinner together every night will always be fond ones. *David Hopkins, Sacramento, California*

TEEN TALK

Some of my fondest family memories are of the outings my parents and I took together. If you want your family to be close, you have to spend time together. Family outings don't have to be all day; even an hour is better than nothing. (Kim, California)

◇

It takes some of us teens a long time to realize that family is important. But we usually come around to this fact. (Aileen, California)

FAMILY TIME ◇ My advice to parents is to do what you enjoy—but remember to bring the kids along as often as possible. *Jim Goodwin, Fremont, California*

DON'T MAKE YOUR INVOLVEMENT WITH YOUR TEEN SEEM LIKE A CHORE TO YOU ◇ A good parent needs to be involved in all aspects of their teenager's life (school, friends, activities, sports, etc.). Let them know that you enjoy being involved with them in their activities. Don't make your active participation seem like it's a chore to you. *Jennie Eccher, Crystal River, Florida*

FAMILY MEETINGS ◇ Short, weekly meetings can build communication and cooperation in a family. We have all learned some effective nonconfrontational problem-solving skills from these meetings. Our rules for family meetings are as follows: attendance is mandatory, the chairperson (who runs the meetings) rotates among us, anyone can add an agenda item to the list on the refrigerator, kids' items are always listed first on the agenda, and all decisions are made by consensus. *Mary Lea McAnally, Stanford, California*

MANDATORY FAMILY ACTIVITIES ◇ One thing that I plan to do differently with my younger children that I did with my eighteen-year-old son is not to let them skip so many family functions. Beginning at about age fourteen, he usually declined to go to restaurants and other places with us. I insisted that he go on vacations. My teen daughter is just entering that same stage, but I more often insist that she go with us. She even has a good time (once she stops pouting!). *J.A.C., Minneapolis, Minnesota*

PARENT SKILL BUILDER

Family Meetings

Many parents credit their weekly family meetings with strengthening their family as a whole, improving individual family relationships, and promoting better communication. For many families, a weekly meeting is a time to make decisions together, give encouragement to each other, solve problems, and make leisure and vacation plans. Some parents also like to review the upcoming schedule for the week and discuss problems that have occurred the previous week.

Have a set time (Sunday evenings are good for many families) to conduct your family meetings each week, and strongly encourage (or require) all family members to attend. Those who miss a meeting without a reasonable excuse will have to live with the decisions made by the rest of the family. Limit the meeting to thirty minutes; otherwise the meetings could go on too long and attendance will begin to dwindle.

It is important to have an agenda for each meeting. Most families have set agenda items as well as an "Other" category where family members can add items they would like to address. The refrigerator door is a good place to post the agenda. The job of moderator, the individual who runs the meeting, can rotate between family members. It should be the moderator's job to make sure that everyone has an opportunity to talk and that everyone listens when others are speaking. The meetings should be upbeat, not just a gripe session about problems. Some families end their meetings by encouraging each member to give at least one compliment to another family member.

FAMILY OUTINGS—WITHOUT FRIENDS ◊ We allow our teens to bring friends along on some of our family outings, but we also reserve some family outings for just family. When friends are along, our children focus on them instead of their family. It's fun to have friends along occasionally, but it's very important to reserve some outings where we all concentrate on each other in the family. *Anne Kirby, Salem, Oregon*

FAMILY TRADITIONS ◊ Continue to celebrate family traditions, even though your teen may complain or protest about them being corny or dumb. Often my fourteen-year-old son would think that he was too old for a particular family tradition, so he would choose to skip it. After it was over he would often admit that he missed it. *Charly Kasal, St. Paul, Minnesota*

ENJOYED MY PARENTS AS MUCH AS MY FRIENDS ◊ I have fond memories of my own adolescence, and now I hope to create those same feelings in my own children. My own parents instilled such a loving, caring, and upbeat atmosphere at home, that I was often content to stay home and do things with my family. My parents and I developed a great friendship just by doing so many fun things together, whether it was going out to dinner or weeding the yard. I had many friends and an active dating life as well, but because of the strong relationship with my parents, my peer group did not have as strong an influence over me as they did over some of my friends. *Kathy Hamm, Apopka, Florida*

PARENT-TEEN DATES

The importance of one-on-one time with a child cannot be overemphasized. Teens enjoy having a parent's attention focused exclusively on them. This is especially true when there are siblings in the home. Sitting home and watching television together doesn't count as a parent-teen date. It's best, say parents, when the activity is something that is mutually enjoyed, something that is done away from the home, and something that will encourage (or at least permit) conversation. Here are some great ideas from other parents.

◇

QUANTITATIVE TIME ◇ Quantitative time is what's needed, not just quality time, to establish a good relationship with your child. Even better is quality, quantitative time. Time is nurturing and it can't be sacrificed by anything else. The best conversations with my sons usually occur one-on-one and during times when I'm on their agenda, particpating in an activity that they enjoy doing. The conversations are always more relaxed and natural. Kids of all ages come to life and are appreciative when we do things they want to do. *Bennett Oppenheim, Mission San Jose, California*

A PARENT-TEEN DATE ◇ Some of the best times my husband and I have had with our teenage children is when we spend time alone with only one child. For instance, if one teen is busy with a school or sport activity during the dinner hour, we'll take our other teen to his favorite restaurant. Our children seem freer to gab with us when they don't have to compete with a sibling. We also enjoy doing this one-on-one, one parent to one teen. All children, regardless of age, enjoy being the parents' center of attention. *Denise Rounds, Tulsa, Oklahoma*

PARENT-TEEN INTERVIEW ◇ Once a month, I try to make a point of having a lengthy conversation with each of my children on a one-to-one basis. We call it an interview because we take turns asking each other questions. We promise each other to be honest with each other. I ask some general questions, like "How are things going?" followed by specific questions about school, activities, friendships, boyfriends/girlfriends, etc. Then it's my child's turn to ask me questions. The most frequently asked questions are about my boyhood and adolescence, with the occasional obligatory inquiry about my job. I answer each question honestly, even the tough ones about the first time I kissed a girl or my worst heartbreak. These interviews promote discussions that we usually don't talk about in our normal interactions. They bring out joys and concerns, problems and issues. It's a great way to stay tuned in to each other in this fast-paced society. *P.R., Billings, Montana*

SURPRISE! TOMORROW IS OUR SPECIAL DAY TOGETHER ◇ Occasionally, I place a card on my teen's dinner plate that reads, "Surprise! Tomorrow is our special day together, so place an X next to your choices." The card lists places to have breakfast, which mall to go shopping at, where to eat lunch, and which movie to see (complete with popcorn and the "works"). I also buy an inexpensive article of clothing or a collectible item for her during our shopping trip as a memento of our day together. By the end of the day, my teen and I have not only had fun together but have had some wonderful conversations—just like best friends. I figure it's OK to act like a pal with her once in a while. She gets to see the human side of me, and I get to see the emerging young adult in her. *Mary Kay Hennings, Omaha, Nebraska*

SPECIAL TIME ◇ I make a point of scheduling special time with my teenage daughter. Our special time together originally began as a mom-daughter dinner out. It was nice getting away from telephones, televisions, dishes, and other distractions. As she has gotten older, we have expanded to other activities: taking a line dance class together, going on long walks, or going to a special event like a play or concert. Afterward, we always go out for dessert. It's amazing what conversations take place when we've had some fun and are relaxed. *Donna J. Carlyle, Austin, Texas*

"LET'S DO LUNCH" ◇ Occasionally, I take each of my teenagers out separately for a meal. They love the one-to-one time alone with me. Sometimes it is an early breakfast or a late dinner, but their favorite is for me to pick them up at school during their lunch break and take them to lunch. *Deborah Burt, Clovis, California*

EYE-TO-EYE ◇ At least for a short time each day, I try to sit down face-to-face with each of my three children and hear about their day or whatever they want to talk about. I do more listening than talking. They seem to

---

TEEN TALK

We like our parents to spend time with us, but we don't like them to "hang out" with us. There is a difference. (Arinn, California)

◇

Similar to most preteens, I was embarrassed by my mother. But in high school and now in college, I find myself bragging about her all the time. Sometimes it takes teenagers a long time to really appreciate all that a parent has done for them. (Kim, California)

---

really appreciate the attention. *Judy Harris, Seffner, Florida*

LUNCH WITH DAD ◇ When my three daughters were in high school, I used to take each one, one at a time, to lunch with me. They could pick the restaurant and order anything (within reason) they wanted. This was their private time with me. They could talk about whatever they wanted, and I would listen. I would give advice *only* if they asked for it, and our conversations were always confidential. I wouldn't even tell my wife what was discussed. Sometimes they had nothing special to talk about, but other times they did. My daughters are all in their twenties now, but they still want their alone time at lunch with Dad. And I still have to pay! *Pastor Don Reed, Omaha, Nebraska*

TIME ALONE WITH EACH CHILD ◇ In large families (we have eight children), it's especially important to spend time alone with each child. This is important to do during all age levels, but is especially crucial during the adolescent years. Teens will tell you many things on a one-to-one basis that they would never tell you if other family members were present. Even my quiet children, the ones who didn't talk quite as openly as the others, opened up and shared many personal things about their life with me. The larger the family, the more important it is to schedule this time in advance, otherwise it may never happen. I have wonderful memories about these times spent together and I think my children do too. *R. Merrill, Orem, Utah*

SHOPPING WITH STYLE ◇ Shopping for clothes with my teenage son has had some hidden benefits for both of us. For my son, he enjoys hanging out together and doing something that he wants to do. For myself, I enjoy the time together, too, but even more important, I discover a lot about my son as we shop. For example, he has taught me about the current styles, what and how his peers respond to in regard to clothing, and what girls like. It was enlightening and I found myself understanding his world a little better. I only wish that I could have explained beads and bell bottoms as articulately to my father as my son explained his styles to me. *Anonymous, Ventura, California*

DAD DATE ◇ Since I work full-time, I don't have the opportunity to see my children as often as my wife, who works full-time in our home. So, as often as possible, I take one child at a time on a "dad date." I let them decide what to do and where to go. During our "date," I focus entirely on them, listening carefully to all they have to tell me about their life. They love the attention and I cherish the conversations we have. *B.B., Bountiful, Utah*

✦✦✦✦✦✦✦✦✦✦✦✦✦✦✦✦✦✦✦✦✦✦✦✦✦✦✦✦✦✦✦✦✦✦✦✦✦✦

MUTUAL RESPECT

✦✦✦✦✦✦✦✦✦✦✦✦✦✦✦✦✦✦✦✦✦✦✦✦✦✦✦✦✦✦✦✦✦✦✦✦✦✦

IT BEGINS WITH YOU ◇ Mutual respect between you and your teen begins with you. *Patricia Stahler, Niles, California*

A RESPECTFUL APPROACH ◇ We try to treat our teenage daughter in the same respectful way that we want to be treated by others. It's a simple principle, but we believe that people will treat you in the same manner as you treat them. *Marsha McAllister, Bossier City, Louisiana*

RESPECT THEIR PRIVACY ◇ Privacy is extremely important to teenagers, especially when it has to do with their bedroom and personal belongings. Their bedroom is their haven. My fifteen-year-old gets very upset if she notices that someone has been snooping around her room or took something that is hers. As long as I am not suspicious or do not have reasonable cause to go looking through her things, I respect her privacy. I also have told all three of my teenagers to respect each other's privacy and personal belongings. *Judy Harris, Seffner, Florida*

AUTHOR'S NOTE: *Teens develop a strong need for privacy during adolescence. Although it can be difficult for parents to accept that their teen has a private life that is not shared with them, it's important to respect their privacy as you would for an adult. Opening a teen's mail, reading his diary, or listening in on his phone conversation without his permission is not advised. Not only is that disrespectful, but it can sometimes do irreversible damage to a previously trusting relationship.*

FAMILY CONFIDENTIALITY ◇ Respect your teenager's request to keep something confidential when they confide in you. Even teenagers have a right to privacy about sensitive issues. If they should hear that you told other people about their secret, even one of your own friends, they may never confide in you again. *L.C., Pleasanton, California*

PRIVACY DURING EXAMS ◇ When my children reached the age of ten or eleven years old, I told them that I would voluntarily walk out of the examination room any time they had to disrobe for their doctor. I also mentioned that, of course, I would stay if they asked me to. I do, however, sit in on all consultations and other exams. I believe that my children have appreciated this courtesy. *Cathy Hairup, Magna, Utah*

COURTESY MESSAGES ◇ We had a rule in our family: always leave a note to let the rest of the family know where you are. My husband and I made it clear that we weren't checking up on them, but we just wanted to know where they were. In turn, my husband and I were always careful to leave notes to let the children know where we were and what time we would return. The refrigerator door was where we posted our notes. *Mary Hopkins, Sacramento, California*

TEEN TALK

Teens appreciate advance notice of plans and family obligations just as adults do. We have schedules too. Learning about an afternoon visit to a relative's house two hours before we leave shows us no courtesy—the same kind of courtesy parents often ask us for. (Amy, Arizona)

TEENS APPRECIATE COURTESY NOTES TOO

◊ As parents, we like our children always to let us know where they are. The teens in my classroom mentioned that parents don't always return the favor of letting their children know where they are when they return home from school or work. Courtesy notes explaining changes in plans, last-minute shopping, or visits to the neighbors are always appreciated, whether we're parents or teens. *Patty McMillan, Long Beach, California*

PARENTS ARE REAL PEOPLE TOO

What a concept for a teen: parents are real people who make mistakes. And they were teenagers once too. Although we parents are all too aware of our shortcomings and past mistakes, our children frequently are not. For them, it's almost inconceivable to imagine that we were once children and adolescents. They tend to always think of us as we are now. Through the eyes of a struggling teenager, an idolized parent can be a tough act to follow. A teen's imperfections and failures will be even more intensified if he compares himself to some mythical perfection. And the more successful parents are, the more this can become an important factor in your son's or daughter's self-image.

Many teens have told me how reassured they were when, for the first time, they began to see a parent as a whole human being, complete with failures and struggles. Besides the relief that teens often feel, there are other benefits in presenting a more complete picture of yourself. The more parents share their true self with their teens, the more likely their teens will reciprocate with disclosures about themselves.

Here are some more thoughts about this subject from teens and other parents.

$\diamond$

WE'RE BOTH ROOKIES—YOU AS A TEEN, WE AS PARENTS OF ONE ◇ My wife and I are not afraid to admit our mistakes to our two sons. We also apologize. In one such situation with our oldest son, I told him, "After all, we've never had a sixteen-year-old son before. We'll make some mistakes occasionally." He seems more willing to cut us some slack when we're honest with him. *R.H., Fremont, California*

PARENTS NEED TO APOLOGIZE TOO ◇ We were late to learn this, but my husband and I apologize to our children for our shortcomings and mistakes. We admit our mistakes, say we are sorry, and ask for their forgiveness. *Dolly Hickey, Clearwater, Florida*

ADMIT YOUR MISTAKES ◇ As parents, we must be willing to admit when we are wrong. A comment like "I didn't handle that very well last night" admits our mistake and helps to restore lines of communication that may have been damaged the night before. If we set an example by admitting when we are wrong and asking for forgiveness, our children will learn to do it as well. *JoAnn Wadley, Spanish Fork, Utah*

TEEN TALK

Teenagers love to hear honest stories about their parents' own adolescence. It helps us to remember that parents are real people who experienced similar things to what we are dealing with now. (Emily, Utah)

◇

I never thought that I could live up to my dad's own personal success. He was very successful in his job and seemed never to have made a mistake in his life. In my late teens he told my brother and me how he had flunked out of his first major in college and struggled with many different jobs. We had never heard these stories before. What a relief it was to know that my dad wasn't perfect. It sure took a lot of pressure off my brother and me. (Anonymous, Colorado)

SIBLINGS

Living in such close proximity to each other, brothers and sisters experience both positive and negative aspects in their sibling relationships. Conflict is usually high between siblings. In fact, the highest amount of conflict within a family is usually between two siblings. But siblings also contribute a great deal to each other's development. They teach each other new things, give each other important feedback, and contribute to each other's socialization.

The first tip in this section is similar to many I received from parents about siblings. "Never compare siblings" they wrote. Good advice. Other sibling topics are addressed here as well.

◇

NEVER COMPARE SIBLINGS ◇ Never compare one sibling to another; they are each unique with their own strengths and weaknesses. *A.R., Bakersfield, California*

WHO STARTED THE FIGHT ◇ Sometimes it's impossible to determine which of your two children started a fight or argument, especially after listening to all of their accusations. ("He said . . ." "She said . . .") against each other. In these cases, I step in between both kids and state, "I don't know who started this, but I just finished it!" If there's any more griping I again state, louder than the first time, "I just finished it." The kids usually resume their activities together. There's no winner or loser with this tactic because the authority figure stays neutral. It's a great way to end an argument quickly. *Jane Barker, Fremont, California*

DOUBLE ALLOWANCE ◇ My daughters share a bedroom, which was the site of many squabbles during one particular phase of their adolescence. To deal with this in a positive way, I told them that they could double their allowance each day (they receive a daily allowance for chores completed) if they didn't fight with each other. If I heard the beginnings of what sounded like a squabble, I would call out, "Is that a fight that I hear?" Then, I would usually only hear silence or two faint voices answering, "No." The extra incentive of the allowance encouraged them to use strategies other than fighting to settle their differences. *Judy Voelker, Palmer Lake, Colorado*

FINED FOR PUT-DOWNS ◇ An effective way to eliminate or cut down on the number of put-downs, name calling, and bad words spoken to another family member is to require the offender to pay a quarter to whom the words were directed. In our house, this rule includes the parents. *Bill and Judy Arnett, McKinleyville, California*

EXPEDITING MORNING SHOWERS ◇ A surefire way to expedite the process of getting everyone ready for school in the morning is to require the last person who showers to clean the bathroom (wipe down the shower, floor, etc.). You'll never see your teenagers scramble faster to get clean! What used to seem like an eternity to get everyone showered in the morning will now set some sort of world record. *Mary McKinley, Reynoldsburg, Ohio*

TO ENCOURAGE ACTS OF KINDNESS AMONG SIBLINGS, SEE THE TIP "REINFORCING ACTS OF KINDNESS" IN CHAPTER 9 (page 138).

FAMILY VACATIONS

Any parent who has spent a prolonged vacation with a sullen, grumbling teenager will appreciate the alternatives offered in this section by other parents. The middle and late teen years are a time when many teenagers balk at being forced to join their family on an extended vacation. As teens get older and responsibilities increase, they covet what little free time they have left. They may also cite a boyfriend or girlfriend, job responsibility, or team practice as the reason for not wanting to participate in the family vacation. Unless you want your home to become "party central," most parents agree that it's not a good idea to leave a teen home alone for an extended period of time. So what do you do?

In this section, parents share some alternatives to the typical family vacation that take into consideration the needs of teenagers.

◇

INVOLVE THE TEENS IN PLANNING ◇ I have learned that when we involved our two teens (twelve and fifteen) in the planning of our summer vacations, we all enjoy ourselves better. Involve your children in the planning of your next trip. Ask them what kind of trip they want to go on (camping, car travel, beach trip, rent a cabin, etc.), what specific place they want to visit, and what they want to do along the way. Bring them along to the travel agent and encourage them to read the travel brochures. Involve them in mapping out your itinerary, selecting travel routes, etc. When the teens are happy on the trip, everyone is happy on the trip! *Becky Martin, Orlando, Florida*

FAMILY VACATION OR SUMMER CAMP ◇ I gave my fourteen-year-old daughter the option of going to summer camp or going with her family on vacation and pretending to enjoy herself. She chose camp and loved it. My husband and I felt comfortable knowing that she was in good hands and having a great time. And we didn't have to listen to her whine for two weeks! *Susan Eisman, Tampa, Florida*

LET TEEN STAY WITH A FRIEND DURING YOUR VACATION ◇ We have always allowed our teenage son to take a friend with us on our annual vacation. There's usually no extra charge for one more teen in a motel room, and the parents often sent along meal and spending money. If there is any inconvenience, it's still much better than bringing an unhappy teenager on your vacation. They can make the vacation miserable for everyone if they choose to. One time my son couldn't find anyone to take with him, so I asked his friend's parents if he could stay with them for one week. He did, and it worked out great. And his friend stayed with us while his parents went on a vacation. *Shawna Hall, Waterford, Michigan*

FAMILY VACATIONS ◇ We always allowed our teenagers to take a friend with them on family vacations if they were isolated by age group from their siblings. The alternative is to spend your entire vacation dealing with an "I don't want to be here" attitude and constantly hearing, "There's nothing to do." *A.B., Bountiful, Utah*

INVITE ANOTHER FAMILY ALONG ◇ When our children were teenagers, we used to go on vacation with another family who also had teenagers. Our teens had companions to hang out with, and my husband and I enjoyed the company of the other parents. Occasionally, one set of parents would stay with the teenagers while the other went out for the evening. Whether it was camping, renting a houseboat, or going on a short cruise, we all had a great time. *I.L.T., Spokane, Washington*

MINIVACATIONS ⬦ My wife and I have learned that, with teenagers, it's easier to think small and have frequent minivacations rather than have one or two grand vacations somewhere exotic. It works best for our teens, too. Although our teens are often reluctant to give up a week or two of their summer vacation to join us on a trip, they appreciate an occasional weekend away. And if they don't want to go with us, they are easy to farm out to friends and relatives for two or three evenings. *G.L., San Jose, California*

Recommended Reading for Parents

Ryan Holladay and Friends, *What Preteens Want Their Parents to Know* (New York: McCracken, 1994).

Recommended Reading for Teens

Alex J. Packer, *Bringing Up Parents: The Teenager's Handbook* (Minneapolis: Free Spirit, 1992).

15

DIVORCE AND STEPPARENTING

Divorce brings with it feelings that are difficult for every family member to deal with.

— EDWARD TEBER

COPING WITH DIVORCE

Over half of all marriages now end in divorce. As a result, many two-parent households have been replaced with a single parent, a stepfamily, or even a blended household composed of children from one or more previous marriages. It's estimated that over 50 percent of children born in the 1980s will spend at least part of their childhood or adolescence in one of these nontraditional family structures. For parents and children alike, transitioning into one of these new forms of family can be a painful experience.

Anyone who has experienced a divorce knows that it's much more than two people ending a relationship. One parent described her divorce as "having her whole life tossed up in the air." Mavis Hetherington, an expert on adolescence and divorce, writes that "divorce and remarriage should not be viewed as single static events but as part of a series of transitions modifying the lives and development of children."[38] This domino effect of divorce can lead to a change in family finances, in residences, in the children's schools, in personal habits and living conditions, and in friendships, just to mention a few. Any one of these transitions by itself can cause a great deal of stress and conflict, but together they can be overwhelming.

Divorce is difficult enough, but with children it can become quite complicated. At a time when many parents feel immobilized and helpless, they are faced with the task of helping their children through this difficult transitional period. It's common for parents to feel lonely, confused, anxious, elated, fearful, hurt, and angry. Parents often have less time but more demands; they may feel relieved but have occasional bouts of depression; and they often feel guilty for interrupting their children's lives, even though they know they did the right thing.

Children of different ages and developmental stages express their reaction to their parents' divorce in different ways. Adolescents are no exception. For many teenagers, a family divorce adds strain to an already stressful time filled with changes and conflicts. For others, a divorce is a welcome relief from years of family tension. Common feelings for teens to express include sadness, anger, confusion, and denial. It's also common for teenagers to exhibit behavior problems both at home and in school, and to have increased anxiety during the transitional period of the divorce. There is also a greater tendency for teens to experiment with drugs during this time, often as a form of escape. These negative behaviors usually diminish as the family returns to a more predictable routine and stable environment.

Edward Teber, author of *Helping Your Children with Divorce,* writes, "One of the strongest determinants of how well a child adjusts to a divorce is whether or not the ex-spouses support each other in their continuing relationship as parents."[39] Children benefit when both parents coexist peacefully and accept that their ex-spouse is important to their children. If you have joint custody of the children with your ex-spouse, try to work out some simple guidelines for your children that you and your ex-spouse can agree on: rules, discipline, curfews, nutrition, etc. Continuity is important to children, especially during and after a family divorce.

Even though the consequences of divorce can be grim, for many individuals it can be an improvement over their former circumstances. A calm and stable single-parent home can be a welcome relief from a conflict-ridden two-parent home. One study reveals that adolescents in divorced families that are typically low in conflict function better than adolescents in intact, never-divorced families that are typically high in conflict.[40]

The following helpful tips are from parents who have been through a divorce with their teenagers. Their tips are followed by a parent skill builder, Helping Children Cope with Divorce.

TAKE CARE OF YOURSELF TOO ◇ It's important to nurture not only your children during a divorce but yourself as well. It's easy to neglect yourself as you concentrate your time and energy on your children. I learned the hard way that if you don't take care of yourself, you will not be very helpful to your children in the long run. Take advantage of your support group (friends, neighbors, coworkers, relatives, etc.) and accept offers of help. Talk to other parents who have been through this painful process before. Counseling for you and/or your children may also help. *L.M., Spokane, Washington*

AUTHOR'S NOTE: *Your phone book or the local mental health facility in your area can assist you in finding professional assistance and counseling, but recommendations from friends are one of the best ways to select a counselor.*

DO NOT UNDERMINE YOUR EX-SPOUSE ◇ After a divorce, treat your ex-spouse with respect and do not undermine his/her actions as they pertain to your children. Children have the right to love both parents, and they should not be exposed to the negative feelings you have about their other parent. If you need to vent, do it with a friend, not your children. *Carolyn Beery, Omaha, Nebraska*

FAMILY COUNSELOR ◇ The transition from a two-parent home to a one-parent home can be difficult for the whole family. To help my three children cope with these transitions in their life, I attached our family counselor's name and phone number to the front of the refrigerator and encouraged my children to call and make an appointment anytime they felt the need. It's sometimes easier for teens to talk to someone outside of the family than to talk to their father or me. My teens have taken advantage of this offer more than once. *J.G., San Ramon, California*

DON'T BURDEN YOUR TEENS WITH YOUR PROBLEMS ◇ Do not burden your teens with your own personal problems and worries. I learned the hard way that you can confide too much in your children. It causes children undue psychological stress during a time when they usually have many concerns and worries of their own. Talk to friends or a professional when you need to dump on someone, not your own children. *L.C., Pleasanton, California*

AGREE ON IMPORTANT ISSUES ◇ It's important for parents to present a united front to their children on important issues. This is even important for divorced parents. Parents should always treat each other with respect in front of their children. *Linda Robinson, Lincoln, Nebraska*

STAYING CONNECTED BY E-MAIL ◇ My son lives with his mother in Indiana during the school year, and with me in Maryland during the summer. He stays in close contact with both of us by electronic mail using our computer. It really helps to lessen the distance. His mother gets an almost daily message from him about all of his activities. She loves it. And during the school year, I love exchanging messages with him. E-mail is also a money saver. Even though we pay a small monthly fee for connecting to an on-line service such as America Online, Prodigy, or CompuServe, it's still much cheaper than long-distance phone calls. *Jim Buie, Takoma Park, Maryland*

TOLL-FREE NUMBER HELPS US TO STAY IN TOUCH ◇ My daughter lives with her mother in another state six months of the year. So we could talk more frequently, I gave her a toll-free number that she can use anytime to call me, without running up her mother's phone bill. We're all happy now; my ex-wife has a lower phone bill, my daughter has a special phone number, and I get to talk to my daughter whenever she gets the urge to hear my voice. Your phone company can give you details about a personalized toll-free number. *B.C., Escondido, California*

CONTACT WITH THE NONCUSTODIAL PARENT ◇ For the benefit of the children, both parents should promote regular contact with the noncustodial parent. Teens tend to get busy with their own lives, filling their calendar with activities and, before they know it, they don't have time to visit or stay with the noncustodial parent. Time with both parents is important and should be a priority. *Vicki Brooks, Rantoul, Illinois*

PARENT SKILL BUILDER

Helping Children Cope with Divorce

ANNOUNCING THE DIVORCE TO THE CHILDREN

1. Tell the children as soon as possible after the final decision has been made.
2. Both parents should participate in the talk.
3. Prepare the children for what will come.
4. Impress upon them that the divorce is not their fault. A divorce is never the fault of the children.
5. Let them know that they are loved and valued by both parents.

What Your Children Will Need

1. Your time.
2. Your understanding. (See Chapter 3, "Talking and Listening to Your Teen.")
3. Continuity. Whenever possible, keep changes to a minimum during and immediately after the divorce. Predictable household schedules help a child cope.
4. Reassurance. Even teens need to hear reassuring words from their parents during this transitional period. Let them know that you will always be their mom or dad, even with the changes in the family structure. Tell them that you will be available for them, then follow through with your promise.

✕✕✕◆✕◆✕◆✕◆✕◆✕◆✕◆✕◆✕◆✕◆✕◆✕◆✕◆✕◆✕◆✕◆✕◆✕◆✕◆✕✕

STEPPARENTING AND
BLENDED FAMILIES

✕✕✕◆✕◆✕◆✕◆✕◆✕◆✕◆✕◆✕◆✕◆✕◆✕◆✕◆✕◆✕◆✕◆✕◆✕◆✕◆✕✕

Ask any stepparents if *The Sound of Music* and *The Brady Bunch* accurately portray the real-life experience of stepparenting, and they will laugh uncontrollably. Ask about their own stepfamily, and they will probably respond that it's been a tough adjustment, but their family seems to be getting by. Then ask them to share their own experiences about trying to involve a teenager in the new stepfamily; they probably won't say a word, just show you the battle scars. Although stepparenting is quite common these days, it's a challenge for all involved. Add a teenager to the equation, and it becomes even more complicated.

Adolescence is a time of many changes, a time to gradually pull away from the family and to establish one's own identity. For a teenager to be asked to integrate into a new family structure at the same time is often too much for him to cope with. If the stepparent has new ideas, rules, and discipline, the situation can become impossible. As a result, problem behaviors can occur. According to parenting experts, adolescents in stepfamilies are more at risk for problem behaviors than adolescents living with both natural parents.

Being a stepparent can also be a frustrating experience. Stepparents often feel rejected by their stepchildren and frequently complain of feeling overwhelmed, insecure, isolated, lonely, angry, and resentful. Feelings of anxiety and depression regarding the functioning of the stepfamily is also a common complaint.

Many new stepparents make the mistake of trying to do the impossible: replacing the biological parent. The relationship between a biological parent and child has evolved over many years. To try to duplicate that relationship is usually destined for failure. Instead, ease slowly into the relationship and gradually let your new role define itself. Most parenting experts agree that a stepparent should defer the stepchildren's discipline and control to the children's biological mother or father for the first year or two of the relationship. Trying to control an adolescent stepchild early on will only hurt the already fragile relationship between a child and stepparent.

Stepparents need empathy, support, and guidance. The best individuals to offer this kind of support are other stepparents. The tips listed in this section are all from experienced stepparents. I especially encourage you to take the advice from the tip titled "Stepparent Support Group" (page 210) and form your own support group. You won't have to look far. There are probably other stepparents right in your own neighborhood who would jump at the opportunity to join an informal group of parents who share similar experiences. I also recommend reading some informative books on the subject of stepparenting and blended families. See the recommended reading list for parents and adolescents at the end of the chapter. The Stepfamily Association of America is also a good organization to join. Their address and phone number are listed at the end of this chapter. Immediately following the parenting tips in this section is a parent skill builder, Enriching Stepfamilies.

$\diamond$

ADVICE FOR NEWLY BLENDED FAMILIES $\diamond$

When my husband and I married, creating a blended family of his kids and mine, I thought that we could function pretty much like any other "regular" family. Wrong! Blended families are usually much more difficult and complicated than the typical nuclear family. If I had just accepted that in the beginning, things would have been easier. Trying to relate to my stepchildren the same way that I relate to my own children didn't work; things that were not issues with my own children were major problems with my stepchildren. I have two points of advice for parents beginning a blended family. First, each parent should be the primary disciplinarian for his or her own children during the first year—whenever possible. Let your spouse take the soft-pedal approach and be the good guy for a while with your own children, and vice versa. That's not to say, however, that you or your spouse should ignore negative behaviors and never discipline each other's children. Second, both spouses should back each other up and present a united front to the children. We have settled into our own version of family life, which seems to suit us fine. Our future looks bright. *Anonymous*

A DOUBLE DOSE OF RESISTANCE ◇ Anger, resistance, and rebellion are expected from teenagers. But if you try blending them into a new family expect a double or triple dose. If you anticipate problems, you will be prepared to deal with them. *Patricia Stahler, Niles, California*

DEALING WITH AN ANGRY EX-SPOUSE ◇ I was not prepared for the competitiveness and anger that my husband's ex-wife had toward me at the beginning of our relationship. Although it's been extremely difficult to refrain from making negative comments back to her, I have. And I'm glad that I did. She needed to let off steam and now, one year later, we at least have a civil relationship with each other. *Anonymous*

A UNITED FRONT IN BOTH HOMES ◇ Teens need consistency in their lives, especially if they live in a joint custody arrangement. Living in two homes is often difficult enough, but when the rules are completely different, it can cause major behavior problems. Whenever possible, parents and stepparents from both households should try to agree on the same rules and standards of behavior. It's often not easy to do, but the rewards are worth it for all involved. *N.J., New York City, New York*

STEPPARENT SUPPORT GROUP ◇ Being a stepparent can be very challenging to say the least. My support group has helped me more than anything else. I found three other stepmothers who were having similar problems and issues, and we meet at a restaurant for breakfast or lunch once a month. It's amazing how we've bonded together and leaned on each other over the years. It's OK to call each other in an emergency, and we've even had special meetings to support one another during family crises. I highly recommend a support group for other stepparents. *L.A., Fremont, California*

TEEN TALK

If you remarry, make sure you take time for the kids. The new relationship can take your time away from us when we need you most. (Robert, Washington)

◊

If I could start over again with my stepmother and stepsisters, I would be more tolerant, less defensive, and have fewer expectations. I'd realize sooner that this blended family is permanent instead of hoping it would go away. (Arinn, California)

INTRODUCING A NEW RELATIONSHIP ◊ As my son's noncustodial parent, I have tried to remain friendly with my ex-wife and continue to be a part of my son's life as much as possible. Three years after our divorce, I remarried. During the time that my second wife and I were dating, I was careful to introduce her to my son in small doses and in very positive circumstances. I sought to avoid a situation where he would feel like she was taking his place in my life. Things have worked out fine so far. *David A. Wilson, Oak Park, Illinois*

"YOU MAY CALL ME MOM OR BECKY" ◊ I explained to my three stepchildren that I would never be able to replace their mother, but I would try to be the best stepmother possible. I gave them the choice of calling me either Mom or Becky. The eight-year-old decided to call me Mom and the preteen and the teenager opted for Becky. It helped to tell them that I couldn't replace their real mother. *B.B.J., Des Moines, Iowa*

SECOND THOUGHTS ◊ Blending our two families (two young children and four teenagers) was so difficult and painful for all of us, but especially the teenagers, that at times I wonder if I would even attempt it again if offered a second chance. It would have been easier to maintain two households. *V.P., Palo Alto, California*

KEEPING MY ROLE STRAIGHT ◊ As a stepmother I have learned that there are some roles that I play and some that my stepdaughter's mother plays. The key is to

PARENT SKILL BUILDER

Enriching Stepfamilies

1. Nurture your couple relationship.
   - Plan to do something away from your household once a week that you both enjoy doing together.
   - Arrange to have twenty minutes of relaxed time alone with each other every day.
   - Talk together about the running of your household for at least thirty minutes each week.
2. Find personal space and time for yourself and each member of the family.
   - Take time to make a special "private" place for everyone in your household (a part of a room, a special shelf, a drawer or closet space for children who come on weekends, etc.).
   - You and your partner should each take two hours a week doing something special for yourselves (having a massage, going bowling, sewing, reading, etc.).
3. Nourish family relationships.
   - Give positive feedback to one another.
4. Maintain close parent-child relationships
   - Do something fun together with each child for fifteen to twenty minutes once or twice a week.
5. Develop stepparent-stepchild relationships.
   - Do something fun together with each stepchild for fifteen to twenty minutes once or twice a week.
6. Build family trust.
   - Schedule family time and events.
7. Strengthen stepfamily ties.
8. Work with the children's other household.
   - Give the adults in the children's other household positive feedback once a month.

Reprinted from *Stepfamilies Stepping Ahead: An Eight-Step Program for Successful Family Living* (1989), with permission from the Stepfamily Association of America, 215 Centennial Mall South, Suite 212, Lincoln, Nebraska 68508.

avoid stepping on each other's toes or trying to compete with each other. For example, I try not to duplicate things that are special between my stepdaughter and her mother. There are also some events that I defer to her mother, such as parent-teacher conferences and other special occasions. Everyone is happy when the stepmother and mother get along. *Anonymous, Toledo, Ohio*

For Further Information

Parents Without Partners, 8807 Coleville Road, Silver Spring, MD 20910 (301-588-9394); provides social and educational functions for single, divorced, and widowed parents in local chapters nationwide.

Stepfamily Association of America, 215 Centennial Mall South, Suite 212, Lincoln, Nebraska 68508 (800-735-0329); provides information and support for stepparents; national advocate for positive stepfamily image.

Stepfamily Foundation, 333 West End Avenue, New York, NY 10023 (212-877-3244); serves stepparents and persons considering becoming stepparents. Offers counseling, referrals, speakers, and publications.

American Association for Marriage and Family Therapy, 924 West 9th Street, Upland, CA 91786; professional assistance of therapists who have completed specialized training in marital and family therapy. Referral service.

Association for Children for Enforcement of Support, 1018 Jefferson Avenue, No. 204, Toledo, OH 43624; refers clients to local chapters of support groups.

Fathers' Rights of America, PO Box 7596, Van Nuys, CA 91409 (818-789-4435); works on child custody, child support, divorce, and fathers' rights issues. Provides seminars and reference services.

Mothers Without Custody, PO Box 56762, Houston, TX 77256-6762; offers local support groups for noncustodial mothers.

Big Brothers/Big Sisters of America, 230 North 13th Street, Philadelphia, PA 19107 (215-567-2748); connects children of single-parent families with same-sex role models. Screens and trains role models before assigning them to children.

Big Brothers and Sisters of Canada, 5230 South Service Road, Burlington, Ontario L7L 5K2. Provides adult volunteers for children.

Recommended Reading for Parents

Fitzhugh Dodson, *How to Single Parent* (New York: Harper & Row, 1987).

Neil Kalter, *Growing Up With Divorce: Helping Your Child Avoid Immediate and Later Emotional Problems,* (New York: Free Press, 1990).

Gerald M. Knox, ed., *Your Child: Living with Divorce* (Des Moines: Better Homes and Gardens, 1990).

Isolina Ricci, *Mom's House, Dad's House: Making Shared Custody Work* (New York: Macmillan, 1980).

Edward Teber, *Helping Your Children with Divorce* (New York: Pocket Books, 1985).

Emily Visher and John Visher, *How to Win as a Stepfamily,* (New York: Avon, 1982).

Judith S. Wallerstein and Sandra Blakeslee, *Second Chances* (New York: Ticknor and Fields, 1989).

Recommended Reading for Teens

Judy Blume, *It's Not the End of the World* (New York: Dell, 1986); recommended for preteens.

Ann Getzoff and Carolyn McClenahan, *Stepkids: A Survival Guide for Teenagers in Stepfamilies* (New York: Walker, 1985).

Kevin Leman, *Living in a Stepfamily Without Getting Stepped On* (Pullman, WA: Nelson, 1994).

16

LOOKING TOWARD THE FUTURE: COLLEGE AND CAREERS

I have found the best way to give advice to your children is to find out what they want and then advise them to do it.

— HARRY S TRUMAN

The number of high school graduates who go on to a post-secondary education has risen dramatically since the beginning of the twentieth century: approximately 50 percent of all graduates enroll in college today as compared to only 4 percent in 1900. Although a record number of young people are enrolling in college, many never graduate. Most freshmen learn this fact during their college orientation when the dean asks them to look at the person on their right, then their left, then to look at themselves. "One of you will not be here by the end of the year," he or she solemnly declares.

College is not for every young person. Some individuals choose to delay their college enrollment for a few years of full-time employment or to begin a family; others are neither interested nor motivated ever to attend. Although college graduates generally earn substantially more income over their lifetime than do noncollege grads (the estimates range from $250,000 to $400,000), there are many individuals who have never stepped on a college campus who have not only survived but prospered in their fields of endeavor. One of the worst mistakes a parent can make is to force an uninterested and unmotivated young person to attend college. I have had many of these young people in my college classes, and I can attest to the fact that it is usually a frustrating experience for the student *and* professor—as well as a waste of money for the parents.

If your son or daughter chooses to attend a technical school, college, or university after high school, your support and guidance will help him or her cope with transitions and stresses during the college years. It's quite common for freshmen to have fears about failing in college, not finding a major they like, or not making any friends. If your child is going to be successful in college, he will have to learn, if he hasn't already, how to manage his time, money, stress, and energy. Possibly for the first time in his life, no one will be holding his hand and guiding him to make the right decisions. This is when you and your children "cash in" on all the time and energy you have spent together in years past.

The best advice you can offer to your child to be successful in college is to enroll in a college survival course during his first semester. Research confirms that students who complete a college survival, freshman orientation, or college study skills course (there are many different names for the same course), have a higher rate of graduation and a higher grade point average than those who do not complete such a course. These classes teach the basic skills needed to be a successful student: note and test taking; and time, money, and stress management. Some courses also cover topics such as drug abuse, responsible sexual decisions, and physical health.

The biggest stressor for most freshmen and sophomores is deciding on a career goal. Part of the difficulty in choosing a major is the number of choices available to students today. *The Dictionary of Occupational Titles,* published by the U.S. Department of Labor, lists more than 20,000 occupations. Compare that to the not-too-distant past when a young man usually worked in the same job as his father and a young woman had few, if any, choices. If your child hasn't decided on a major yet, he is in good company. The vast majority of freshmen and many sophomores haven't chosen a major yet either. And there's a good chance that those who do have a major will end up changing it before they graduate.

Unfortunately, many college students today pick their major because of the potential earning power of that profession or because of pressure from parents, even though they have no personal interest in that field. As a college counselor and professor, I try to persuade my students to find their passion in life—what gives them great joy—and then discover how to be paid for it. People who do this, I tell my students, are those who will most enjoy life and prosper at their work.

The decision to either go away to college or to stay home and attend a local campus is also a difficult one for many parents and their teen. There are advantages and disadvantages to both options and many factors to consider, including cost, maturity of your child, and, above all, your child's wishes. Teens who go off to college tend to have improved relationships with their parents. One study revealed that going away to college not only increases the individual's independence but also improves the relationship with parents. Students who boarded at college were more affectionate with their parents, communicated better with them, and were more independent from them as compared with those students who remained at home while attending college.[41]

This chapter is divided into two sections: Planning and Attending College and Careers. There is also a special parent skill builder, Planning for College Begins in Junior High (page 221).

✖✖

PLANNING AND ATTENDING COLLEGE

✖✖

NEVER TOO EARLY TO TALK ABOUT COLLEGE ◇ From an early age and throughout adolescence, talk about the importance, the fun, the independence, and the stimulating environment of college life. If you do,

chances are it will be something your child truly looks forward to. *John Cornett, High Rolls, New Mexico*

COLLEGE PLANNING BEGINS EARLY ◇ If your
teen aspires to attend a good college or university, make
sure she is getting good counseling advice in high school.
College entrance exams and specific high school courses
are often prerequisites for applying to most universities.
Good academic planning begins in middle school. *Mary
Hopkins, Sacramento, California*

SCHOLARSHIP CELEBRATION ◇ When our daughter announced to my husband and me that she had just
been awarded a substantial scholarship for college, we
gave her $500 for a spending spree of her choice. We fig-
ured that we had saved a substantial amount of money on
college expenses. It was a good way to show our appreciation for her hard work and determination in getting good
grades, which made the scholarship possible. *Karen
Dombek, San Diego, California*

COLLEGE CAMPUS VISIT ◇ I highly recommend vis-
iting the college campuses your teen is considering for admission. My daughter and I were both glad that we visited
her first and second choices before we sent in the applications. After spending a half day on each campus and taking the tour, the second choice became the first choice.
Each campus has a different ambience and feel to it,
which is important to consider before spending four years
there. *S.A., Chicago, Illinois*

VACATION DOUBLES AS CAMPUS TOUR ◇ We
used our summer family vacation before my son's senior
year of high school to visit three college campuses that he
was considering. We saw the sights in each of the cities
where the campuses were located as well as all the tourist
attractions in between. The entire family enjoyed the car
trip, and my son was able to prioritize his choices of campuses after our visit. We learned that you never really
know a campus until you visit it. Brochures just don't tell
the whole picture of campus life. *J.M., Spokane, Washington*

MUST MAINTAIN GOOD GRADES ◇ My husband
and I thought it was reasonable to expect decent—not

spectacular—grades in college if we were going to pay for tuition and expenses. We set a very fair GPA for each child to maintain in college, or all support from us would get cut off. It helped to provide extra motivation to get good grades. *K.S.D., Pittsburgh, Pennsylvania*

A COMPUTER IS A MUST ◇ Colleges and universities increasingly require new students to have a personal computer. Many campuses are now wired for computer networks, which allow students to communicate directly with their instructors, send in assignments on-line, and even do research from their dorm room. Before buying a computer system for your son or daughter, ask the college representative which system and components they recommend. Also, inquire about the special computer discounts available for students in the campus bookstores. My daughter insists that she couldn't survive on campus without her computer. *R.C.R., Los Angeles, California*

TOOLS TO GO ◇ Before my two daughters went off to college, I prepared a compact tool box for them. I bought an open-topped plastic tool box with one sliding drawer and filled it with essential tools: small hammer, pliers, screwdrivers, wrench, measuring tape, small container of WD-40, and nails and screws of various sizes. It's been years since they graduated from college, but they still have their tool boxes, which they claim have been very useful. *Neil McCallum, Tahoe City, California*

A NEW RELATIONSHIP ◇ Now that my son has entered his twenties, I realize that I have not lost a child—I have gained a friend. *Deborah Burt, Clovis, California*

COLLEGE CONTRACT ◇ My husband and I signed a *written* agreement with our college-bound teenagers: we will pay for all expenses toward a bachelor's degree for *four years*. Any costs for a B.A. degree after four years will be the responsibility of our children. These agreements help to put a cap on our costs in case our children decide to turn a four-year degree into a six-year degree. Graduate school, if desired, will be negotiated later. *Karen Dombek, San Diego, California*

A "CALL ME" CARD ◇ A wonderful gift for your teen at home or college-bound child is a "call me" card. Available through your phone company, a "call me" card will allow your child to call your home number only. No other phone numbers can be dialed using the "call me" card. Your child can always call home, especially in emergencies, without worrying about change for pay phones. *F.E.S., San Jose, California*

AUTHOR'S NOTE: *Another similar service adds an 800 number to your existing phone line for a nominal monthly fee. Only your family has access to your 800 number, which can be used from any phone in the country. One such service is provided by Call Home America (1-800-594-3000).*

STAYING CONNECTED—ON LINE ◇ If you have a computer and a modem, an effective and inexpensive way to stay in touch with your children when they move away to college is to use one of the on-line computer services. My wife and I signed up with America Online, then we signed-up our daughters who are scattered across the country. Each of our daughters either owned a computer or had access to one which they use for college work. We intend to leave messages with each other via E-mail, and at least once a week we will all go on-line at the same time and chat via the computer. The whole family will feel "connected" to each other, and the only expense is the computer time charged by the on-line company. The phone calls to connect to the service are all local calls. Our daughters also enjoy the convenience of having an updated encyclopedia and other research aids available on-line for their studies. *Michael Stahler, Niles, California*

PARENTS' RIGHT TO SEE COLLEGE GRADES
◇ Parents have a right to see their child's college grades if they are paying for the tuition and/or the child's living expenses while in school. While most colleges don't automatically send grades to parents, most colleges have a special form that the student and parent must sign giving consent to mailing grades home to the parents. *K.S.D., Pittsburgh, Pennsylvania*

PARENT SKILL BUILDER

Planning for College Begins in Junior High

8th Grade Meet with junior high counselor to determine the curriculum for the 9th grade. Inquire about college prep courses.

9th Grade Meet with high school counselor to determine the basic college entrance requirements, *including the necessary high school courses.* Helpful college guides are available at most high school and city libraries. The entrance requirements for many colleges and universities far exceed the minimum high school graduation requirements. Many prestigious campuses require three to four years of advanced placement or honors classes to be completed in high school.

Courses completed from the 9th through 12th grades will be on the school transcript sent to colleges and universities.

10th Grade This is a good time to attend college fairs sponsored by the school district or local community college. Request literature from specific colleges and universities. Some colleges will even send you a video about their campus.

11th Grade Items listed above for 10th grade are also pertinent for the junior year.

Encourage your son or daughter to take the PSAT/NMSQT (a preliminary test) for practice. It is usually given in October.

Inquire about test dates for the Scholastic Aptitude Test (SAT) and/or the American College Test (ACT). Most students also require one or more subject tests. If scores on either the SAT or

ACT are lower than expected, both tests can be repeated in the senior year. There are courses, software programs, and books available to help prepare for the SAT and ACT.

If possible, visit the campuses that are being considered. Campus tours should be arranged in advance.

12th Grade Repeat SAT, ACT, and/or subject tests in the fall if necessary.

Begin requesting admission applications in August or September. Some campuses have admission deadlines as early as November. It is advisable to apply to at least three campuses.

Community College Option: Most community colleges offer a quality education and are a good option for students on a limited budget, students who did not complete the high school prerequisites for freshman admission to a university, students who decide at the last minute that they want to go to college, or students who want to take time to explore career options before transferring to a university. Besides offering vocational programs, most community colleges offer the full spectrum of transfer courses (both general education and lower-division) for the freshman and sophomore years. After completing the transfer requirements, students are eligible to transfer to most four-year colleges and universities where they can complete the junior and senior years.

XX

CAREERS

XXXXXXXXXXXXXXXXXXXXXXXXXXXXXXXXXXXXXXXXXXXXXX

HELP DISCOVER THOSE SPECIAL TALENTS AND ABILITIES ◇ Help your children discover one or more of their special abilities, interests, or talents. Then do all you can to support and encourage them in those endeavors. Help them find outlets for these interests. For example, our son loved acting and the theater, so we encouraged him to join a few local theater productions. Our two teenagers were so busy pursuing their interests, they never had time to get into trouble. It's a natural solution to the issue of keeping your teen occupied and inspired. *Ann Nichols, Tucson, Arizona*

WORKDAY WITH DAD ◇ Once a year I took my children to work with me, one at a time. I enjoyed focusing my attention on just one child and they seemed to enjoy learning more about Dad's job. It was a good time to talk about work and careers and the importance of enjoying what you do. I always impressed upon them that their own career could be anything they wanted it to be, as long as they worked hard to attain that goal. *Dave Hopkins, Sacramento, California*

TEEN TALK

Beware of the subtle negativity you may cast on a talent your child is naturally drawn to simply because it is not something you would have chosen for him/her. (Anonymous, New York)

◇

If you disagree with the career or college major choice of your son or daughter, explain to them your concerns, but respect and support their choice. (Monica, California)

EVERYONE HAS A SPECIAL TALENT ◇ All kids are good at something. Let *them* find what it is and go for it. *Ray and Pam Powers, Papillion, Nebraska*

WHAT'S YOUR PASSION? ◇ Don't try to mold your teen into something they're not. You'll both be unhappy in the end. Instead, discover what their interests and passions are and encourage those. That Ivy League college may be important to you and would offer bragging rights to your friends, but your son may want to be a plumber. *F.E.S., San Jose, California*

VOLUNTEERING HELPS FIND CAREER ◇ When I was a young teen, I volunteered at the local hospital for something to do. The experience exposed me to many different occupations and had a major influence on my career choice. By the time I was ready to apply for a job after college, my résumé already looked very impressive. Volunteering as a teen also kept me from being bored and boosted my self-esteem. Hospitals, veterinarian clinics, schools, and many other businesses actively recruit teen volunteers. *B.G., Miami, Florida*

JOB SHADOW ◇ If your teen is interested in a specific career, encourage her to talk to as many people as possible who work in that profession. Most people love to talk about their job, especially if it's with a young person who is considering the same field. There's always a chance that your teen will be invited to come and job shadow that individual. You can only learn so much from books and career guides about occupations. There's no substitute for talking to people and learning firsthand what it's like to work in a specific profession. *A.S., Wilmette, Illinois*

For Further Information

Job Corps, 200 Constitution Avenue NW, Washington, DC 20210 (202-535-0550). Provides education, vocational training, and work experience for disadvantaged youth sixteen to twenty-one years old.

Junior Achievement of Canada, 1 Westside Drive, Toronto, Ontario, M9C 1B2 (416-622-4602). Provides practical business education and experience to Canadian youth.

Recommended Reading

Karen Levin Coburn, *Letting Go: A Parents' Guide To Today's College Experience* (Chevy Chase, MD: Adler and Adler, 1988).

William Hopke (Ed.), *The Encyclopedia of Careers and Vocational Guidance* (Chicago: J. G. Ferguson, 1981). A good reference for career development and vocational choice.

Richard Bolles, *What Color Is Your Parachute?* (Berkeley: Ten Speed Press, 1995). An excellent book on career planning and job hunting.

TEN THINGS YOU CAN DO TO IMPROVE THE LIVES OF TEENS

Besides being a good parent, there are other ways to improve the lives of teenagers in our society. Here are a few ways you can help:

1. *Volunteer your time* There are many schools, churches, and community-based organizations serving young people in your community that could use your help. You have a skill they can use, whether it's as a tutor, recreation leader, mentor, fund-raiser, counselor, or Big Brother/Sister. Even an hour or two of your time each week can help make a difference in your community.

2. *Does your community have a teen council?* Encourage your community leaders to create a teen council if you don't already have one. The council should be composed of a cross-section of youth from your community who can advise the city and civic leaders on the local needs of youth.

3. *Teens need a safe and fun place to hang out* Encourage your community leaders to provide teen facilities for recreation and sports programs. Teens should be consulted as to the equipment purchased and the activities, games, and programs offered. A teen center should be a safe, upbeat place for teens to spend time. Some centers have large-screen televisions, areas to do homework, comfortable conversation areas, and games such as pool, table soccer, and Ping-Pong.

4. *Get the media involved* Ask your local newspaper and television news station to balance their usual negative portrayal of teenagers (sex, drugs, pregnancies, violence, gangs, etc.) with positive stories about teens in your community. Give them examples of the type of coverage you and other parents would like to see.

5. *Lower teen violence*

- Stricter laws: Help initiate or support stricter laws and penalties for violent behavior. Support strict handgun control, buy-back-gun programs, and special task forces dealing with teen gangs.
- Curfews: Encourage your community to adopt and enforce a reasonable teen curfew. Many communities who have such a curfew claim that it lowers juvenile crime and victimization.
- Media: Stop patronizing theaters that show violent movies. Encourage local video and music stores to stop selling videos and music that promote violence.

6. *Help fight teen drug and alcohol abuse*

- Teen support groups: Encourage the appropriate community-based groups to sponsor more teen twelve-step programs. Teens are more willing to attend and follow through with programs that are geared with their special needs in mind.
- Stricter laws: Help initiate or support stricter laws and penalties for teen substance abuse and for selling and manufacturing illegal drugs. Many communities have implemented tough alcohol and tobacco ordinances that place a high fine on merchants who sell these products to minors.
- Drug education: Support drug education programs in schools, including the highly successful DARE (Drug Abuse-Resistance-Education) program.

7. *Support new laws for teen driving*

- Graduated licensing programs: To reduce the number of teen traffic fatalities each year, encourage your state legislators to adopt a "graduated" or "three-tier" licensing program for teenagers if they haven't already done so. These programs require more driving practice for teens and usually include a learner's permit, provisional license, and a full license. This licensing procedure is recommended by the National Highway Safety Administration.
- Zero tolerance for drinking and driving: Encourage your state legislators to adopt a zero tolerance policy for teens who drink and drive. Most zero tolerance laws state that anyone under the age of twenty-one who is caught driving under the influence of alcohol

or drugs (any amount) receive an immediate one-year suspension of their driving license. Many states have already adopted such a program and claim it to be successful in lowering the number of teens killed each year from drinking and driving.

8. *Help your schools*

- Counselors: Support efforts to increase the number of junior and high school counselors. School counselors assist teens with academic issues, college and career planning, and guidance with personal problems. There are many negative results when schools have no counselors or a high counselor-to-student ratio.
- Youth job training and apprenticeship programs: Encourage local schools to offer youth job training and apprenticeship programs. We need to provide better support and training for the millions of teenagers who do not go to college.
- Parenting and life skills classes: Encourage local high schools to teach mandatory parenting and life skills courses during the junior and senior years.

9. *Propose new policies for businesses*

- Support for families: Encourage local businesses to adopt policies such as paid maternity leave, job sharing, part-time and flexible work hours, and telecommuting.
- Apprenticeship programs: Encourage local businesses to offer much-needed youth job training and apprenticeship programs (see number 8, above).

10. *Begin a program titled "The Year of the Child"*

Encourage your city or county leaders to adopt a year-long program titled "The Year of the Child" or "Putting Kids First," which enlists businesses, government, and community groups to make an all-out effort to address the plight of young children, teens, and families.

NOTES

1. Jerry Ceppos, "A Vision of the *Mercury News* of the Future," *San Jose Mercury News*, Jan. 15, 1995, 1C.

2. D. Offer, E. Ostrov, K. I. Howard, and R. Atkinson, *The Teenage World: Adolescents' Self-Image in Ten Countries* (New York: Plenum, 1988).

3. R. E. Frisch, "Puberty and Body Fat." In R. M. Lerner, A. C. Petersen, and J. Brooksgunn (eds.), *Encyclopedia of Adolescence* (New York: Garland, 1991).

4. J. Tanner, "Sequence, Tempo, and Individual Variation in Growth and Development of Boys and Girls Aged Twelve to Sixteen." In J. Kagan and R. Coles (eds.), *Twelve to Sixteen: Early Adolescence* (New York: Norton, 1972).

5. Judy Blume, *Are You There God? It's Me Margaret* (New York: Bradbury Press, 1970). Reprinted with permission of Simon and Schuster Books for Young Readers.

6. D. Elkind, "Egocentrism in Adolescence." *Child Development* 38, (1987), pp. 1025–34.

7. Erik Erikson, *Identity: Youth and Crisis* (New York: Norton, 1968) p. 245.

8. C. R. Cooper, H. D. Grotevant, *Individuality and Connectedness in the Family and Adolescents' Self and Relational Competence.* Paper presented at the meeting of the Society for Research in Child Development, Kansas City, 1989.

9. H. S. Bernard, "Identity Formation in Late Adolescence: A Review of Some Empirical Findings," *Adolescence* 16, (1981), pp. 349–58.

10. E. Greenberger and L. Steinberg, (1986) *When Teenagers Work: The Psychological Social Costs of Adolescent Employment* (New York: Basic Books, 1986) and (1981) *Project for the Study of Adolescent Work: Final Report,* Report prepared for the National Institute of Education, U.S. Dept. of Education, Washington, D.C.

11. Laurence Steinberg, *Adolescence,* 3rd edition (New York: McGraw-Hill, 1993), p. 170. Reprinted with permission.

12. Ibid., pp. 182–83.

13. Barbara Vobejda, "As Kids Age, Parents' Role at School Wanes," *Washington Post,* printed in the *San Jose Mercury News,* Sept. 5, 1994, p. 1.

14. G. Csikszentmihalyi and R. Larson, *Being Adolescent.* (New York: Basic Books, 1984), p. 63.

15. Ibid.

16. "Kids: TV Preaches Sex, Lying, Violence," *San Jose Mercury News,* Feb. 27, 1995, 1A. A report on a study conducted by Children Now, a national children's advocacy group.

17. L. A. Tucker, "Television, Teenagers, and Health," *Journal of Youth and Adolescence* 16, (1987), pp. 415–25.

18. Scripps Howard, "Top Educator Talks about TV," reprinted in *The Argus,* Sept. 8, 1994, p. A-1.

19. Betsy Bates, "Latchkey Kids Need Supervision Even from Afar," *Los Angeles Daily News,* reprinted in the *San Jose Mercury News,* July 14, 1993, p. 1D. The study was conducted by the University of Southern California.

20. G. Gallup and D. Poling, *The Search For America's Faith,* (New York: Abington, 1980), p. 16.

21. A. W. Astin, K. C. Green, and W. S. Korn, *The American Freshman: Twenty-Year Trends* (Los Angeles: UCLA Higher Education Research Institute, 1987), and A. W. Astin, W. S. Korn, and E. R. Berz, *The American Freshman: Twenty-Year Trends* (Los Angeles: UCLA Higher Education Research Institute, 1990).

22. Barbara Vobejda, "Study Finds More Teens Using Birth Control," *Washington Post,* reprinted in the *San Jose Mercury News,* July 7, 1994.

23. H. D. Thornberg, "Sources of Sex Education Among Early Adolescents," *Journal of Early Adolescence,* 1981, p. 174.

24. American Social Health Association, *"Becoming an Askable Parent: How to Talk with Your Child about Sexuality,"* 1994, p. 2.

25. Associated Press, "Three Stages Are Sought for Drivers' Licenses," *Boston Globe,* Sept. 9, 1994, p. 14.

26. "How Teens Can Drive Up Cost of Auto Insurance," *Colorado Springs Gazette Telegraph,* Aug. 28, 1994, W2.

27. "Teenagers at Risk for Auto Accidents, Research Shows," Medical Tribune News Service, *Daily News of Los Angeles,* July 2, 1994, L16.

28. Gary Blonston, "Teen Drug Use Rising for First Time in a Decade," *San Jose Mercury News,* a report on the 1994 University of Michigan Study, Feb. 1, 1994, 1A.

29. Centers for Disease Control (CDC), "Alcohol and Other Drug Use Among High School Students—United States, 1990," *Morbidity and Mortality Weekly Report,* Nov. 1991, p. 776.

30. Gary Blonston, "Teen Drug Use Rising for First Time in a Decade."

31. Office of the Inspector General (OIG), U.S. Department of Health and Human Services (HHS), "Youth and Alcohol: A National Survey. Drinking Habits, Access, Attitudes, and Knowledge," Washington, D.C., June 1991, p. 11.

32. Public Health Service, HHS, "Healthy People 2000: Na-

tional Health Promotion and Disease Prevention Objectives," Washington, D.C., 1990, p. 97.

33. OIG, HHS, "Youth and Alcohol," p. 6.

34. National Council on Alcoholism and Drug Dependence, Inc., "The Scholastic/CNN Newsroom Survey on Student Attitudes about Drug and Substance Abuse," *Fact Sheet: Youth and Alcohol,* New York, 1993.

35. *New York Times,* "Study Finds Girls' Self-Image Is a Casualty of Adolescence," reprinted in *San Jose Mercury News,* Jan. 9, 1991, 1A. The study was commissioned by the American Association of University Women.

36. Laurence Steinberg, *Adolescence,* (New York: McGraw-Hill, 1993), p. 120. Reprinted with permission.

37. D. Baumrind, "Current Patterns of Parental Authority," *Developmental Psychology Monographs* 4 (1971), pp. 1–103; and D. Baumrind, "Effective Parenting During the Early Adolescent Transition" in P. A. Cowan and E. M. Hetherington (eds.), *Advances in Family Research (Vol. 2)* (Hillsdale, NJ: Erlbaum, 1991); and "Parenting Styles and Adolescent Development" in J. Brooks-Gunn, R. Lerner, and A. C. Petersen (eds.), *Encyclopedia of Adolescence,* Vol. 2 (New York: Garland, 1991).

38. E. M. Hetherington, M. Stanley-Hagan, and E. Anderson, "Marital Transitions: A Child's Perspective," *American Psychologist* 44, (1989), pp. 303–12.

39. Edward Teber, *Helping Your Children with Divorce: A Compassionate Guide For Parents* (New York: Pocket Books, 1985), p. 134.

40. S. M. Bishop and G. M. Ingersoll, "Effects of Marital Conflict and Family Structure on the Self-Concepts of Pre- and Early Adolescents," *Journal of Youth and Adolescents* 18, (1989), pp. 25–38.

41. K. Sullivan and A. Sullivan, "Adolescent-Parent Separation," *Developmental Psychology* 16, (1980), pp. 93–99.

INDEX

KNOW A GOOD TEEN TIP?

Do you know a tip that was not included in this book? If you do, I want to hear from you. And so do the thousands of parents who could read your tip in the next edition of *Teen Tips: A Practical Survival Guide for Parents with Kids 11 to 19.*

Please let me know if you would like to have your name or initials and your city printed with your tip.

If you have a tip or comment about the book, write to:

PARENTING TIPS
P.O. Box 3395
Mission San Jose, CA 94539
(Please use form on next page)

Or call the TIPS fax/answering machine:

925-461-6080 (24-hours)
(VOICE MESSAGES OR FAXES)

or contact me on-line:

kidtips@aol.com

MY TIP IS . . .

_____

_____

_____

_____

_____

_____

I give my permission to reprint my tip(s) in all editions of the parenting books and newspaper columns authored by Tom McMahon and any derived uses therefrom or in any other manner, subject to necessary editing.

☐ Please list my name or initials, city, and state as listed below with my tip(s).

_____
(please print clearly)

☐ Please do not print my name or initials.

_____ *signature*

_____ *print name*

_____ *mailing address*

_____

_____ *phone number*

Mail this completed form to:
Parenting Tips
P.O. Box 3395
Mission San Jose, CA 94539

Use additional paper for tips if necessary